# HIKING
## THE GULF ISLANDS
## OF BRITISH COLUMBIA

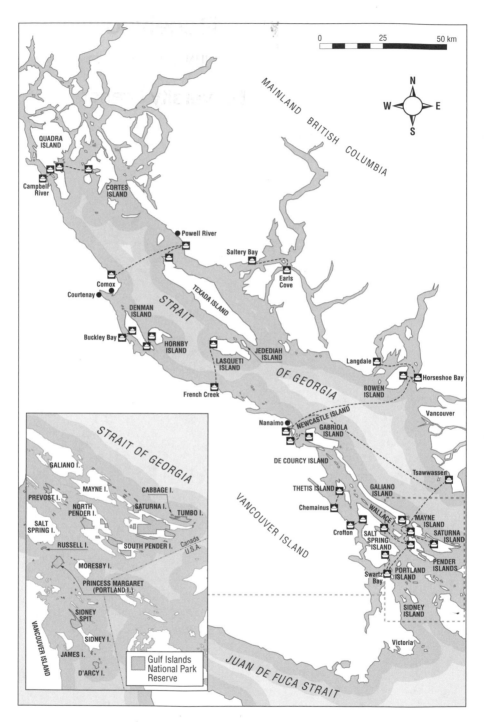

# The Gulf Islands

🚢 ---- Ferry routes

# HIKING
## THE GULF ISLANDS
## OF BRITISH COLUMBIA

Charles Kahn

HARBOUR PUBLISHING

Published by
Harbour Publishing Co. Ltd.
P.O. Box 219, Madeira Park, BC V0N 2H0
**www.harbourpublishing.com**

Text design by Martin Nichols
Cover design by Teresa Karbashewski
Cover photo: Sandstone shoreline and arbutus grove at Malaspina Point,
    Gabriola Island, by Chris Jaksa for All Canada Photos
Back cover photo: View from Mount Maxwell, Salt Spring Island
Edited by Margaret Tessman
Maps by Nick Murphy
Photos by Charles Kahn and Judy Norget unless credited otherwise
Printed and bound in Canada

THE CANADA COUNCIL | LE CONSEIL DES ARTS
FOR THE ARTS | DU CANADA
SINCE 1957 | DEPUIS 1957

BRITISH
COLUMBIA
ARTS COUNCIL
Supported by the Province of British Columbia

Harbour Publishing acknowledges financial support from the Government of Canada through the Canada Book Fund and the Canada Council for the Arts, and from the Province of British Columbia through the BC Arts Council and the Book Publishing Tax Credit.

**Library and Archives Canada Cataloguing in Publication**

Kahn, Charles, 1945-

    Hiking the Gulf Islands of British Columbia / Charles Kahn. – Expanded 3rd ed.
Includes bibliographical references and index.

ISBN 978-1-55017-511-0

    1. Hiking—British Columbia—Gulf Islands—Guidebooks. 2. Gulf Islands (B.C.)—Guidebooks. I. Title.

GV199.44.C22G84 2011      796.5109711'28      C2011-900278-7

# Contents

*For*
*Judy Norget*

# Preface

In its most limited sense the term "Gulf Islands" refers only to the cluster of islands hugging the Vancouver Island shore from Nanaimo south to the US border. Some consider it a stretch even to include Denman and Hornby. But this book uses the term in its broadest sense, which includes all the above plus Lasqueti, Texada, Quadra, Cortes and Bowen. The main criteria for inclusion were the quality of hiking opportunities and public access: almost all the islands included have walking/hiking trails and are accessible by BC Ferries, although several marine parks that can only be reached by private boat are also included.

Population figures are from the most up-to-date government sources at time of writing. For historical information, I consulted materials provided by tourist offices, local newspapers, written histories and word-of-mouth accounts, but relied mainly on previously published materials, most of which are acknowledged in the resource section at the end of the book. Of course, whenever more than one island history exists, there is often disagreement on details.

As well, island information is constantly changing: new roads are built; new stores open and old ones close; new trails and shore accesses are developed while older ones become overgrown or vanish because of new development. I apologize for any discrepancies caused by such changes and for any errors or omissions.

*Brooks Point Regional Park is typical of Gulf Islands picturesque.*
Capital Regional District Parks

*The beautifully contorted arbutus tree keeps its leaves year-round but sheds its thin outer bark to reveal the trunk.*

# How to Use This Book

This book is designed to be user-friendly. The first section introduces you to the Gulf Islands and provides information on their natural features, history, wildlife and what you can expect to find when you're there. I've also included information on hikers' responsibilities, what to bring when hiking, some safety considerations and information about public parks and Crown (government-owned) land.

The main part of this book—the islands and their walks and hikes—is arranged alphabetically, beginning with Bowen and ending with Thetis, with a supplementary section on marine parks. In addition to information on the different walks and hikes, you'll find information on island history, how to get to each island, accommodation and services. A separate section in each chapter highlights the more gentle walks, and for those who want to combine exploring on land with exploring on the water, each chapter concludes with paddling suggestions.

You'll find a map that provides an overview of the island at the beginning of each chapter, although only main roads and those mentioned in the text are labelled. This map also identifies the location and often a simple trail outline of the hikes (by number), the main shopping area(s), public shore accesses, parks, Indian reserves and, often, Crown land. Additional maps are provided for the more involved hikes. These are simply schematic diagrams to give you an overview of trail systems; while they are often based on GPS data, they rarely include topography or physical features. Because the maps are necessarily small, their scales are approximations, and you will find the distances provided in the hike descriptions more reliable. Wherever you can, try to obtain larger-scale maps than can be provided in a book of this size. These will be available from a variety of sources, including realtors, parks and recreation commissions, chamber of commerce information centres, hiking clubs and bookstores.

To help you decide which hikes to take, at-a-glance information is provided for each hiking trail described. This information includes a short description of the hike, its length, the time required to hike it, its degree of difficulty, how to access it and any cautions. Of course, the amount of time necessary for each hike will vary with your speed, how much time you have available and your interest in stopping to smell the Nootka roses. My estimates are based on about 4 kilometres per hour on flat ground and 2 kilometres per hour in hilly terrain, with additional time allowed for stops and for enjoying views and flora. A full description of each hike and its special features follows the summary. Individual trail maps have been provided for difficult-to-follow trails. To further help you choose which hikes to take, each is rated on the following five-star system:

| | |
|---|---|
| ★ | One-star hikes are the least interesting or beautiful. |
| ★★ | Two-star hikes are fairly pleasant but nothing spectacular. |
| ★ ★ ★ | Three-star hikes are definitely worth doing. |
| ★ ★ ★ ★ | Four-star hikes are really special but lack the variety of the five-star hikes. |
| ★ ★ ★ ★ ★ | Five stars are reserved for the most outstanding hikes: Bodega Ridge on Galiano; Mount Warburton Pike on Saturna; Mount Maxwell and Ruckle provincial parks on Salt Spring; Helliwell Provincial Park and the Cliff Trail on Mount Geoffrey on Hornby; Nugedzi Lakes on Quadra; and Kw'as Park Trails on Cortes. |

Keep in mind that everything is relative: even a one-star hike in the Gulf Islands is special when the great out-of-doors gives you pleasure.

Many of these hikes require a half or full day to complete, although there are many shorter walks. Shore and road walks are also listed for each island. For simplicity, all measurements are given in metric units (1 kilometre = 0.6 mile; 1 metre = 39.37 inches; 1 centimetre = 0.4 inches; 1 hectare = 2.5 acres).

You will find a resource section and an index at the end of the book. I hope you enjoy using the book as much as I enjoyed researching and writing it. Happy hiking!

## DISCLAIMER

The writer, editors and publisher of *Hiking the Gulf Islands* have made every effort to ensure the accuracy and completeness of the descriptions contained in this book, as well as the reader's awareness of accessibility, hazards and level of expertise involved in the activities described, but your own safety is ultimately up to you. We can take no responsibility for any loss or injury incurred by anyone using this book. If you spot any inaccuracies, please let us know.

# Introduction

A paradise to residents and visitors alike, the Gulf Islands are graced with the grandeur of mountains and sea, lush temperate rain forests and a climate that is rarely too cold, too hot, too wet or too dry. When I first discovered them two decades ago, I was captivated by their charms and I remain entranced.

Whether you are a laid-back nature lover or a hard-core trekker, the Gulf Islands have it all—from gentle walks through exquisite old-growth forest to rugged hikes with breathtaking views. As you follow the hikes in this book, you are certain to come across many of the natural features that make these islands unique: sandstone shores worn by wind and water into sculptural shapes, twisting arbutus trees and towering Douglas-fir, rolling farmland where sheep graze, rocky sun-kissed ridges, forest floors covered in thick layers of bright green moss and, in the spring, meadows dotted with wildflowers.

## SERVICES AND ACCOMMODATION
Services and accommodation vary with the seasons. If you come in the off-season (roughly from Thanksgiving in October through to the May long weekend), expect fewer accommodations, restaurants and shops to be open. If you come in the summer, be sure to reserve well ahead, as accommodations, including bed and breakfasts and campgrounds, are quickly filled. (Even in the off-season, reservations are useful, as campgrounds are often closed—especially on islands with no provincial parks—and many bed and breakfasts close for the season.)

In any season it's possible to buy food and find accommodation on every Gulf Island with ferry service. All the islands in this book have at least one restaurant, although it may not be open during weekdays in the off-season. Most islands also have at least one real estate office, which is often the best place to obtain a free map that notes local services and points of interest. As well, most of the islands have a service station (or gas pump), an ATM, a pub, a liquor outlet and at least one excellent bakery. Many also have a small RCMP detachment and stores that sell items such as hardware and clothing. All have arts and crafts shops and studios, which are open in season.

## A BRIEF HISTORY OF THE GULF ISLANDS
The Gulf Islands is actually a misnomer. When Captain George Vancouver charted the Strait of Georgia in 1792, he made a slight mistake. He at first thought he was sailing in a gulf, so he named it the Gulf of Georgia and the

islands in it became known as the Gulf Islands. Although Vancouver soon discovered the land mass that formed the western shore of his supposed gulf was a large island, the naming error wasn't corrected until 1865, when Captain George Henry Richards was surveying the area and renamed the gulf correctly as a strait. However, no one bothered to change the name of the islands—after all, "the Strait Islands" doesn't sound nearly as appealing.

Almost all the Gulf Islands share a similar history. For thousands of years they were inhabited by First Nations people, many of whom lived a semi-nomadic life, moving with the seasons and gathering, hunting and fishing the abundant flora and fauna along the coast. Our knowledge of their lives and settlements is derived mainly from the research of anthropologists who studied the people, and from archeological work connected with the many middens (shell and ash deposits) and other remains that have been found.

On July 15, 2010, a poignant ceremony took place in Esquimalt, BC, to commemorate the naming of a section of the waters around Vancouver Island the Salish Sea in honour of the First Nations peoples who have lived here for millennia. The Salish Sea encompasses the Strait of Georgia, Strait of Juan de Fuca and Puget Sound. It extends as far north as Desolation Sound in the Strait of Georgia and as far south as Tumwater, Washington, in Puget Sound. While both the Canadian and US governments have approved the name, the Salish Sea is meant to be an umbrella term for the bodies of water within it, and the original names will still be found on maps and marine charts.

The first non-aboriginal settlers arrived in the Gulf Islands in 1859. Under the Land Ordinance Act of 1870, settlers were allowed to pre-empt, or claim, up to 160 acres (65 hectares) of land if they lived on it for four years and made improvements equal to $2.50 per acre. When these requirements were met and the land had been surveyed, they could purchase it for a mere $1 per acre. The ownership almost completely ignored traditional First Nations claims to the land and many aboriginal people were displaced, though not without resistance.

Settlers did not have an easy go of it. Before they could begin farming they needed to clear the land of trees, and the rocky soil and lack of water made cultivation particularly challenging. Transportation problems added to the difficulties: there were no public wharves or roads for many years and settlers had to rely on their own boats to get their crops to market. However, many farmers did succeed, especially in the south. Well before orchards were developed in the Okanagan, Mayne and Salt Spring were known for their bountiful crops of fruit.

Communities grew more rapidly in the 1900s. Steamship service, and ultimately ferry service, linked some islands to Vancouver Island and others to the mainland; electricity and improved roads modernized island life; and the development of the islands began in earnest.

In recent decades tourism and the acquisition of recreational property have been strong factors in the development of most of the Gulf Islands. With improved services and the best climate in Canada, the islands now attract more newcomers each year, including many recent retirees seeking to spend their golden years in a golden locale. Tourism brings tens of thousands of visitors each year, which puts great pressure on available services and resources, especially water, which is in short supply on most Gulf Islands. As a result, growth is the greatest concern facing these islands in the 21st century.

## FLORA AND FAUNA

### Flora

The Gulf Islands lie in the rain shadow created by the mountains of Vancouver Island. While much of Vancouver Island and the mainland coast receive great amounts of precipitation, the Gulf Islands are relatively dry on a year-round basis. Most of the precipitation comes as rain during the fall and winter (from November to March), while drought conditions are often common during the summer. Because of the effect of the rain shadow the vegetation on the Gulf Islands is more diverse than the west coast of Vancouver Island.

Conifers such as giant Douglas-fir, grand fir, western hemlock and western red cedar are common to the islands. Sitka spruce and the occasional stand of western white pine and lodgepole pine can also be found. Among the islands' deciduous trees are the contorted Garry oak; the fascinating, evergreen arbutus (also known as madrone or madrona) with large, shiny leaves and drooping clusters of white flowers; and the expansive bigleaf maple. In areas where the forest has been cleared, coniferous cedar and fir are often naturally replaced by deciduous bitter cherry and red alder, which seem to grow quickly in wet organic areas. Garry Oak grows in dry, sunny, rocky areas, mainly along the coast from southern California to southwestern British Columbia.

Gulf Island shrubs include the evergreen hairy manzanita, which grows on wind-swept mountain slopes and has reddish bark, small, pink, urn-shaped flowers and coffee-coloured berries. Ocean spray, a tall shrub of the rose family, grows particularly well in sunny areas at the edge of the forest and has large clusters of tiny, creamy-white flowers.

*Prickly pear cactus is very common in the Gulf Islands.*

Salal and Oregon grape accompany Douglas-fir in drier areas, and sword fern is associated with cedar in wetter areas. A wide variety of mosses, lichen and fungi grow in moist forest habitats. The hardy skunk cabbage, with its distinctive yellow bloom and distinctive springtime odour, grows in marshy areas.

Visitors to the Gulf Islands are amazed by the variety and beauty of the wildflowers in the spring, perhaps the most beautiful season in the islands. At this time of year look for trilliums, rattlesnake plantain, vanilla leaf and calypso orchids in shady forests; Easter lilies, spring gold, blue camas, death camas, sea blush, shooting star, field chickweed, blue-eyed Mary, paintbrush, western buttercup and chocolate lily in sunny, open, dry, grassy and rocky areas along the coast and in arbutus and Garry oak meadows; star flowers in dry, open woods; broad-leaved stonecrop in rocky crevices on outcrops; and yellow monkey flower and skunk cabbage in wet areas.

## Fauna

One of the treats of being in the Gulf Islands is the opportunity to view wild-life in its natural habitat. Most of the easily observable animal and bird life on the Gulf Islands can be found in either the sea or the air. Large animals such as cougars, bears and wolves were systematically exterminated from the Gulf Islands years ago, although wolves and cougars have been reported on Quadra and Cortes and the occasional cougar or bear manages to swim across from Vancouver Island to other islands from time to time. The largest wild animals you are likely to see in the Gulf Islands are the blacktail deer, common enough in island gardens to act as a stimulus for the local fencing industry. Joining the deer in the forests and along the shores are such smaller animals as mice, squirrels, raccoons, mink, otters, muskrats, beavers and, of course, the giant, oozing banana slugs and their smaller, shiny black cousins.

Bald eagles are common in the Gulf Islands, where they are especially visible in the spring when they are rearing their young (look up to the tops of large, often dead trees, particularly near the sea). Among other large birds, vultures, ravens, hawks, owls, woodpeckers, grouse, jays, quail and crows are common. Ospreys are seen here and there. Among the more frequently

*One of Texada Island's many osprey nests.* Norman MacLean

seen smaller birds are wrens, towhees, sparrows, nuthatches, juncos, varied thrushes, band-tailed pigeons, kingfishers, hummingbirds, chickadees, robins and swallows.

Geese and ducks of many species, loons, sandpipers, cormorants, gulls, black oystercatchers and herons can all be spotted, especially during the colder months. In the winter the Gulf Islands become a birdwatchers' paradise, with large collections of waterfowl in the estuaries and bays that provide the birds with winter havens.

Gulf Island waters are home to seals, otters, sea lions and even dolphins and killer whales, as well as an abundance of sea life along the shore and in tide pools. When the tide goes out you might see oysters, mussels and little squirts of water from buried clams on some beaches. Look in the water for crabs and around rocks for black barnacles and purple, coral and white sea stars.

## RESPONSIBLE HIKING

The future of hiking in the Gulf Islands is really up to us, those who walk the trails, the shoreline and the roads. Some trails are on rights-of-way across private land and will remain available only as long as hikers respect the property rights and concerns of the owners and their neighbours. And while it is true that you might only "pass this way but once," others will follow you. If we are to continue using many of these trails, it is imperative that we treat the environment with care and behave responsibly.

Responsible hiking means respecting both the land and its owners— whether it is private property, Crown land or a national, provincial, regional or local park. In general, this often-given advice is still the best: take nothing but photographs; leave nothing but footprints.

Here are some guidelines for responsible hiking:

**Garbage in, garbage out:** Waste is a problem throughout the Gulf Islands. Few of the islands have their own landfills, so garbage must be transported off-island. Make sure that you leave nothing on the trails, and take as much of your garbage as possible off the island, where it can be disposed of without cost to the locals. Many hikers carry a spare plastic bag in which they collect any garbage they see along the trail.

**Be fire safe:** Fire is a constant and very real threat on the Gulf Islands, especially in the dry period from June to October. Most islands have only volunteer firefighters, and water to fight fires is often unavailable, especially on forest trails. Fires, even on beaches, are not allowed during the summer on many islands. As well, trails in the Gulf Islands are sometimes closed if the threat of fire is severe. Be sure to check for trail closures if you are visiting an island during hot weather.

It's best to avoid fires altogether or to restrict them to beaches below the high tide line. If you do build a fire, follow these BC Forest Service guidelines:

*Wildflowers are abundant on the Gulf Islands in the spring.* Lynn Thompson

- Prepare your campfire site by removing all leaves, twigs and other flammable material from an area extending at least 30 centimetres around the fire and down to mineral soil.
- Never light a campfire when strong winds are blowing.
- Build your campfire at least 3 metres from any flammable structure, slash or flammable debris.
- Equip yourself with a shovel and a full pail of water before you light your campfire.
- Keep the cooking fire small and hot for best results.
- Attend your campfire at all times and be certain it is extinguished before leaving.
- Report any suspicious fires you see to a forest ranger, property owner, the RCMP or call 1-800-663-5555 (a free, province-wide, forest fire emergency number) or *5555 from your cellular phone.

**Leash your dog:** Dogs should be leashed at all times. It is unfair to subject other hikers, local residents or wildlife to the boisterous or possibly aggressive behaviour of your dog. As well, sheep graze widely throughout the Gulf Islands and are easily spooked by dogs.

**Don't pick the flowers:** Resist picking any wildflowers, which is illegal in public parks. Bring a camera and take photos instead.

**Keep the noise down:** Hikers are seldom loud but it's worth noting that sound carries easily in the forest. Be especially wary about noise levels on trails that border private property.

**Take care with bikes and ATVs:** The increased popularity of mountain bikes, off-road motorcycles and all-terrain vehicles (ATVs), and their use on hiking trails, is a concern for many hikers. However, some trails in this book are open to both cyclists and hikers, and this combined interest group actually strengthens the lobby for the maintenance and extension of trails. If you ride a bike, use only trails on which bikes are permitted. In many places ignoring this advice may cause irreparable destruction of the land.

**Be aware of camping rules:** Camp only in designated campgrounds.

**Don't disturb trail markings:** The trails described in this book were either well marked or self-evident at time of writing. There should be no need to add your own markings to help you find your way back. However, if you are afraid of getting lost and decide to do this, do not blaze (slash) trees. Instead, tie surveyor's ribbon to branches and remove these ribbons on your return. Never remove trail markings already in place. In general, it is best to neither add nor remove trail markings to avoid misleading other hikers.

**Keep to the trails:** Trails in the Gulf Islands often run across land that is vulnerable to erosion and the destruction of fragile mosses, ground cover and wildflowers. Some trails are on or skirt private property and their continued existence depends on the goodwill of local property owners. For these reasons hikers should stick to the trails at all times and avoid creating shortcuts.

**No trespassing on private land:** If you are hiking on private land, be sure that you have the property owner's permission. If you are on public land, do not venture onto private land. If you are hiking along beaches, stay below the high tide line. (In Canada, generally all the foreshore—the land between the high and low tide lines—is public.) While this book contains occasional references to private properties that landowners have generously allowed hikers to use in the past and that might even be signed as if they were public, trails on such land are not described, and I recommend that you secure the landowners' permission before using their land.

All Indian reserves, and there are several in the Gulf Islands, are private. Permission to hike on First Nations land may be granted if you contact the relevant band. Contact information is included on page 320.

**Respect the middens:** Middens, indicated by soil containing broken shells, often mixed with ash-black dirt, can be found fronting the shore throughout the Gulf Islands. These indicate places where aboriginal people once lived. As with petroglyphs (rock carvings) and pictographs (rock paintings), middens are of great interest to archeologists and are protected by the Heritage Conservation Act. There are penalties for disturbing them.

## WHAT TO BRING

I can say with some assurance that you'll never have everything you want with you when you go hiking. Still, if you're like me and lug along everything but the kitchen sink, you'll come pretty close to having everything you need.

**Footwear:** Good footwear is essential. Although I have come to prefer the security of waterproof hiking boots, for most of the hikes described in this book running shoes with good treads would be fine, except in wet conditions.

I like wearing a pair of thick woollen or synthetic hiking socks. Most hikers avoid cotton socks because they don't wick away perspiration, take longer to dry and remain cold when wet.

**Clothes:** Good synthetic or merino wool fabrics have generally replaced cotton for most vigorous activities because of their ability to stay relatively dry and to dry quickly when they do become wet. I always wear a hat for protection against cold and the sun. In any season I like the layered approach because it lets you peel off clothes as you warm up and put them back on when you cool off or when it begins to rain. In cooler weather I wear a lightweight fleece and a dry-shell jacket. I keep a pair of gloves, a small hat or toque, paper and pencil and plastic bags (for garbage) in my pockets.

**Daypacks:** You'll probably want to carry a daypack for extra clothes, including a bathing suit (in case the weather co-operates and there's a good place to swim). My lunch also goes into my daypack, sometimes in a plastic container to keep my food from getting horribly squashed. Don't forget to include water or another thirst-quenching drink (lots on a hot day!). I also carry a small, collapsible umbrella on really threatening days.

*Other than cotton shorts, everything I'm wearing is synthetic, lightweight and comfortable. My backpack contains a first-aid kit and most of what's listed in the "What to Bring" section of this book.* Craig Carpenter

**Walking sticks:** Many hikers like to carry a walking stick or pair of poles. Poles help you maintain your balance, especially when going downhill. They are also useful for deflecting stinging nettles, thistles and spider webs.

**Miscellaneous items:** My fanny pack or daypack contains a lot of extra stuff. You'll want to bring along this guidebook, of course, and any maps for the area you're hiking. My pack and pockets also contain:

- a compass
- sunscreen
- a sewing kit (like the ones provided by travel agents or hotels)
- a first-aid kit, including moleskin or liquid bandage (to put on at the first hint of a developing blister)
- a Swiss army knife (the kind with useful tools)
- surveyor's tape (to tie to trees to mark the path, so you don't get hopelessly lost on your return trip)

- a small flashlight (for evening walking or for exploring caves)
- a small pair of binoculars
- carabiners to attach things (like a jacket) to your pack
- pens, pencils, paper, elastics, paperclips, Post-its (for leaving messages)
- extra shoelaces or string
- tissues and biodegradable toilet paper (just in case)
- sunglasses, reading glasses or extra glasses and a strap to hold them on
- a sweatband and a pack towel (which takes up almost no room and is incredibly effective for those spur-of-the-moment swims)
- waterproof matches/fire-starting kit
- snacks (e.g., granola bars, chocolate bars, trail mix, packages of salt and pepper, teabags)
- a GPS (Global Positioning System) receiver and extra batteries
- a cellphone for emergencies (NB: they do not work everywhere in the Gulf Islands)
- a wallet and a digital camera
- a plastic poncho for absolute downpours (especially when you aren't wearing a waterproof jacket)
- a whistle or other noisemaker
- a thermal blanket (garbage bags can also help you conserve body heat and stay dry in cold or wet weather)
- plastic or foam for sitting on wet ground
- a large orange garbage bag for an emergency shelter and to help rescuers find you if you're lost
- a tide table
- field guides to plants and birds (if not too heavy)

This is my personal list. At some time or other I've used almost every item on it. Undoubtedly there are different lists to suit individual needs, but this should give you some ideas.

One final word about first-aid kits. Some people feel they are essential. I have started carrying a selection of the following items:

- antacid tablets
- antibiotic ointment, anti-itch ointment
- alcohol swabs
- ASA tablets/Tylenol/ibuprofen, antihistamine tablets
- cotton swabs, absorbent cotton
- tensor bandage

- sterile gauze dressings, roll of 2.5-centimetre adhesive tape
- tongue depressors (for use as finger splints)
- matches or a lighter (for sterilizing)
- tweezers, scissors, safety pins, elastic bands
- variety of bandages/dressings
- an oral thermometer

Even if you never use these things yourself, you will find someone who needs them, and that's a great way to make new friends.

## SAFETY CONSIDERATIONS

Hikers frequently get lost. I certainly have—and you might, too. If you do "misplace" yourself, you'll probably manage to find your own way out. However, it's wise to take precautions to prevent getting lost and to avoid discomfort, injury or even death. Take responsibility for your own safety. Here are a few suggestions:

- Know your limits. Don't attempt a hike that is beyond your ability, strength or the time you have available.
- Before you leave, ensure that you know where you're going. Read the maps and trail descriptions carefully and take maps and a compass along, since directions are often difficult to determine, particularly on cloudy days in a BC forest or when trail markings are limited.
- Let someone know where you're going, how long you'll be, the number of people in your party and when you plan to return, so there's someone who has enough information to know where to look for you if you're not back at a reasonable time.
- Don't hike alone. You're much safer with a partner.
- Don't leave too late in the day; be sure there's ample time to return before dark. This is especially important in the fall and winter, when there's less daylight.
- Keep to designated trails. Some are recognizable only by the pathway created by the passing of many hikers, while others may be marked by surveyor's ribbon, plastic or metal markers, or slashes or spray paint on trees. In some places cairns are used where it is difficult to mark the trail in any other way. Cairns may also be used to indicate a change in direction. Where alternative trails exist, stones and branches are often placed to block them off, indicating a side trail. Deadfalls can often obscure main trails, and other trail markings are easily removed, naturally or otherwise. Take great care to follow the correct trail.

- Wear appropriate clothes and footwear for the area. It's also important to carry extra clothes, even if it's quite warm when you leave home. Hypothermia is one of the most common causes of distress, and even death, for lost hikers.
- Carry emergency equipment as suggested under What to Bring, page 19.
- If you do get lost, keep calm and remain in a place where rescuers can see you. Do not leave the trail, even if it's obvious you're on the wrong one. It's much more difficult to find a hiker who has taken off through the bush.
- In addition to mosquitoes and wasps, hikers should beware of ticks, especially from early spring to late summer. Hikers can discourage tick bites by wearing long-sleeved shirts and full-length pants secured at the ankles. If you suspect that you are hiking in a tick-infested area, be sure to check for them when you return from your outing. If hiking with a dog, you should also check your pet. Bites by coastal ticks seldom create complications, although they may cause infection or a condition called Lyme disease. If you experience a circular rash or flu-like symptoms following a bite, see a doctor immediately.
- Be cautious of eating any shellfish before first checking for possible contamination areas with Fisheries and Oceans Canada (1-866-431-3474; www.pac.dfo-mpo.gc.ca/psp).
- Never pick and eat any wild mushroom without being able to identify it with absolute certainty. Unwary pickers are killed every year from eating poisonous mushrooms.

## A NOTE ABOUT TIDES

As so many of the shore walks in this book are possible only at low tide, you should know something about tides. In general, you can expect two high tides and two low tides each day in the Gulf Islands. Depending on the time of year, the difference between high and low tide may range from nothing to 4 metres. In general, a tide that is at its lowest when you start your hike will be at its highest approximately 6 hours later, and the beach trail you followed may have completely disappeared. Unless you are on Crown land or in a park, this can force you to trespass on private property to make your way back. Worse, you may be completely stranded. For this reason it is essential to check the tide tables before starting out and schedule your movements accordingly if any part of your hike crosses the intertidal zone.

*The sandstone along Gulf Islands' shores is an infinitely fascinating series of sculptures best viewed from the water.*

## PUBLIC PARKS AND CROWN LAND

Most of the trails described in this book are found in public parks, which are in some of the most beautiful spots on the Gulf Islands. These parks are managed by several different jurisdictions and have been established for different reasons.

**Community parks:** Many Gulf Islands have parks and recreation commissions that administer local parks. Increasingly, new local parks, usually for day use only, are being created under provincial laws that require up to 5 percent of all new developments to be dedicated to public use. These new parks often include trail networks. Local parks and recreation commissions also obtain statutory rights-of-way over shore accesses, which are often outfitted with a bench or picnic table.

**Regional parks:** Regional governments maintain these parks for a variety of recreational uses. They are open year-round and are usually larger than municipal parks and often more accessible than provincial parks.

**Provincial parks:** The province's parks, many of which are marine parks (usually accessible only by water), provide users with outdoor recreational opportunities, while conserving the natural environment. No mineral exploration or commercial development is permitted inside any of the parks described in this book at time of writing. Provincial parks are administered by the Ministry of Environment. You can find information on provincial parks on the BC Parks website, www.env.gov.bc.ca/bcparks. Provincial parks are considered Crown land and currently make up over 14 percent of all the land in British Columbia.

**Crown land:** The provincial government manages Crown (or public) land. A significant portion of this land—including provincial parks, ecological reserves and Ministry of Forests land—is available for public recreational activities, such as camping and hiking. Some of the trails described in this book have been developed co-operatively by the Ministry of Forests and members of the community. Crown lands that have not been designated as provincial parks or ecological reserves are often referred to as "vacant" or "unallocated," which means that no decision has been made as to how they may ultimately be used. Outdoor enthusiasts hope the government can be persuaded to convert this land into parks to protect it for future public use.

Anyone has the right to enter vacant Crown land. A Ministry of Forests resource officer explained that the general rule for Crown land is "use it but don't abuse it, and don't steal from it." For our purposes this means that you can camp and hike on this land. However, you are not allowed to remove anything (mushrooms, firewood, cedar boughs, etc.), especially for commercial purposes.

There are well-established trails, used by local residents, on Crown land throughout the Gulf Islands. Where possible, these trails are described in this book. Crown land is often surrounded by private land and can be accessed only by crossing private property. If this is the case, you must first get permission of the landowners.

**Ecological reserves:** Ecological reserves have been established on selected pieces of Crown land to preserve representative and special natural ecosystems, rare and endangered plants and animals, and unique, rare or outstanding features and phenomena. They are not created for outdoor recreation. Although most ecological reserves are open for non-destructive observational uses such as wildlife viewing and photography, recreational use is discouraged. The primary uses of ecological reserves are research and educational

*Stunning views from Salt Spring Island are the reward for a steep climb up Mount Erskine.* Bob Davidson

activities. While the government does not encourage hikers to walk in ecological reserves, hiking is allowed in them.

**The Gulf Islands National Park Reserve (GINPR):** This national park was officially established in May 2003 to protect a representative portion of the Strait of Georgia Lowlands Natural Region—one of Canada's 39 distinct natural regions. The park currently includes properties on 15 islands, plus numerous small islets and reef areas. With a total area of 36 square kilometres (including a 25-metre intertidal zone), it is Canada's fifth-smallest national park. The park reserve will continue to grow as additional lands are purchased or donated. An additional 26 square kilometres of adjacent waters, generally extending 200 metres from the mean low tide mark, are also protected and managed by Parks Canada. The park's main office is in Sidney, and there are smaller field offices on North Pender and Saturna islands.

At time of writing the services and facilities for visitors in the park reserve included two drive-in campgrounds—McDonald Campground close to the Swartz Bay ferry terminal on Vancouver Island (near the town of Sidney) and Prior Centennial Campground on North Pender Island—and walk-in campsites at McDonald Campground, Narvaez Bay on Saturna, Beaumont on South Pender Island and Sidney Spit (via pedestrian ferry from Sidney). Boat-in camping is also possible in the latter three sites as well as on D'Arcy Island, Isle-de-Lis (Rum Island), Portland Island (Princess Margaret), Prevost Island and Cabbage Island. Organized picnic facilities exist at Georgina Point and Bennett Bay on Mayne Island, Winter Cove on Saturna Island, Roesland on North Pender Island, Russell Island and Sidney Spit. Mooring buoys for boaters are provided at Sidney Spit, Beaumont and Cabbage Island, and an overnight dock is available at Sidney Spit. In the summer months national park personnel conduct interpretive programs. For more information about the park, visit www.pc.gc.ca/gulf.

# Bowen

**R**esidents of Bowen view their island as a rural paradise within commuting distance of Vancouver. One of the larger and more populated of the Gulf Islands, Bowen is about 52 square kilometres and home to around 3,700 full-time residents, with another 1,800 visitors in the summer. Most of the island's amenities, including a general store, restaurants and craft shops, are centred in quaint Snug Cove, the location of the ferry terminal and a magnet for Vancouverites seeking a quick escape from the "Big Smoke."

*Snug Cove, Bowen's capital, from the ferry.*

From Snug Cove you can walk to beaches, Killarney Lake or into lush forest. Because of its steep terrain and shortage of good farmland, the centre of the island is largely undeveloped and you can easily spend a day walking its paths in quiet contemplation. Promoted by locals as the Island of Walks, Bowen has established trail networks in Crippen Regional Park and Mount Gardner, and hiking enthusiasts are working to connect these with the rest of the island.

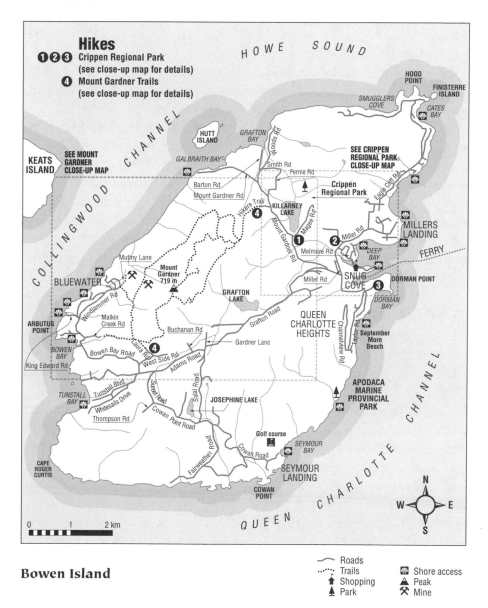

**Bowen Island**

## HISTORY

For centuries, the Squamish people visited the island they called *Xwlil'xhwm*—"fast drumming ground"—to hunt and fish. In 1791 Spanish explorers named it Isla de Apodaca in honour of a Spanish naval officer. Less than 70 years later the British renamed the island after one of their naval heroes, Rear Admiral James Bowen. Bowen's first settlers established farms on the island in the 1870s and supplemented their income by fishing, hunting and logging. From the 1890s on, cottage communities began to develop at Snug Cove, Bluewater, Eagle Cliff, Hood Point, Cowan Point, Miller's Landing, Tunstall Bay and Deep Bay.

Early industry included two brick factories in Deep Bay and an explosives factory in Tunstall Bay. In the early 1900s numerous unsuccessful attempts were made to mine gold and copper but, as Captain John A. Cates discovered when he began a ferry service between Bowen and Vancouver around the turn of the century, recreation was the island's real pay dirt. For more than 20 years Cates brought vacationers to his resort in Deep Bay. In 1920 Cates sold the resort to the Union Steamship Company, which went on to build a small tourism empire that included a hotel, stables and bridle paths, tennis courts, a bowling green, a tea room, a dance pavilion, cottages, a store and picnic grounds. Until the company was sold in 1962, Bowen was like a company town centred around Snug Cove. Today, despite its relatively large number of year-round residents, the Municipality of Bowen Island retains its rural charm.

## GETTING THERE

There are hourly 20-minute ferry sailings, from early morning to late night, from Horseshoe Bay (near Vancouver) to Snug Cove on Bowen Island. For information, obtain a BC Ferries schedule or contact BC Ferries (see page 320).

English Bay Launch Ltd. provides a 30- to 35-minute service from both Granville Island and Coal Harbour in Vancouver to Snug Cove. For more information call 604-484-8497 or visit http://englishbaylaunch.ca/. Cormorant Marine (604-250-2630 or 604-947-2243) offers a late-night water taxi service between Snug Cove and Horseshoe Bay.

## SERVICES AND ACCOMMODATION

Bowen's shopping area is relatively small but includes a good range of stores, restaurants and services. Most businesses are either in Snug Cove or Artisan Square, a short walk from the ferry dock. Bowen has many bed and breakfasts and rental cottages, including some of the original Union Steamship cottages; however, the island has no camping facilities. The Bowen Island Historians Museum and Archives (1014 Miller Road; 604-947-2655; www.bowenhistory. ca), funded and managed by volunteers, is open to visitors four days a week.

The Bowen Island Community Shuttle's two routes (Bluewater and Eagle Cliff) connect with incoming and outgoing ferries. Although there might be long periods of time to wait, the shuttle does make it possible to get around most of the island without a car (check www.translink.bc.ca or call 604-947-9775 or 604-947-0229). As well, most of the hikes described in this chapter can easily be reached on foot from the ferry.

*The Bowen Map and Guide*, which includes maps and trail information, is available from the Bowen Island Chamber of Commerce (604-947-9024; e-mail: info@bowenisland.org; or www.bowenisland.org). A visitor's information centre is open in Snug Cove during the summer. You can also obtain information on Bowen from the island's municipal website, www.bimbc.ca.

## ESPECIALLY FOR WALKERS

There's lots of walking within easy reach of the Snug Cove ferry terminal and marinas. In addition to the shore and road walks described below, try Crippen Regional Park (see hikes 1 and 2). You might also explore the Bowen Island Greenway, which now connects Crown land on Mount Gardner with Crown land to the southwest. The main access is off Sunset Road, 1.3 kilometres from Adams Road. Parking is on the right-hand side of the road. This trail network is under development and may eventually connect to trails around Cape Roger Curtis. Contact the Bowen Island Parks and Recreation Commission (604-947-2216 or biprc@bimbc.ca) for information.

## HIKES on BOWEN

Bowen's main hikes are on trails within 240-hectare Crippen Regional Park (12.5 kilometres of trails) and on Crown land on Mount Gardner. A brochure on Crippen Regional Park is available from the Bowen Island Tourist Info Centre, or from the Metro Vancouver Regional District Parks Department's website, www.metrovancouver.org/services/parks_lscr/regionalparks/Pages/Crippen.aspx. You can also view the trails on the illustrated map showing the location of all of Bowen's trails on the information board in front of the Bowen Public Library (once the Union Steamship Store) to your right as you leave the ferry.

## 1. Killarney Lake Loop Trail (Crippen Regional Park) ★★★

| | |
|---|---|
| Trail length | 4-kilometre round trip |
| Time required | 1.5 hours, including time to enjoy the vegetation |
| Description | This pretty walk around a shallow lake passes through boggy areas and over boardwalks through marsh. |
| Level | Easy |
| Access | Either from the picnic area at the intersection of Magee Road and Mount Gardner Road or from 800 metres farther north on Mount Gardner Road on the west side of the lake |
| Cautions | Wear waterproof shoes or boots, as parts of the trail can be swampy. |

*Note: This hike can be combined with either the Killarney Creek Trail (see hike 2) or the Cedar Trail (see map, page 33), both of which run southeast from Magee Road.*

*Bowen retains many old-growth trees as testified by this giant cedar with its intriguing cavity that invites exploration.*

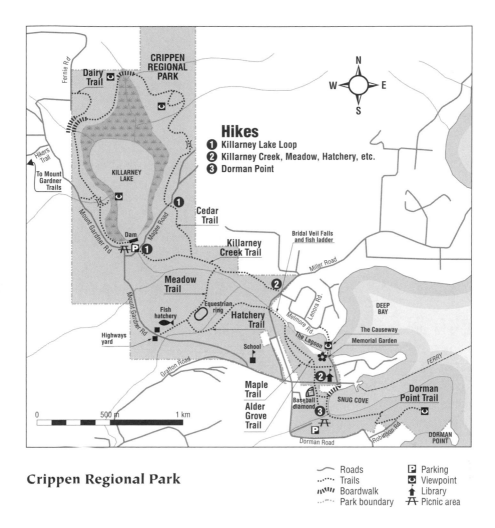

**Crippen Regional Park**

| | Roads | | Parking |
|---|---|---|---|
| | Trails | | Viewpoint |
| | Boardwalk | | Library |
| | Park boundary | | Picnic area |

Walking east from the picnic area, you pass a dam that controls the lake's water level and the flow of water to the fish ladders in Killarney Creek. Follow Magee Road for a short distance until you regain the trail (on the left), which follows the east side of the lake. There are several creeks and some small falls within the lake area.

The trail climbs steadily to the northeast and passes a flooded area before reaching a boardwalk that crosses a marsh at the northern tip of the lake. At the western end of the lake is a drowned forest, where you'll find stands of Sitka spruce. Labrador tea, sundew, western bog laurel and sweet gale grow in the low-lying areas along this part of the trail. Keep your eyes open for waterfowl, especially in the spring.

| 2. Killarney Creek, Meadow, Hatchery, Alder Grove, School and Maple Trails (Crippen Regional Park) ★★★ | |
|---|---|
| Trail length | About 3.5 kilometres of trail in total, depending on route taken |
| Time required | 1-2 hours, depending on route taken |
| Description | These interconnecting trails pass through lovely red cedar forest, as well as by a waterfall, a fish hatchery and a fish ladder. |
| Level | Easy |
| Access | From two points on Magee Road near Killarney Lake; two points on Miller Road; near the municipal works yard on Mount Gardner Road; and near the Bowen Island Library in Snug Cove |

The Killarney Creek Trail runs between Miller Road (from an access opposite Lenora Road) and Magee Road. It passes through a forest of alder, maple, cedar and hemlock. The Meadow Trail, branching off the Killarney Creek Trail to the southwest, crosses a swampy meadow, passes through alder, nears an equestrian ring and ends a short distance past a fish hatchery. From between the equestrian ring and the hatchery, the Hatchery Trail leads back to Miller Road through dense red cedar forest, which also contains western hemlock and Sitka spruce.

Across Miller Road the trail leads to a fish ladder and Bridal Veil Falls. The trail branches slightly south of here. If you go left (southeast) along Alder Grove Trail toward the Memorial Garden, you can descend to a trail that leads to the causeway dividing a pretty lagoon from Deep Bay. Along the way there is a lovely view of the entrance to Deep Bay. The lagoon is a great place to observe waterfowl and, nearby, you'll find an access to the beach on Deep Bay.

From the lagoon the trail climbs to Melmore Road. Turn left on Melmore Road, then left on Lenora Road to rejoin Miller Road. Alternatively, you can follow the trail back down to the library, cross the road and follow the board-walk to the Dorman Point Trail.

## 3. DORMAN POINT TRAIL (CRIPPEN REGIONAL PARK) ★★★

| | |
|---|---|
| Trail length | 2 kilometres return |
| Time required | 1 hour |
| Description | The trail climbs steadily to a point above Snug Cove that overlooks West Vancouver. |
| Level | Moderate, with one fairly steep ascent |
| Access | From the boardwalk on the left (south) side of the main street at the first intersection you reach after leaving the ferry (opposite the library). Park in the lot beside the boardwalk. There's a second access to the point from the end of Robinson Road. |
| Cautions | The climb is very steep, especially from the end of Robinson Road. The cliffs at the top fall off steeply, so don't get too close to the edge. |

The trail was originally built to service a microwave repeater tower used for communication on the Howe Sound portion of the BC Rail line, but has since been decommissioned. It ascends the hill partly on stairs and partly along an old logging road that begins at the end of Robinson Road. The picnic area at the trailhead is very pretty, as are the views of the arbutus-clad summit of Whytecliff Park in West Vancouver and the Point Grey neighbourhood of Vancouver in the distance. Ferries pass back and forth below.

## 4. MOUNT GARDNER TRAILS ★★★★

| | |
|---|---|
| Trail length | 8 kilometres for the loop described here |
| Time required | 5 hours round trip, allowing time for lunch and long looks at the spectacular views |
| Description | The trails—partly old logging roads—climb fairly steeply. Depending on the route taken, there are excellent views of the Sunshine Coast to the west and Vancouver to the east. The trail signage on the mountain has been recently improved. Look for descriptions carved into signposts at major junctions. |

| Level | Moderate to strenuous |
|---|---|
| Elevation | 719 metres |
| Access | A. From the ferry follow the signage to Killarney Lake. The main access is 500 metres up Hikers Trail Road, a gravel road that runs west off Mount Gardner Road (between electrical poles 490 and 491) about 500 metres past the entrance to Crippen Regional Park at Magee Road (Killarney Lake). The trailhead is about 3 kilometres from the ferry dock. |
| | B. There are two access points to the trails on the west side of the island in Bluewater. Take the bus or drive to the end of Windjammer Road where you will find Mutiny Lane, a short, bumpy dirt road that takes you to the signboard at the trailhead. Mine Trail, on the right side of Mutiny Lane, rises steeply and soon passes an old mine shaft on the left about 100 metres along from the trailhead. Bluewater Trail begins about 300 metres farther, on the right side of the water storage tank. |
| | C. On the west side of the island the Laura Road trailhead, at the end of Laura Road (off West Side Road), is the steepest access to the summit. It is known locally as Bowen's Grouse Grind. Follow the orange metal signs on trees to avoid trespassing on private property. You will find a map kiosk in the parking area near the trailhead. You can reach this access by bus from the ferry at certain times of the day. |
| Cautions | Follow the Mount Gardner trail map carefully, as the mountain is honeycombed with old and new trails and many old logging roads. |

This description assumes that you start from access A. From Mount Gardner Road it's about 500 metres (15 minutes) up Hikers Trail Road to a steel gate. Almost immediately look for a "Skid Trail" sign on the left. The trail is

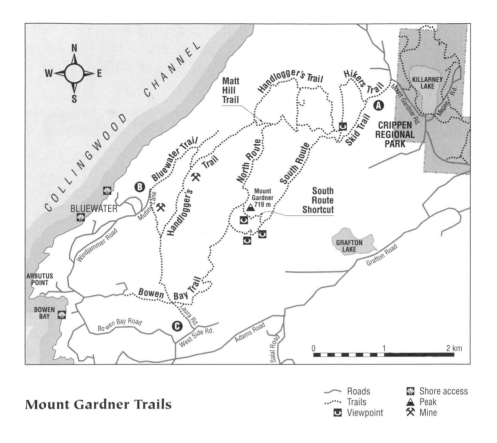

**Mount Gardner Trails**

Roads — Shore access
Trails ···· Peak ▲
Viewpoint ◙ Mine ✗

flagged with red metal markers on trees. It crosses a stream and begins to climb almost immediately. After another kilometre (about 15 minutes), the trail reaches a junction. Continue straight up Mount Gardner South Route.

Continue for about 2 kilometres (about 1 hour) until you reach another junction. The trail to the right is a shortcut to the summit but it's very steep. I recommend that you continue straight ahead. Within a few minutes you reach a great viewpoint and then a wetland. About 500 metres farther you reach another junction. Continue straight ahead (north) to reach the summit. The trail to the left descends to Bowen Bay.

The trail to the summit actually descends before rising again. Just before the summit you reach another junction where the north and south routes meet. Go right to reach the north summit. Here you have views from two helipads used to service the communications towers that dot the mountain-top. The first helipad you'll reach faces south and west toward Vancouver Island and the Gulf Islands. The second helipad faces north toward Gambier Island and up the Squamish Valley. The Sunshine Coast is to the west.

From the summit retrace your steps to the junction of the north and south routes. Continue right on the north route until you regain Hikers Trail Road (the old logging road). Stay on the right at the fork on this road and return down to the trailhead.

## SHORE AND ROAD WALKS

**Trans Island Pathway System (TIPS):** The Bowen Island Parks and Recreation Commission has been developing a trans-island pathway. The gravel trail starts at the top of Tunstall Boulevard and runs toward Snug Cove, along the north side of the road edge. Where sections of the trail are not complete, hikers walk along the road's narrow shoulder. Coming from Snug Cove, you'll find the beginning of the trail across the street from the community school.

**Tunstall Boulevard and Bay:** Walk along Tunstall Boulevard down to Tunstall Bay on the southwest side of the island. When you reach the sea, you can walk along the beach at low tide for a short distance. You will pass the remains of a brick chimney from the explosives factory that once operated on this site. Behind it is the Tunstall Bay Community Association recreation centre. There is an outhouse at this shore access.

**Cromie Road Trail:** A 10–15-minute trail from opposite 1410 Adams Road descends to Cromie Road, a lane that leads to Whitesails Drive. From here you might continue to the shore access at the bottom of Tunstall Boulevard to check out the remains of the explosives factory on the beach (see Tunstall Boulevard above).

**Quarry Park trails:** (see map on page 39) Bowen municipality's first community park (15.4 hectares) is accessed from a signed trailhead off Cowan Point Drive, about 500 metres southeast of its intersection with Thompson Road, as well as from a signed trail at the end of Thompson Road. The 700-metre walking trail circles a pond and will take you about 20 minutes to complete. Another trail continues past a rocky sculptural installation created by the Bowen Island Garden Club and into the neighbouring parcel of Crown land. The trails on the Crown land are not signed and are quite slippery and wet much of the year, so use caution if you walk them. Quarry Park is part of the Bowen Island greenway, which ultimately will allow hikers to walk from Mount Gardner to the ocean.

**Headwaters Park Trail:** This loop trail starts opposite Quarry Park off Cowan Point Drive, about 500 metres southeast of Thompson Road. The pretty trail crosses a pond that feeds Terminal Creek and a lovely bridge over a cattail-filled wetland. You can combine this short walk with the walks in Quarry Park.

**Cowan Point development and golf course trails and Seymour Bay shore access:** There are many trails along the forested roads in this development at the end of Cowan Point Drive, as well as a trail along the perimeter of the golf course. There's also a trail to a shore access on Seymour Bay, just past the golf course.

**Buchanan Road Trail:** There are two trails: the first starts opposite 1257 Adams Road and reaches a tiny playground after about 5 minutes; the second starts about 150 metres along Buchanan Road (off Adams Road). This 1.2-kilometre loop trail can also be accessed from Gardner Lane and includes 700 metres along the road. The latter section is part of the Bowen Island Trans Island Pathway System, which is often no wider than the shoulder of the road.

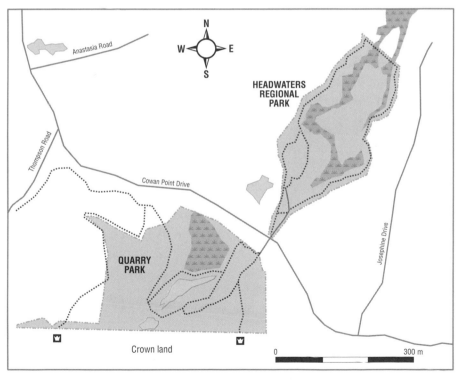

**Headwaters Park and Quarry Park**

Roads
Trails
Park boundary
Crown land

**Bowen Bay:** Another pretty beach at the junction of Bowen Bay Road and Windjammer Road boasts an outhouse, a wheelchair-accessible path and an extensive parking area. Walk along the driftwood-strewn gravel beach, by rocky outcrops and past the many summer cottages that line this shore.

**Malkin Creek Trail:** This 25-minute loop trail through pretty forest can be accessed from the driveway at 1621 Malkin Creek Road (at its end and the intersection of Amelia Lane) or from Bowen Bay Road just north of Holdings Road. Turn right at each of the first two junctions you meet. These take you into Evergreen Estates, where the trail follows the development roads or the paths beside them. When you see a trail to the left of Amelia Lane, take it down to Malkin Creek Road where you began. You will cross the creek near this point in the walk.

**King Edward Bay:** A short trail leads to this shore access at the end of King Edward Road (off Windjammer Road).

**Windjammer Road:** Windjammer Road, in the same neighbourhood as Bowen Bay, makes a pleasant road walk. At the northern end by power pole number 873 (near the driveway of 974 Windjammer Road), a path leads to steps that descend to the beach. A stream enters the sea at this beach. Farther along, if there has been sufficient rainfall, another stream cascades to the ocean as a small waterfall.

**Queen Charlotte Heights:** The Queen Charlotte Heights area provides views of Vancouver. To access a trail to September Morn Beach, follow Hummingbird Lane to the cul-de-sac at the end of the road. Stairs lead down to a pebble beach with views of Vancouver and West Vancouver.

**Snug Cove:** The walking around Snug Cove is delightful. Follow a trail to the viewpoint at Dorman Point (see hike 3) or a trail that climbs to Melmore Road, passing a lagoon on the left and the Deep Bay beach on your right. In the fall you might see salmon trying to climb the fish ladder into the lagoon. The roads in this area offer water views and are interesting to explore. Melmore connects to Lenora Road, which joins with Miller Road.

**Miller Road:** Miller Road passes a wide variety of houses and provides many views of the sea. It's possible to descend to Miller's Landing, but you can't walk along the shore.

**Dairy Trail:** Dairy Trail leaves the northwest corner of the Killarney Lake Loop Trail and connects with Fernie Road (turn right), which soon turns into

Smith Road. This multi-use trail is shared by hikers, cyclists and equestrians. To make a good walk, turn left on Woods Road and then right on Mount Gardner Road to eventually reach the Mount Gardner dock on Galbraith Bay. From the parking lot at Killarney Lake, this excursion would take you about 90 minutes return.

**Hood Point:** Be sure to take Eagle Cliff Road north to Hood Point and visit the beach at Cates Bay. Park near the private tennis courts (on the left) and continue east along a flat, straight trail that accesses a staircase to the beach. Hood Point was originally a completely private cottage development. Although many of the cottages have been replaced by large, modern homes, the Hood Point development still looks like a cottage area. Respect private property by keeping to the road, trail and beach.

## AND IF YOU PADDLE . . .

Paddling around Bowen is not for beginners. There can be a fair bit of traffic, as well as strong currents in Queen Charlotte Channel between Bowen and the mainland. Before heading out be sure to check your tide and current tables carefully. This said, the Bowen shore is beautiful and fairly accessible. You will not want to miss Apodaca Provincial Park. This 8-hectare marine park, bordered by private property, is a beautiful spot to walk. The rocky cliffs that line the shore invite exploration. The pristine gravel beaches make great picnic sites and you can climb the banks for views over Queen Charlotte Channel.

Here are some launching sites:

**Tunstall Bay or Bowen Bay:** These neighbouring beaches both have good access, outhouses and ample parking. You can paddle to the left (southwest) along Bowen's relatively undeveloped shore to Cape Roger Curtis. This is also the best access to the popular group of islands around Pasley Island off Bowen's west side. Paddlers should be aware that there are few places to pull out between Bluewater and Galbraith Bay to the north.

**Galbraith Bay:** The government dock (Mount Gardner dock) is a good place to launch. From here you can explore Bowen's northern shore, as well as nearby Hutt Island. Parking is very limited in this area during all but the winter months.

**Hood Point:** From the access on Cates Bay at Hood Point, explore the northern tip of Bowen, including tiny Finisterre Island just offshore. There's no road access to the shore to the west until you reach Grafton Bay.

**Deep Bay:** This is a good spot to launch at high tide. It gives you access to Bowen's busiest waters, so paddle carefully. Keep well away from the ferry, which docks in Snug Cove to the south, and be careful of its wash. Farther south, the shore around Dorman Point and down to Cowan Point is well worth paddling. Plan to stop on one of the small beaches at Apodaca Provincial Park and climb a trail to one of the viewpoints for a picnic lunch. The Deep Bay ocean access has an outhouse at Sandy Beach and is only a 5-minute walk from the ferry.

**Snug Cove:** While the ferry and heavy boat traffic can make paddling here stressful, people can wheel their kayaks off the ferry and launch from the nearby government dock. Kayakers should stick close to the shore and time their arrival and departure so as not to coincide with the ferry. From here you can paddle south toward Cowan Point or explore Deep Bay to the north.

*Many of Bowen's shorter trails afford outstanding views like this one of Bowen Bay with Pasley Island behind and Keats Island in the distance. This photo was taken from one of the trails in Evergreen Estates.*

# Cortes

*A*lternately grouped with the Discovery Islands and the Northern Gulf Islands, Cortes is located immediately east of Quadra. About 25 by 13 kilometres at its longest and widest points, respectively, it covers an area of 130 square kilometres. With a population of approximately 1,000, Cortes has a remote feel, although there is daily ferry service and public roads linking the main settlements: Mansons Landing (the largest); Whaletown; Squirrel Cove; and an area known as the Gorge. With the superb Kw'as Park trails and the fabulous kayaking provided by the island's intricate coastline, Cortes is well worth visiting.

## HISTORY

Cortes lies within the traditional lands of the Klahoose and Sliammon First Nations, and the Klahoose First Nation still occupy a large reserve in Squirrel Cove. Cortes Island was named by Spanish naval commanders Galiano and Valdes after Hernando Cortez, who conquered Mexico. (The island to the southeast is named Hernando, also after Cortez.)

One of the first activities that caused non-Native people to stop at Cortes was whaling. Whales were once numerous in the Strait of Georgia, and a whaling station flourished briefly at Whaletown from 1869 to 1871. Shetland Islander Michael Manson started the first permanent non-Native settlement in 1886, establishing a trading post at present-day Mansons Landing. A post office opened in 1893 and the first school, a two-room building near Gunflint Lake, opened in 1895 with 12 students. There were also communities at Von Donop Inlet, Gunflint Lake, Squirrel Cove, Smelt Bay, Seaford, Gorge Harbour and Carrington Bay. Ferry service began in 1969 and electricity arrived in 1970. Early settlers tried sheep ranching and fruit farming but, as elsewhere, logging was the chief occupation. An important industry today is clam, mussel and oyster aquaculture, reputedly valued at $10 million per year.

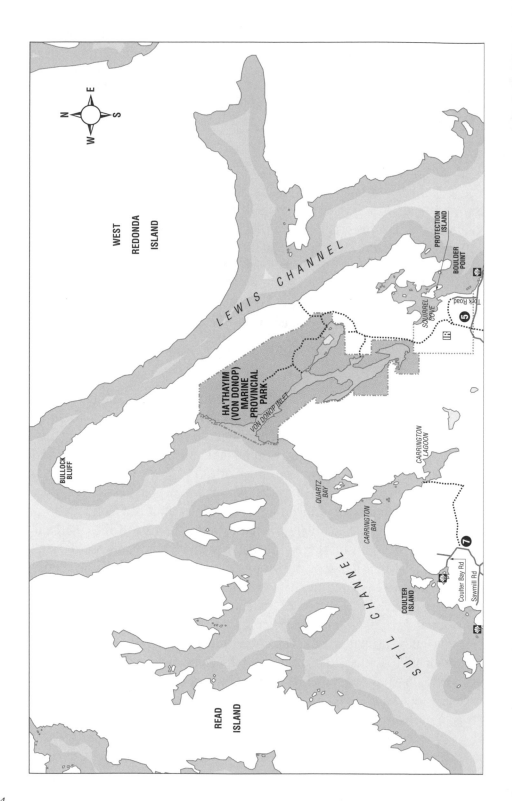

WEST
REDONDA
ISLAND

LEWIS CHANNEL

PROTECTION
ISLAND

BOULDER
POINT

SQUIRREL
COVE

Tork Road

⑤

HA'THAYIM
(VON DONOP)
MARINE
PROVINCIAL
PARK

VON DONOP INLET

BULLOCK
BLUFF

CARRINGTON
LAGOON

QUARTZ
BAY

CARRINGTON
BAY

COULTER
ISLAND

Coulter Bay Rd

Sawmill Rd

⑦

SUTIL CHANNEL

READ
ISLAND

# Cortes Island

**B.C. MAINLAND**

TIBER BAY

MARY POINT

THREE ISLETS (COD ROCKS)

CORTES BAY

Easter Bluff ❹

Red Granite Road

Squirrel Cove Road

Cortes Bay Rd

Cortes Bay Rd

GUNFLINT LAKE ❸

Larson's Meadow Rd

Whaletown Road

NUTSHELL LAKE

Green Mountain ❻

Gorge Harbour Road

MANSONS LANDING

HAGUE LAKE

SEE KW'AS PARK CLOSE-UP MAP ❶

HANK'S BEACH

Bartholomew Rd

SISKIN LANE

IR

Sutil Point Road

TWIN ISLANDS

BAKER PASSAGE

Kw'as Bay Road

Hague Lake Road

Smelt Bay Road

SMELT BAY

SMELT BAY PROVINCIAL PARK

SUTIL POINT

MANSON BAY

MANSONS LAGOON

MANSONS LANDING PROVINCIAL PARK ❷

GORGE HARBOUR

Olmstead Road

Robertson Rd

Hunt Rd

Whaletown Rd

Carrington Bay Road

WHALETOWN

WHALETOWN BAY

Seavista Road

Harbour Road

UGANDA PASSAGE

MARINA ISLAND

FERRY

**Hikes**

❶ Hank's Beach
❷ Mansons Landing Provincial Park
❸ Kw'as Park Trails (see close-up map)
❹ Katimavik Trail to Easter Bluff
❺ Ha'thayim (Von Donop) Marine Provincial Park
❻ Green Mountain Loop
❼ Carrington Bay

5 km

0

Roads

Trails

Park boundary

IR Indian Reserve

Shopping

Park

Shore access

# See text

**Cortes Island**

## GETTING THERE

From Campbell River on Vancouver Island, take the ferry to Quathiaski Cove on Quadra Island, then make your way across the island to Heriot Bay to catch the 45-minute sailing to Whaletown Bay on Cortes. For information obtain a BC Ferries schedule or contact BC Ferries (see page 320).

## SERVICES AND ACCOMMODATION

Since the island has long attracted boaters to its many naturally protected harbours, Cortes has all the basic services. There are general stores near the docks at Squirrel Cove, Gorge Harbour and at "downtown" Mansons Landing, which also has a motel and a credit union with a 24-hour ATM. The island also has a couple of seasonal restaurants, several bed and breakfasts, a lodge, kayak rentals, the well-known Hollyhock retreat centre and other services, many of them seasonal. There's camping at Smelt Bay Provincial Park and an RV park and marina at the Gorge Harbour Marina Resort. For more information, check www.cortesisland.com, www.northcentralisland.com or the excellent information brochure available locally.

## ESPECIALLY FOR WALKERS

Although some of the hikes described below are fairly strenuous, there are also many easy walks on Cortes, suitable for boaters wanting to stretch their legs. In addition to most of the shore and road walks described below, walkers might try one or more of the trails in the following areas:

- Hank's Beach Regional Park (see hike 1 below)
- Mansons Landing Provincial Park (see hike 2)
- Ha'thayim (Von Donop) Marine Provincial Park (see hike 5)
- Carrington Bay (see hike 7)

You might also try the first bits of the Kw'as Park hike from either of the two accesses (see hike 3). You will find the going quite easy for a while, and when it gets too strenuous, you can return the way you came and try something else—or just go for coffee.

## HIKES on CORTES

Although one of the larger islands described in this book, Cortes is one of the least developed. The following are descriptions of a few of the more remarkable and accessible places to hike. Pets must be leashed at all times on these trails to reduce wildlife conflict.

## 1. HANK'S BEACH ★★

| | |
|---|---|
| Trail length | 3 kilometres |
| Time required | 60 minutes, depending on how many trails you do and how long you spend on the beach |
| Description | An easy walk along fairly level logging roads to a beautiful beach |
| Level | Easy |
| Access | A. Westgate Trail: On the south side of Bartholomew Road, 200 metres east of Hague Lake Road |
| | B. Eastgate Trail: On the south side of Bartholomew Road, 300 metres east of Hague Lake Road |
| Cautions | Park in the designated parking area at the Westgate trailhead completely off the road, but not in front of the gate that provides emergency vehicle access. |
| | Do not walk on neighbouring private property, even if you find trails leading to them. |
| | Dogs must be leashed at all times, and this property is subject to seasonal restrictions on pets to reduce wildlife conflict. |

*Note: This property was donated primarily to preserve as a forest conservation area, which protects ecologically significant lands and wildlife corridors. The property is covenanted with the Land Conservancy of BC, and public access is restricted to the trails and beach.*

Hank's Beach derives its name from Henry Herrewig, who homesteaded here in the 1920s and was affectionately known as Hank. The 62-hectare property was logged in Hank's day and then fairly extensively by MacMillan Bloedel, which owned it from about 1965 to 1999. It was purchased for the community by the Tides Foundation in 2007 and was slated for designation as a regional park at time of writing.

There are three trails to walk: the Eastgate and Westgate trails are logging roads that head south through mature second-growth forest. They join a trail that curves down to the beach from a third gate that does not provide access

*Hank's Beach, a favourite picnic spot on Cortes, is largely made up of smooth, round stones with intricate designs created by nature's artists.*

to the property because it is between the public property and a parcel of private property. It will take you about 20 minutes to reach the beach if you take the most direct route.

One of the most beautiful beaches on Cortes, Hank's Beach is littered with a collection of driftwood and some of the loveliest smooth round stones imaginable. Each has a speckled pattern of its own and an assortment of unique colours. This spot is a great place for a picnic, for watching the sea and the expansive view, or just for meditating on how wonderful life is with places like this to visit. The view is directly east: to Cod Rocks and Mary Point on Cortes and Sarah Point on the Malaspina Peninsula on the mainland. If you return from the beach along Eastgate Trail to Bartholomew Road, keep to the left when you see a junction. The trail to the right ends up on private land.

## 2. Mansons Landing Provincial Park ★★★

| | |
|---|---|
| Trail length | About 3 kilometres in total, depending on route taken |
| Time required | An hour or more, depending on pace |
| Description | A pleasant walk through open woods to a sand spit, along the beaches of a large and beautiful lagoon and through forest trails to a lake |
| Level | Easy |
| Access | At the end of Sutil Point Road (about 15 kilometres from the ferry). Look for signs to the right of the government dock for a trail leading to a sand spit. From the spit, you can follow a beach trail along the lagoon. |
| Cautions | Dogs must be leashed at all times to reduce wildlife conflict. |

Walk along the soft sand spit, an ancient midden site, until you reach the narrow opening to the lagoon. This is a popular place to snorkel in the current created by the tide coming in and out of the lagoon. Observing the colourful sea life as you float over it is a fantastic experience. This is also a great place to picnic, swim or watch the sun set.

Continue along the lagoon until the rocks block your way, then duck into the forest on a trail along an old logging road. This trail takes you across Seaford Road to Hague Lake, one of Cortes residents' favourite swimming spots. Paths run both ways along the lakeshore, but neither is very long. There are a number of great spots in the park for a picnic, the best being the sand spit and the beach at Hague Lake.

## 3. KW'AS PARK TRAILS ★★★★★

| | |
|---|---|
| Trail length | 12 kilometres in total |
| Time required | 2-3 hours for the north loop (access A); 1-1.5 hours for the south route (access B). There are also a number of shorter trails within the north loop area. |
| Description | Vigorous hike through a mature forest, with views of Hague and Gunflint lakes |
| Level | Moderate to challenging and definitely strenuous if you combine it with hike 4 |
| Access | A. North entrance: east side of Seaford Road on the south side of a sharp bend in the road just south of the Cortes Island Motel. There's very limited parking here. |
| | B. South entrance: south side of Kw'as Bay Road off Hague Lake Road. There's a parking lot here. |
| Cautions | Stay on the trails to protect ecologically significant lands. Dogs must be leashed at all times to reduce wildlife conflict. |

The Regional District of Strathcona's labyrinth of trails is on 70 hectares of well-forested Crown land between Hague (Kw'as) and Gunflint lakes. The trails are well marked and maps are posted throughout the trail system. Most of the inspiration for these extraordinary trails came from the late Pierre de

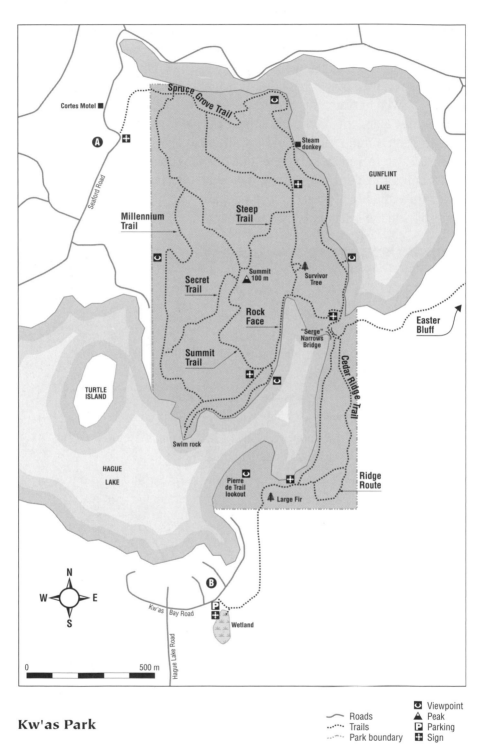

Cortes Motel

Ⓐ

Sealord Road

Spruce Grove Trail

Steam donkey

GUNFLINT LAKE

Millennium Trail

Steep Trail

Secret Trail

Summit ▲ 100 m

Survivor Tree

Rock Face

"Serge" Narrows Bridge

Easter Bluff

Summit Trail

TURTLE ISLAND

Cedar Ridge Trail

Swim rock

HAGUE LAKE

Pierre de Trail lookout

Large Fir

Ridge Route

Ⓑ

N
W E
S

Kw'as Bay Road

Hague Lake Road

Ⓟ

Wetland

0                500 m

| | Viewpoint |
| Roads | ▲ Peak |
| Trails | Ⓟ Parking |
| Park boundary | ✚ Sign |

## Kw'as Park

Trey, who thought up the interesting names for land formations, wrote all the signs and built the bridges, ladders and other aids you'll find on the trails.

Starting from Seaford Road (access A), you quickly enter a forest where everything seems upholstered with green moss. As you walk over a tangle of roots, you'll notice huge stumps with "gardens" sprouting out of them, remnants of the early logging that took place here. Some of this area is wetland, complete with skunk cabbage and other swampy vegetation. The Spruce Grove Trail to the east follows the shoreline of Gunflint Lake for some way. You pass the "Inca Ruins," a massive rock wall that looks as though Inca stonemasons could have constructed it. There are a number of access points to the lake, including one on which you'll find an old steam donkey that exploded in the fall of 1923, bringing logging in this area to an abrupt halt.

It will take you at least 35 minutes to reach the fanciful bridge over Serge Narrows (see the accompanying map). From here you can take a 2-hour side trip to Easter Bluff (see hike 4), continue on the south trail loop that leads to Kw'as Bay Road (a 60- to 90-minute walk) or continue on the trails in the north loop. The trail to the south loop meanders for about 1.5 kilometres through mature second-growth trees with some old-growth Douglas-fir and western red cedar. The largest tree, a Douglas-fir with a circumference of 8.4 metres at its base, is just 500 metres from the Kw'as Bay Road access (access B). There's a swamp at the access, and if you walk onto the viewing float provided you can see a beaver lodge.

*This tree in Kw'as Park, with a circumference of 8.4 metres at its base, is the largest I've seen in the Gulf Islands.*

Once back on the north loop, I stayed on the trails on the circumference as much as possible, but did take a short detour to see the Survivor Tree, a huge fir with a large dead cedar hung up on it. I continued on the Summit Trail (see map), which climbs an impressive rock face (in one place by way of a ladder) high above the lake. There is a fine view of Hague Lake and the trail passes groves of manzanita and pine trees before descending to a swimming spot (Swim Rock) on Hague Lake. The Millennium, Secret and Steep trails all meander through stands of old-growth Douglas-fir. A short side trail from the Millennium Trail leads to a viewpoint overlooking Marina and Vancouver islands. A memorial trail has been created in honour of the trail builder who made this park unique. Named the Pierre de Trail, it starts near the park's largest fir (close to access B), climbs to a lookout over Hague Lake to Swim Rock and then descends back to the main trail.

This exceptional trail system has sufficient variety to keep you enchanted and well exercised for most of a day. There are plenty of great picnic spots, too, so don't forget your lunch.

*After admiring the view from Easter Bluff you may wish to hike down to Gunflint or Hague Lake for a swim.*

## 4. KATIMAVIK TRAIL TO EASTER BLUFF ★★★

| Trail length | 9 kilometres return (2 kilometres if you begin at access B) |
|---|---|
| Time required | 2 hours (45 minutes if you begin at access B) |
| Description | Rocky up-and-down trail leading to an excellent viewpoint |
| Level | Moderate |
| Access | A. The trail starts at Serge Narrows Bridge in Kw'as Park (see the map on page 50). The Kw'as Bay Road access (access B) to the park is the shortest access to the trailhead. |
| | B. The trail crosses Cortes Bay Road 1.5 kilometres from its intersection with Bartholomew Road or 800 metres from its intersection with Seaford Road. You can park on the edge of the road and take the trail in either direction—to Kw'as Park (35 minutes) or to Easter Bluff (10 minutes). |
| Cautions | Respect private property and the protected area by keeping on the trail at all times and keeping your dogs leashed. |

*Note: Easter Bluff and Linnaea Farm lands (127.5 hectares), which the trail crosses, are covenanted by the Linnaea Farm Society to protect ecologically significant lands and species.*

This trail, built by volunteers and Katimavik students led by Pierre de Trey, will give you a fair bit of exercise as it goes up and down over rocky terrain. It follows the south shore of Gunflint Lake for some distance, crosses a private driveway and Cortes Bay Road and then climbs to the top of legendary Easter Bluff, where early settlers are said to have hidden Easter eggs for their children. The westward view encompasses Gunflint Lake below, Marina Island and the Vancouver Island mountains in the distance.

## 5. HA'THAYIM (VON DONOP) MARINE PROVINCIAL PARK ★★

| | |
|---|---|
| Trail length | 6 kilometres each way (more if you explore off-shoot trails) |
| Time required | 4-6 hours |
| Description | A network of grown-in logging roads through mixed young and mature forest, often leading to the shore of Von Donop Inlet and on to Cliff Peak |
| Level | Easy |
| Access | On Whaletown Road, 5.7 kilometres from its intersection with Gorge Harbour Road and 1.2 kilometres west of Tork Road. You will see a large sign advertising the Klahoose Salmon Enhancement Project on the north side of Whaletown Road. Follow the driveway to the right of the sign to the parking area and the trailhead marked by a BC Parks signboard. |
| Cautions | This area is considered backcountry and wildlife takes priority. It is therefore not advisable to take pets in this area. |

To reach the park from the parking area, walk about 2.5 kilometres through the Klahoose reserve on a gentle old logging road. The route is well signed by BC Parks, with helpful distance signs every 500 metres. Stay on the main logging road/trail at least until you're in the park. Remember: reserve land is private land.

It takes about 40 minutes to reach the water's edge. This is a lovely spot but there is really nowhere to walk along the water. A signed path near the outhouse heads 1 kilometre east to a little bay in Squirrel Cove. Another path heads north for 3 kilometres (40 minutes), ending at another of Von Donop Inlet's many bays. This beautiful spot was deserted when I visited. There is no beach trail and you must return the way you came.

There are endless old logging road paths to explore in this way, and you could easily meander for hours on trails similar to those described here. One of these goes to Cliff Peak and provides a view of Lewis Channel and Teakerne Arm.

## 6. GREEN MOUNTAIN LOOP ★★

| | |
|---|---|
| Trail length | 4 kilometres |
| Time required | 70 minutes return |
| Description | Hike up a logging road to a pleasant loop trail overlooking Gorge Harbour. |
| Level | Moderate |
| Elevation | 310 metres |
| Access | The unmarked logging road is off Whaletown Road, 200 metres east of Gorge Harbour Road and 500 metres west of Larson's Meadow Road. |
| Cautions | Pets should be leashed at all times to prevent wildlife conflict. |

This hike on Crown land is familiar to locals but can be confusing to visitors. You can start walking at the beginning of the logging road or you can drive up the road for 300 metres, just past a private driveway on the left, to a small parking space. Do not drive farther, as it is extremely rough.

The hike will take you 35 minutes each way. You will spend 15 minutes on the logging road before branching off to the left, for 5 minutes, on a pretty little trail that leads to the attractive Green Mountain loop. This loop provides views of Gorge Harbour and the Vancouver Island peaks in the distance.

There are a number of side trails off the loop, including a trail to the east that leads down to Nutshell Lake—still on Crown land. The main trail is marked by cairns, but the side trails are not well marked, so take a compass and be careful not to trespass on the nearby private land.

## 7. CARRINGTON BAY ★★★

| | |
|---|---|
| Trail length | 3 kilometres each way |
| Time required | 45 minutes each way |
| Description | A pleasant walk on logging roads through mature second-growth, mostly cedar forest |
| Level | Easy |

| Access | Take Harbour Road from the ferry to Carrington Bay Road. Turn left and drive past Sawmill Road on your left and Olmstead Road on your right to the two accesses—1.5 kilometres and 1.7 kilometres from Harbour Road. I used the second access because the off-road parking was better. Look for the accesses after you pass a house at the top of a rise around 1642 Carrington Bay Road; the second access is 400 metres from here. |
| --- | --- |
| Cautions | This area is considered backcountry and wildlife takes priority. It is therefore not advisable to take pets in this area. |

If you start on the second access as I did, you will pass an old homestead, marked by an orchard, almost immediately. You will soon meet the road from the first access. Turn left.

After about 15 minutes from the start you will reach another junction. This time turn right. There's another old homestead here. You'll reach a third junction in another 15 minutes. This is a major junction with signs for a gravel pit to the east, Coulter Bay Road to the west and Carrington Bay Lagoon entrance to the north. Turn left (north) and continue straight on this road for another 15 minutes and you'll reach the point where Carrington Bay feeds into or drains Carrington Lagoon.

This is a very pleasant spot to spend some time. A picnic table and other amenities have been established by people who come here to party. There are also great views of the bay and warm water for summer swimming. Note the remains of a dam between the bay and the lagoon; it was built to raise the water level in the lagoon so that logs could be boomed here and then sluiced one by one into the bay.

When you return to the big junction, go back to the main road the way you came and then walk west to where you parked on Carrington Bay Road.

## HIKING ON NORTHERN CORTES

Some of the best hiking on Cortes is on the old logging roads and informal bush trails on the undeveloped north part of the island. Much of this wild land is Crown-owned and some private. At time of writing much of the privately owned land belonged to Island Timberlands, which allowed the public to hike and picnic (no camping or fires) on its property when there was no forestry activity. For more information and to avoid disappointment if the land is being used for forestry, contact the company at 4th Floor, 65 Front Street, Nanaimo, BC V9R 5H9; 250-755-3500, or visit www.islandtimberlands.com.

# SHORE AND ROAD WALKS

There are pleasant walks along the roads bordering Gunflint and Hague lakes and along the ocean in Smelt Bay Provincial Park. One especially pleasant walk is beside an enchanting forest on Hunt Road, which leads to Gorge Harbour Marina.

You will find some very attractive public trails and a community park administered by the Strathcona Regional District in a relatively new subdivision called Siskin Lane. There are several access points: four of them are off Sutil Point Road both east and west of Highfield Road; another is off the end of Hayes Road on the west side of the development. You can also access the trails off Cemetery Road from the park on the north side of the development. A map is available on the Siskin Lane website, www.cortesisland.com/renewal.

Closer to the ferry, you should not miss Whaletown. Although you can't walk for very long here, Whaletown is arguably the prettiest settlement on the island, with its tiny local library (private and run by volunteers) and quaint little church. The government wharf is a good place to watch the comings and goings of the community, especially as many residents come to the island by private boat.

Several beach walks on Cortes are worth exploring.

**Seavista Road (first left from the ferry dock):** The beach at the end of the road is quite rocky, but you can scramble over it at low tide.

**Red Granite Road (near the Seattle Yacht Club's Cortes Bay Outstation):** At the end of the road, there's a beach of rocky pink granite. You can walk both ways along the water at low tide, clambering over the large rocks that litter the shore.

**Smelt Bay Provincial Park:** This is a fantastic place to watch the sunset and it has great views, as does Sutil Point. It is also possible to collect oysters and dig for clams along parts of this long beach (for information on shellfish, see page 23). The pebble beach can be walked north as far as Mansons Landing and south around Sutil Point (a.k.a. Reef Point), and then for quite a way north along the eastern shore. Along the way to Mansons Landing a petroglyph on a 2-metre-high boulder can be found on the beach.

## AND IF YOU PADDLE . . .

Cortes Island's intricate coastline offers its own fine paddling, and makes a great jumping-off point for exploring Desolation Sound, one of BC's prime paddling areas. The shoreline here is generally protected, but sudden changes in weather can make any exposed crossing hazardous, so the usual precautions should be observed, especially at the south end of Cortes around Sutil Point. Strong currents can be encountered entering narrows in Gorge Harbour, Squirrel Cove, Carrington Bay, Von Donop Inlet and Mansons Landing. In most cases the government docks are the best places to launch. They are also usually accompanied by parking places and telephones. Here are a few suggestions:

**Squirrel Cove:** Launch either from the government dock or (by permission) from the Klahoose Band beach. You can also pay the Squirrel Cove store to

*Cortes Bay is a popular launching point for paddlers headed into Desolation Sound. Many also come to explore its unique buildings and shore.*

launch from its ramp beside the Cove Restaurant. Explore the cove's labyrinthine shoreline, Protection Island at the mouth and the nearby coast. This is a popular launching spot for paddlers heading for Desolation Sound.

**Cortes Bay:** Explore the bay, the nearby shoreline, Three Islets (Cod Rocks) just offshore and Twin Islands to the south.

**Gorge Harbour:** Launch from the government dock at the end of Robertson Road or the marina at the end of Hunt Road. The Gorge is a large, busy harbour and interesting to explore. If you decide to go through the narrow entrance, be aware that the current runs up to 4 knots. The pictographs halfway down the cliff wall are best seen at high tide.

**Smelt Bay:** Launch at Smelt Bay Provincial Park or anywhere along the extensive beach north of the small park. While this is an easy place to put in, the paddling is somewhat monotonous.

**Mansons Landing Provincial Park:** Put in at the government dock and then explore Mansons Bay, the small islands just outside it and, at a high tide, Mansons Lagoon. The tidal rush at the entrance may force even strong paddlers to portage during tide changes. The island-studded shoreline north to Gorge Harbour is also interesting to explore.

**Coulter Bay:** Launch from the end of Coulter Bay Road. From here you can explore Coulter Island, then continue north to tour Carrington Bay and Quartz Bay. Note that Coulter Bay is a big mud flat at low tide; if you launch at high tide and come back at low tide, you will have to hike over the mud flat to get to the shore. As well, more than one vehicle has been stuck in the mud while trying to launch a boat at low tide!

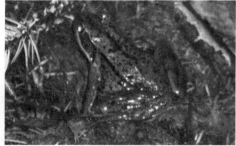

*Small lizards and frogs like these are common on all the Gulf Islands, but are often missed. These were spotted on a Cortes trail.*

# Denman

*L*ocated just off the coast of Vancouver Island halfway between Nanaimo and Campbell River, Denman Island is a low-key and relatively undeveloped island. Denman covers an area of 51 square kilometres and is home to a close-knit, artistic community of about 1,100 residents. Referred to by some as the speed bump on the way to Hornby Island, it has fewer natural attractions than its more popular neighbour. The shoreline is mostly unindented and the island's highest point is a mere 120 metres above sea level. There are, however, pleasant walks on trails in both Fillongley and Boyle Point provincial parks, along beaches and on country roads. While parts of Denman were badly scarred from clear-cutting that occurred between 1997 and 2001, these areas are now recovering, and the rest of the island is quite pastoral, with many productive farms on possibly the best agricultural land in the Gulf Islands. Almost all of the island's services are a short walk from the ferry terminal in Denman Village.

## HISTORY

Denman Island is named after Rear Admiral Joseph Denman, commander-in-chief of the Pacific station from 1864 to 1866. For centuries the K'omoks First Nation had summer camps on Denman where they hunted and fished. Beginning around 1870 several Scottish families moved to Denman from the Orkney Islands. By 1878 the island had a post office and a school, and a church and store quickly followed, although it wasn't until 1897 that a community hall—the sign of an established community—was built.

Agriculture, especially dairy farming, was always a significant industry on Denman but, as elsewhere, locals supported themselves through a variety of means including salmon fishing and logging. This latter activity was so popular that by 1950 most of the island was logged. From 1908 to 1915 some islanders were employed at an ill-fated local sandstone quarry, which shut down after it was discovered that the stone, used in buildings in Victoria, streaked as it weathered. Today, oyster farming is an important local industry, and much of Denman's sheltered western foreshore is leased for this purpose.

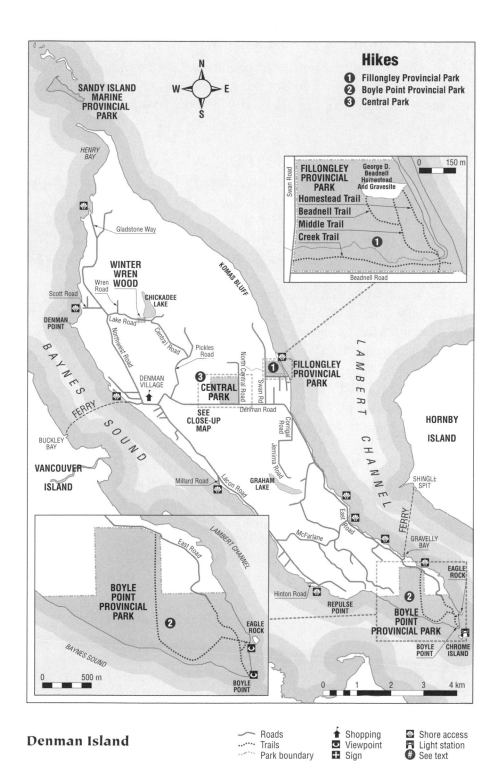

## Hikes

1 Fillongley Provincial Park
2 Boyle Point Provincial Park
3 Central Park

SANDY ISLAND MARINE PROVINCIAL PARK

HENRY BAY

Gladstone Way

KOMAS BLUFF

WINTER WREN WOOD

Wren Road

CHICKADEE LAKE

Scott Road

Lake Road

DENMAN POINT

Northwest Road

Central Road

DENMAN VILLAGE

Pickles Road

North Central Road

Swan Rd

FILLONGLEY PROVINCIAL PARK

CENTRAL PARK

SEE CLOSE-UP MAP

Denman Road

LAMBERT CHANNEL

HORNBY ISLAND

BUCKLEY BAY

VANCOUVER ISLAND

BAYNES SOUND

FERRY

Corrigal Road

Jemima Road

Millard Road

Lacon Road

GRAHAM LAKE

McFarlane

East Road

SHINGLE SPIT

FERRY

GRAVELLY BAY

LAMBERT CHANNEL

East Road

BOYLE POINT PROVINCIAL PARK

EAGLE ROCK

Hinton Road

REPULSE POINT

BOYLE POINT PROVINCIAL PARK

EAGLE ROCK

BOYLE POINT

CHROME ISLAND

BAYNES SOUND

BOYLE POINT

FILLONGLEY PROVINCIAL PARK

George D. Beadnell Homestead And Gravesite

Homestead Trail
Beadnell Trail
Middle Trail
Creek Trail

Swan Road

Beadnell Road

0    150 m

**Denman Island**

| | | |
|---|---|---|
| Roads | Shopping | Shore access |
| Trails | Viewpoint | Light station |
| Park boundary | Sign | See text |

0    500 m

0   1   2   3   4 km

## GETTING THERE

The 10-minute ferry to Denman leaves Buckley Bay on Vancouver Island (about 20 kilometres south of Courtenay) almost hourly. For specific ferry information, obtain a copy of the latest BC Ferries schedule or contact BC Ferries (see page 320).

## SERVICES AND ACCOMMODATION

All of Denman's stores are located in Denman Village, a short stroll from the ferry terminal. These include the general store dating from 1910 (with a gas pump and liquor outlet), a café, a craft store, a bookstore, the community centre and a museum and art gallery. Denman has about a dozen bed and breakfasts, and there is a small public campground at Fillongley Provincial Park.

A combined visitor's guide to Denman and Hornby that includes a map of each island is produced yearly and is available on the ferry and at other outlets. A wealth of tourist information is also provided on the Denman website, www.denmanisland.com.

## ESPECIALLY FOR WALKERS

Denman has fewer public hiking trails than most Gulf Islands. However, because the island is so flat, all of them are suitable for most walkers. One of the easiest is the very short but very pretty interpretive nature walk in 2.4-hectare Winter Wren Wood at the southwest corner of Chickadee Lake. There are also numerous shore and road walks to enjoy. Opportunities for walking will increase soon as a result of changes to the island, which include a large provincial park planned for part of the area logged from 1997 to 2001, an extension planned for Boyle Point Park at the south end of the island and a small new regional park at the northwest tip of the island. Trail information on these new parks will soon be available.

# HIKES on DENMAN

## 1. FILLONGLEY TRAILS ★★★

| | |
|---|---|
| Trail length | About 2 kilometres in total |
| Time required | Plan to spend at least an hour in this beautiful, tranquil park. |
| Description | Lovely walks through old-growth forest and along a stream that flows into the sea, from where you can walk along the beach in both directions |
| Level | Easy |
| Access | The route to the park is well signed. From the ferry drive east along Denman Road, turn left (north) on Swan Road and then turn right (east) at Beadnell Road. The park runs from the corner of Beadnell and Swan down to the sea. It's about 5.5 kilometres from the ferry. |

The 23-hectare Fillongley Provincial Park was once the oceanfront estate of George David Beadnell, whose parents bought the property in 1889. George and his wife, Amy, developed a park-like property that included paths, a bowling green, gates and trellises, a lily pond, rockeries, birdhouses and flowerbeds filled from the estate's greenhouses. The Beadnells deeded the property to the province in 1953, and it became a provincial park after George's death.

Information shelters in the park display a map of the park trails, as well as a couple of articles on the Beadnell family. You can easily walk all the short, scenic paths described below in an hour or so, but you'll probably want to spend more time in this peaceful spot.

**Creek Trail:** This path parallels Beadnell Road from just beyond the camping area to Swan Road, passing through stately old-growth forest along the edge of Beadnell Creek.

**Homestead Trail:** One of three that lead to the remains of the Beadnell home and gravesite, this 400-metre trail starts just outside the camping area. It crosses a bridge over the creek, continues up through the forest and enters a meadow—perhaps a lawn in an earlier incarnation—in which you can see the base of a fountain from the old estate, as well as the wide variety of trees planted by the Beadnells and a profusion of flowers in the spring. George Beadnell's grave is at the entrance to the field.

**Beadnell Trail:** To the west of the Homestead Trail and running off it, this trail is prettier than its counterpart and overlooks the creek in places.

**Middle Trail:** A short trail that connects the Beadnell and Homestead trails.

**Shoreline Trail:** Begins just beyond the turnaround for vehicles in the camping area. It parallels the shore, following a midden between the creek and the sea. This is a splendid walk on a sunny day with the trees reflected in the creek. The stream enters the ocean about a 10-minute walk north from the campsites. After crossing the stream, which is dry by mid- to late summer, you can walk almost indefinitely along the beach. You can also return to the camping/parking area by way of the beach instead of the path.

## 2. BOYLE POINT PROVINCIAL PARK ★★

| | |
|---|---|
| Trail length | 2-3 kilometres round trip |
| Time required | 30 to 60 minutes, depending on route taken |
| Description | A pleasant hike through some second-growth forest to the sea, with views of picturesque Chrome Island light station and Eagle Rock offshore |
| Level | Easy |
| Access | The end of East Road |

This 190-hectare provincial park has no facilities, except for the park signboard that displays a map of the simple trail system. The main trail starts beside a stream bed and is fairly straightforward, leading to a steep cliff overlooking Chrome Island light station. This is a good spot to stop and sit on the bench provided and enjoy a picnic lunch. On your return from the viewpoint, look for a marked trail to the right (east) that leads to a view of Eagle Rock around the point. Visitors used to explore the shore here, clambering down the steep cliff to the beach below, where it is possible at very low tides to walk right out to Eagle Rock. However, BC Parks has placed a fence here and advises against doing this because of the danger.

# DISASTER AT CHROME ISLAND

Chrome Island's first lighthouse was established on the east end of the island in 1891, and a second (the one used today) was built at the west end in 1898. The British originally named the island Yellow Island because of its light colour. Aside from its Alcatraz look—a flat tabletop with sheer cliff edges falling straight down to the sea—Chrome Island's main claim to fame was a spectacular shipwreck that took place during a gale on December 16, 1900.

The British merchant steamer *Alpha* was heading for Union Bay on Vancouver Island to pick up coal before it started on its journey to Japan with a cargo of coal and canned salmon. The ship foundered on the rocks on the east end of the island and sank. Although most of the crew were able to reach safety, the captain and eight crew members went down with the ship. The story does not end there, however. In the days following the disaster, cases of salmon were salvaged by Denman residents. Reportedly, one case contained rum, rather than salmon, and the fellow who found it drank himself to death.

*Like most light stations, Chrome Island is small, rocky and hard to access but still crowded with small buildings whose construction defies the imagination.* Kate Dunsmore

Once you've retraced your steps to the Chrome Island Trail, you can return to East Road the same way you came or take the unmarked trail a little south to Eagle Rock. This 3-kilometre trail leads through lovely open forest, following an old logging road in 65 hectares of land recently added to the park. While this trail is fairly easy to follow, there are a few offshoots, including one leading to a beach, that are not as well maintained: some people have gotten lost here. Carry a compass and make sure that you're heading in the right direction. If you have any doubts, retrace your steps and exit via the established park trail. The alternate trail emerges on East Road about 2 kilometres northwest of the park entrance. Turn right (southeast) to return to the park entrance.

| 3. Central Park | |
|---|---|
| Trail length | About 4 kilometres in total |
| Time required | 60 minutes to walk all trails |
| Description | A 60-hectare block of land containing three long wetlands that was logged around 2000 |
| Level | Easy |
| Access | On the north side of Denman Road across from the Old School Centre |

Purchased by the Denman Conservancy Association in 2006, this conservation parcel was fancifully named after New York City's Central Park, acknowledging that Manhattan and Denman islands are approximately the same size, and that both parks fall roughly in the middle of the island.

Three long, narrow wetlands extend from northwest to southeast across the park. Trees are regenerating well after recent logging and will eventually mature as a coastal Douglas-fir forest, which is increasingly rare in this region. The open areas of Central Park are home to two endangered butterfly species, and the marsh is the winter home of trumpeter swans. An extensive and increasing network of multi-use trails criss-crosses the area; a trail guide is displayed at the southern entrance on Denman Road.

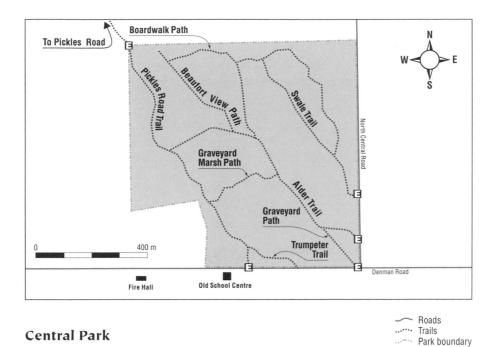

**Central Park**

Roads
Trails
Park boundary
E Entrance

# SHORE AND ROAD WALKS

There are many well-signed oyster leases along Denman's shoreline. Respect the signs and do not threaten the livelihood of the oyster farmers by walking on the leased area or by picking oysters between the posted signs.

The following shore accesses can be walked comfortably only at low tide:

**Scott Road (at the end):** North of the ferry terminal.

**Millard Road (at the end):** Off Lacon Road, about 3 kilometres south of the ferry dock. This particularly lovely shore access is down a good but very steep road that is impassable at certain times of the year (you could find it impossible to get back up). You'll find yourself on a little promontory from which you can walk along the beach in both directions. On a clear day you will have excellent views of the Beaufort Mountains on Vancouver Island across Baynes Sound.

**Gladstone Way (at the end):** From Denman Village take Northwest Road for about 6 kilometres until you reach Gladstone Way. A public walkway follows a fence to the beach. At low tide you can walk along the beach for some distance in both directions, although walking north requires crossing a stream that swells after heavy rainfall. If you head north, you can walk along Henry Bay to the north tip of the island. Sandy Island Marine Provincial Park is accessible by foot from here, but only at low tide.

**Fillongley Provincial Park:** This wonderful beach is as fine as any on Denman. You can walk along this beach in both directions for quite some distance.

**East Road:** There are several shore accesses off East Road.

**Central Road:** Near Chickadee Lake, this is a pretty, narrow, level road, one of the most pleasant to walk on Denman. The southeastern end of it and Pickles Road go through a ferny woods.

## AND IF YOU PADDLE . . .

Denman has a smooth shoreline with few bays and beaches, but with lots of rocks in the shallow water along its coast.

**Beadnell Road:** It's easy to launch a boat at the end of Beadnell Road near Fillongley Provincial Park on Denman's east side. From here you can paddle to Sandy Island Marine Provincial Park (about 4 nautical miles or 7.4 kilometres) and explore its sand beaches.

**Gravelly Bay ferry terminal or Bill Mee Park:** Launch at the ferry terminal to Hornby Island or at the boat launch in Bill Mee Park on East Road south of the ferry terminal. Head south and paddle around Eagle Rock and Chrome Island, where you can observe cormorant colonies, seals and sea lions and Boyle Point Provincial Park above you.

**North of the ferry dock from Vancouver Island:** Launch at one of the shore accesses north of the ferry dock and paddle to Sandy Island Marine Provincial Park, where you can birdwatch or swim. This park is accessible from Denman by foot at low tide.

# Gabriola

*J*ust a 20-minute ferry trip from Nanaimo, Gabriola is the second most populous southern Gulf Island, with around 4,500 residents, and is one of the largest, at some 53 square kilometres. The settlements near Descanso Bay, Degnen Bay, Silva Bay and Taylor Bay are equipped with most amenities, including many craft studios. The island is laced with country roads, surrounded by walkable beaches and blessed with several fine parks with developed trails. Gabriola is famous for its honeycombed sandstone grottoes, one of which, the historic Malaspina Galleries, is a provincial landmark. Known as the Queen of the Gulf Islands, Gabriola's gentle topography, park-like Garry oak and arbutus groves, snug harbours, spectacular ocean vistas and its atmosphere of pastoral balm make it an excellent choice for anyone wishing to sample the storied enchantment of BC's Gulf Islands in one easy trip.

## HISTORY

Gabriola's name is adapted from the Spanish name Gaviola; Spanish explorer José Maria Narvaez, master of the *Saturnina*, named the east end of Gabriola Punta de Gaviola in 1791. Gabriola is in the traditional territory of the Snuneymuxw (Nanaimo) people, who decorated the soft sandstone, both inland and on the shore, with the intriguing petroglyphs reproduced at the Gabriola Museum, where visitors can make their own rubbings. Many of the island's first non-aboriginal settlers were Scots who farmed, mined coal in Nanaimo or worked in the sandstone quarry near Descanso Bay, producing stone for buildings in Victoria and the enormous pulp mill grindstones that now decorate some island yards. A brickyard operated from 1895 to 1945 near Brickyard Hill, providing employment for many local families and Chinese labourers; old broken bricks can still be seen along the high tide line at Brickyard Beach. By 1906 the island had about 200 residents, some of whose descendants live there still. In the 1920s summer cottagers began to arrive from the cities, a trend that continues today.

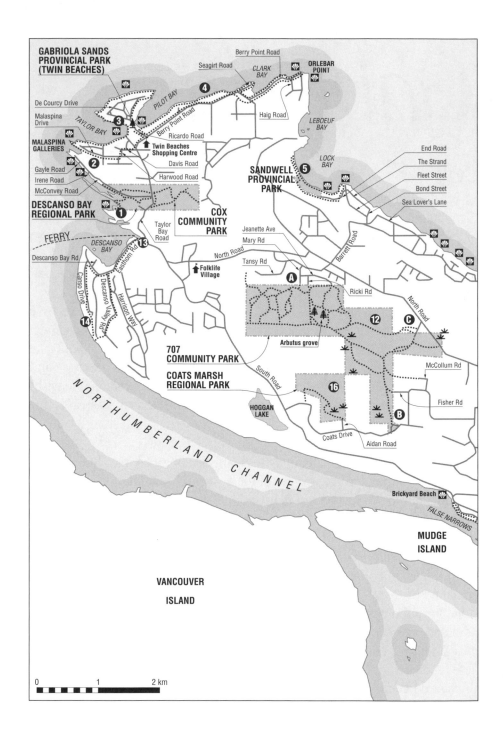

**GABRIOLA SANDS PROVINCIAL PARK (TWIN BEACHES)**

Berry Point Road
Seagirt Road
*CLARK BAY*
**ORLEBAR POINT**

De Courcy Drive
*PILOT BAY*
Haig Road
*LEBOEUF BAY*

Malaspina Drive
*TAYLOR BAY*
Ricardo Road
Twin Beaches Shopping Centre

**MALASPINA GALLERIES**
Davis Road
*LOCK BAY*

Gayle Road
Harwood Road
**SANDWELL PROVINCIAL PARK**
End Road
The Strand
Fleet Street
Bond Street
Sea Lover's Lane

Irene Road
McConvey Road

**DESCANSO BAY REGIONAL PARK**
**COX COMMUNITY PARK**
Taylor Bay Road

Jeanette Ave
Mary Rd

*FERRY*
*DESCANSO BAY*
North Road
Tansy Rd
Ricki Rd

Descanso Bay Rd
Folklife Village

*Canso Drive*
*Descanso Valley Rd*
*Eastholm Rd*
*Harrison Way*

**707 COMMUNITY PARK**
Arbutus grove
*South Road*
McCollum Rd

**COATS MARSH REGIONAL PARK**
Fisher Rd
*HOGGAN LAKE*

Coats Drive
Aidan Road

**N O R T H U M B E R L A N D   C H A N N E L**

Brickyard Beach
*FALSE NARROWS*

**MUDGE ISLAND**

**VANCOUVER ISLAND**

*Barrett Road*
*North Road*

0    1    2 km

## Gabriola Island

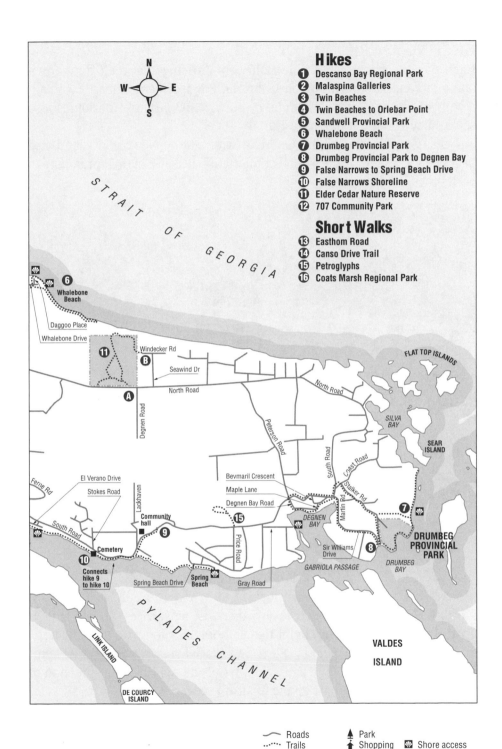

# Hikes

1. Descanso Bay Regional Park
2. Malaspina Galleries
3. Twin Beaches
4. Twin Beaches to Orlebar Point
5. Sandwell Provincial Park
6. Whalebone Beach
7. Drumbeg Provincial Park
8. Drumbeg Provincial Park to Degnen Bay
9. False Narrows to Spring Beach Drive
10. False Narrows Shoreline
11. Elder Cedar Nature Reserve
12. 707 Community Park

# Short Walks

13. Easthom Road
14. Canso Drive Trail
15. Petroglyphs
16. Coats Marsh Regional Park

Roads
Trails
Park boundary

Park
Shopping
See text

Shore access
Marsh

## GETTING THERE

Each day the ferry makes almost hourly crossings between downtown Nanaimo and Descanso Bay on Gabriola. For specific information, obtain a copy of the BC Ferries schedule, or contact BC Ferries. Gabriola is also serviced by Tofino Air (see page 320).

Note: Consider combining Gabriola with nearby Newcastle Island (see pages 305–7) as they make a good combination because of their proximity to each other.

*Crashing storm waves sculpt Gabriola's sandstone shores and remind islanders of their isolation.* Mark Kaaremaa

## SERVICES AND ACCOMMODATION

Most of the island's services are located at or close to Folklife Village on North Road, 1 kilometre from the ferry dock. Other services can be found in Twin Beaches Mall on Berry Point Road, about 2.5 kilometres from the ferry, and at Silva Bay. From Victoria Day to Thanksgiving, a farmers' market takes place every Saturday from 10 a.m. to noon outside Agi Hall at the junction of North and South roads, just up the hill from the ferry.

There's a Visitor Information Centre at Twin Beaches Mall (250-247-9332; www.gabriolaisland.org). Information is also available from www.gabriolaonline.ca. A free brochure, including a detailed map of the island, is produced annually and is available in local stores and at the Gabriola ferry terminal in Nanaimo. The Gabriola Land and Trails Trust (GaLTT) publishes a hiking brochure with excellent information on the hikes on the island. The 2010 version I used was called *23 Walks on Gabriola*. An interactive, up-to-date version of the island map is available on the GaLTT website, www.galtt.ca/trails.htm.

Gabriola has three provincial parks, two regional parks and many community parks and trails. The island's only public campground at Descanso Bay Regional Park has 32 sites. Many of the island's shore accesses are well marked with yellow concrete blocks and often yellow paint on trees as well.

## ESPECIALLY FOR WALKERS

One of the highlights of Gabriola is the accessibility to easy walking and hiking along the shoreline. These walks are on sand and gravel beaches, on sandstone shelves and along the curves of bays and headlands. Almost all beach walks should be hiked only at low tide.

The island's country roads and many woodland trails through parks are pleasant to explore at almost any time of the year. In many cases walks along the shore, the roads and occasionally through forest can be combined to make long, satisfying outings. Almost all the walks and hikes described in this chapter are accessible to walkers of almost any ability. The provincial parks contain some of the most beautiful shoreline on the island.

Nature lovers and photographers will be kept busy on these walks. There is rich intertidal life and the birdwatching is good year-round, especially at Gabriola's newest park, Coats Marsh Regional Park (see walk 16). The walks around the shoreline that parallels Berry Point Road can offer stunning sunsets. And be sure to walk the trails lined with old-growth cedar and fir in Elder Cedar Nature Reserve (see walk 11).

## HIKES AND WALKS on GABRIOLA

Of the walks described in this chapter, those along the beautiful sandstone shoreline are best from late spring to early fall when the tides are lower. If you try them in the winter months, note the cautions listed for each hike, as the sandstone shore is very slippery in the winter. To make the most of the walks, be sure to check the tide tables before starting and plan your walks around low tide.

The first ten walks are listed clockwise around the island starting from the ferry terminal, so they can easily be grouped together to make a longer day out.

In addition to the hikes, routes and walks suggested here, you might want to join the Gabriola Walking Group, which has regular weekly outings at 10 a.m. on Wednesdays. For more information consult the *Sounder* (www.soundernews.com), one of the island's two free weekly newspapers, which lists the group's current and upcoming activities.

### 1. Descanso Bay Regional Park to Cox Community Park ★★★

| | |
|---|---|
| Trail length | About 4.5 kilometres |
| Time required | 60 minutes |
| Description | A well-signed trail allows easy access to two bays and headlands. |
| Level | Easy |
| Access | Left off Taylor Bay Road, 900 metres north of the ferry. A gravel road leads to a parking area near the beach. |
| Cautions | Stay on the groomed trail in the winter months or after rain, as slippery rocks make this hike hazardous. |

The trail starts just right of the notice board in the parking area of the park's day-use section and leads up a gentle slope. Keep to the right at all forks and you'll soon see a plaque that provides a history of the park. To your right is the original home of the McDougall family. The headland just beyond the house provides a view of Descanso Bay, with Protection and Newcastle islands across the channel and Nanaimo and Mount Benson beyond. In the spring you'll find a mass of wildflowers and flowering shrubs along the rocky bank below. In summer locals like to watch the sunset from the smooth, warm sandstone shoreline.

Continue clockwise around the headland with the house to your right. The trail descends to a footbridge that leads to a split rail fence at the head of the bay. Cross the footbridge and, at the end of the fence, look for a narrow trail that winds up to some amazing rock formations. Taking great care of the steep drop-off, follow the trail to the top, where you reach McConvey Road. Turn right and walk back toward Taylor Bay Road.

The "Yogi" rock figure you'll see on the bank at Taylor Bay Road was erected by the Youth Organization of Gabriola Island in the 1960s. Continue a few metres to the left and cross the road to the signed trailhead into Cox Community Park. From here the trail passes through typical coastal forest terrain. Turn right on Yogi Trail, walk for about 10 minutes to another junction and turn left on River Place Trail. You'll soon see a majestic stand of bigleaf maples at an "S" turn. This area is resplendent with the vibrant colours of the maples in the autumn and the deep greens of the mosses, lichen and ferns of the rain forest in the winter.

You will soon reach a junction and a choice:

• The trail on your left leads up a steep slope and returns the way you came. Keep left at all forks until you reach the clearing where you started the Yogi Trail. Take it and turn right when you reach the T-junction at the end; Taylor Bay Road is only a few metres away. Cross the road to return to the starting point of the walk via the gravel access road into Descanso Bay Regional Park.

• If you take the trail straight ahead, you will soon reach a fork. The left fork leads into private property and is closed off. Take the right fork along a winding forest trail for about 700 metres to a bridge that spans a marshy wetland. Beyond the bridge the trail winds up a short hill to the River Place entrance to the park. You can take other longer, circular walks from here, but to complete this hike simply return the way you came to the junction with the return route described above.

## 2. MALASPINA GALLERIES TO TWIN BEACHES AND RETURN ★★★

| | |
|---|---|
| Trail length | About 3 kilometres |
| Time required | 60 minutes or more, as the galleries are particularly beautiful |
| Description | A walk that follows a unique sandstone shelf to a sandy beach, offering panoramic views and intertidal life |
| Level | Easy |
| Access | The Malaspina Galleries Community Park parking area at the end of Malaspina Drive (off Taylor Bay Road) |

| Cautions | Be careful of the steep drop-off near the starting point. Do not walk on the unstable ledge above the galleries or inside the galleries where you might be endangered by falling rock. Slippery rocks and high tides make the sandstone ledge from Malaspina Galleries Community Park to Gabriola Sands Provincial Park hazardous from late September to mid-May. |
| --- | --- |

*Note: This hike can be combined with hikes 3 and 4 to make a magnificent large loop. Take a picnic lunch and allow four hours to complete the loop.*

This spot is a must-see: a community park on a beautiful little point that includes an unusual natural phenomenon—a hooded sandstone ledge sculpted by the elements. For about 100 metres at the edge of the sea, the rounded sandstone overhang extends several metres out from the solid rock cliff from which it was formed.

This rare geological feature was originally named Galiano Gallery after the Spanish explorer Dionisio Alcalá Galiano, who visited the area in 1792 and described the galleries in his reports. The galleries reminded the Spaniards of the cloisters commonly found in Europe, but with floors of honeycombed, pockmarked rock and ceilings of smooth, curved sandstone.

Take the short access trail from the parking area, through trees to an open sandstone clifftop. Walk to your left and out to the edge of a sheer drop to the sea below. Be very careful, especially if you are with small children. To view the galleries walk out toward the headland and down the sandstone slope. You must view the galleries from the beach as the area above them is unstable and there's a danger of falling rock if you enter them.

After leaving the galleries, go out to the headland for spectacular views, especially at sunset. From the headland, continue right along the sandstone ledge to Taylor Bay, about 1.2 kilometres to the east. The sandy beach at Taylor Bay is part of Gabriola Sands Provincial Park (known locally as Twin Beaches).

From here you can continue with hike 3 and/or 4. If you wish to return, either retrace your steps along the shoreline to the Malaspina Galleries or take an alternate route along the country roads by crossing the open grassy area behind the beach to Ricardo Road. Turn right on Ricardo Road and walk to Berry Point Road. Turn right on Berry Point Road and, at the next intersection, turn right again on Davis Road and then left on Harwood Road. This route returns you to Malaspina Drive, where you turn right and walk to the end of the road where you began.

*The Malaspina Galleries—also known as the Galiano Galleries—formed by wind and salt spray over past millennia, attract hundreds of visitors every year. A famous portrayal of the galleries by Jose Cardero hangs in the Museo Navel in Madrid.* Carolyn Davey

## 3. TWIN BEACHES HEADLAND LOOP ★★★

| | |
|---|---|
| Trail length | About 3 kilometres |
| Time required | 45 minutes |
| Description | A walk along beaches and a sandstone shore offering panoramic views, rock formations and intertidal life |
| Level | Easy |
| Access | The parking area at Gabriola Sands Provincial Park toward the end of Ricardo Road |
| Cautions | Slippery rocks make the sandstone ledge too hazardous from late September to mid-May. |

*Note: This hike can be combined with hikes 2 and 4 to make a large loop. Take a picnic lunch and allow four hours to complete the loop.*

Gabriola Sands Provincial Park (Twin Beaches) spans two sandy beaches on either side of a narrow neck of land. This hike starts on the beach at Taylor Bay, which is the end of hike 2. From the Gabriola Sands parking area, walk over the grass field to Taylor Bay beach. Walk to the north end of the beach and follow the rocky shelf close to the high tide line. For the first 100 metres or so you have to pick your way among the rocks, but will soon find yourself on a smooth sandstone shelf.

Follow the sandstone ledge around the headland. On a clear day you can see Mount Benson behind Nanaimo, and as you round the first headland you get a panoramic vista to Lasqueti and Texada islands to the north. Continue along this north ledge until you round the next headland. In the distance to the east you'll see the Entrance Island lighthouse. Continue a further 100 metres toward Pilot Bay and look for a yellow marker on your right indicating a public-access wooden stairway. Climb the stairs and follow the short trail to Decourcy Drive. Turn left and follow the road, turning left again at Ricardo Road to return to your starting point at Gabriola Sands Provincial Park.

## 4. TWIN BEACHES TO ORLEBAR POINT ★★★

| | |
|---|---|
| Trail length | About 8 kilometres |
| Time required | 2 hours |
| Description | A walk along a sandstone shore and a scenic road, with views, rock formations and interesting intertidal life |
| Level | Moderate |
| Access | From the parking area at Gabriola Sands Provincial Park (see hike 3) |
| Cautions | Slippery rocks make the sandstone ledge too hazardous from late September to mid-May. |

*Note: This hike can be combined with hikes 2 and 3 to make a large loop. Take a picnic lunch and allow 4 hours to complete the loop.*

Start from the shore at Pilot Bay, to the east side of the parking area. Turn right along the shore and follow the sandstone ledge, heading northeast toward the lighthouse on Entrance Island. Continue along the sandstone ledge for about 2.5 kilometres to a headland at the end of Seagirt Road.

To get to the sandstone ledge on the other side of Clark Bay, you must take a short diversion along Seagirt and Berry Point roads. To find the trail to Seagirt Road, stand at the headland with your back to the lighthouse. Walk along Seagirt Road and then turn left onto Berry Point Road. Follow the path along Berry Point Road.

After about 150 metres, you'll see several beach-access trails down to the sandstone ledge. Follow the sandstone shelf toward the lighthouse. Alternatively, you can stay on the road, which runs parallel to the seashore. Either way, it is about 1.2 kilometres farther to Orlebar Point, a good place to rest and view the lighthouse.

To return to where you started, either retrace the beach route or follow Berry Point Road all the way back to Ricardo Road, opposite the Twin Beaches Shopping Centre. Follow Ricardo Road down the slope to your starting point at Gabriola Sands Provincial Park.

If you are returning to the starting point of hike 2, instead of turning onto Ricardo Road, continue along Berry Point Road to Malaspina Drive. Then refer to the directions for hike 2.

| 5. AROUND SANDWELL PROVINCIAL PARK ★★★ | |
|---|---|
| Trail length | About 3 kilometres |
| Time required | 45 minutes |
| Description | This trail leads to a sandy beach where you can walk at low tide. |
| Level | Easy, although there is one short, steep section on the trail |
| Access | The parking area at the end of the Strand |
| Facilities | Pit toilets, picnic tables |
| Caution | Shore access is limited to periods of low tide. |

From the parking area, take the trail into this 12-hectare park. The trail—an old logging road—is flanked by high rocky cliffs to the west and the sea, below the trail, to the east. Just a few minutes into the trail, you'll notice stairs down to the beach. These are a good alternative to the steep shore access 1 kilometre along the trail. Either way, take care going down. At the bottom of the slope continue straight to an open meadow area. At the end of the meadow look over the fence at the small, marshy area, a wintering site for the many species of ducks that start arriving in late September and stay until April.

Follow the fence down to the beach and walk along it as far as the private residence at the north end of the bay. If the tide is high, return by the trail you took into the park. If the tide is low, continue south along the sandy beach around the bay. You'll know you're out of the park when you round a point and reach another small bay with residences beside the beach.

At the south end of this bay, make your way over the sandstone ledge to a straight stretch of mixed sandstone shelf and shingle beach. Look for a community boat launch about 100 metres along this beach and take it up to End Road. You'll find a large parking area at the top. Walk to the next road (the Strand), turn right and continue about 400 metres along the road to the starting point of the hike.

## 6. AROUND WHALEBONE BEACH ★★★

| Trail length | About 2 kilometres |
|---|---|
| Time required | 30 minutes |
| Description | A short walk on a pebble beach, a sand beach and a woodland trail |
| Level | Easy |
| Access | At the end of Whalebone Drive |
| Caution | Shore access is limited to periods of low tide. |

Walk back along Whalebone Drive to just past Daggoo Place, where you'll find a signed trail on the right (east) leading to a community park. This trail opens onto a grassy area and ends at steps that descend to the beach. Turn right on the beach and walk along the high tide line. Just offshore is a rock outcropping that is home to a colony of harbour seals. After about 500 metres you'll round a headland that opens onto Whalebone Beach. Walk along the beach toward the cliffs at its east end. At low tide you can reach an extensive sandy beach with tide pools.

To return, walk back along Whalebone Beach, looking for steps up the bank to a trail at the top of the beach. At time of writing this spot was marked by a rope swing hanging from a tree near the high tide line. At the top of the steps you'll join a woodland trail that follows the top of the bank. Turn right and take this trail until you reach your starting point on Whalebone Drive.

There are a number of community parks along Whalebone Drive, all with marked accesses and steps down to the beach. You can make this hike longer by exploring these parks.

It's also possible to walk all the way from Sandwell Provincial Park to Whalebone Beach at low tide. But beware: the loose, round beach stones make for tough going. At low tide it's easier, and more interesting, to walk along the rock ledges and sandy beaches at the water's edge. Locals consider the rocky shore walk more of an endurance test than a pleasant stroll.

| 7. Drumbeg Provincial Park ★★★★ | |
|---|---|
| Trail length | 2.6 kilometres in the park; 4.8 kilometres if you add the beach walk |
| Time required | At least an hour |
| Description | A walk along established park trails and a picturesque sandstone shoreline |
| Level | Easy |
| Access | The end of Stalker Road or from the park's parking area off Stalker Road |
| Facilities | Pit toilets, picnic tables |

*Note: This hike can be combined with hike 8.*

The trail runs from Stalker Road to the northern boundary of this 20-hectare park. It follows the shore, which is made up of sculptured sandstone shelves weathered into fascinating formations. You can walk along the Garry-oak-lined trail or, at low tide, along the sandstone shore, which can be reached by carefully descending the step-like rocks at the north edge of the park. Try going along the trail one way and returning by the shore, or vice versa.

At low tide you have the option of continuing north for 1.2 kilometres along the beach beyond the park boundary to the channel between Gabriola and Sear Island (one of the Flat Top Islands) and then retracing your steps to Drumbeg Park. On your return along the beach you can loop back to where you started by following the shore access about 200 metres from the park (it's on a grassy knoll between two houses and is marked by a yellow stone marker and yellow paint on trees). This woodland walk will take you back to Stalker Road about 50 metres east of the park entrance. (Turn left at the road to return to the parking lot.) There's one junction on this trail where you must turn left to reach the road. If you decide not to do the loop, return the way you came.

Be sure to walk the trail west in the southern part of the park, between Stalker Road and the parking area. This will give you a chance to see the strong tidal current through narrow Gabriola Passage, which can reach as high as 7 knots. To the south across the passage is Valdes Island.

From Stalker Road continue along the path outlined in hike 8 or return to the parking area.

*Located next to Gabriola Passage, Drumbeg Provincial Park has a bit of everything—a lovely trail through a grove of huge Garry oaks, sandstone formations, and views of the busy boat traffic through the Flat Top and Passage Islands.*

## 8. DRUMBEG PROVINCIAL PARK TO DEGNEN BAY ★★★

| Trail length | 7 kilometres |
|---|---|
| Time required | 90 minutes |
| Description | A walk along sandstone shoreline and country roads |
| Level | Easy |
| Access | The end of Stalker Road or the parking area in Drumbeg Provincial Park |

*Note: This hike can be combined with hike 7.*

Take the trail onto the beach from the end of Stalker Road and walk right (southwest) along the high tide line for 100 metres. Look for steps made out of old car tires. At the top of the steps continue on the trail that leads away from the beach. Follow the trail signs.

The trail goes through low bush and enters onto what appears to be a private driveway, but is actually an undeveloped section of Sir Williams Drive. Continue to your right (northwest) for 150 metres until you reach a gravel road (Martin Road). Turn right and follow the road for about 1 kilometre, at which point you will see Degnen Bay to your left.

Continue along Martin Road until you reach the paved road (South Road), where you turn left. On the opposite side of South Road is a large Garry oak with a "Gossip Corner" sign nailed to it. Early settlers on this end of Gabriola Island would gather here to await the mail delivery by boat into Degnen Bay. Continue past the oak tree and turn left onto Bevmaril Crescent. After 100 metres turn left again onto Maple Lane, which ends 50 metres farther at the top of a bluff. Take the narrow trail that starts beside a fire hydrant supply line and descends to Degnen Bay Road on Degnen Bay. This trail is eroding and is slippery and treacherous when wet. Proceed with caution; a fall over the bluff could be terminal. If you walk on the government dock, you will soon feel the ambiance of this historic harbour, which serves both commercial and pleasure vessels.

Turn right (west) on Degnen Bay Road and follow it until you reach South Road. Turn right and walk along South Road for about 1.2 kilometres past Gossip Corner until you reach Coast Road. Turn right (east) on Coast Road and continue until you reach Stalker Road, then turn right once again. Follow Stalker Road until it reaches the sea at Drumbeg Provincial Park, where you began your hike.

## 9. False Narrows to Spring Beach Drive ★★★

| | |
|---|---|
| Trail length | About 6 kilometres |
| Time required | About 2 hours return |
| Description | A beach walk with views of De Courcy and Mudge islands |
| Level | Easy |
| Access | From the Gabriola Community Hall parking area on the north side of South Road, just east of Lackhaven Road |
| Caution | This walk should be done at low tide. |

*Note: This hike can be combined with hike 10.*

Turn right (west) on South Road and continue down the hill toward the shoreline until you reach a shore access (stairs down to the shoreline) indicated by the usual yellow marker and yellow paint (800 metres from the community hall and just past a small dilapidated metal shelter). Once on the beach, turn left and walk east. (There is another shore access that you may see before you reach the stairway. It's just past the bottom of the hill about 500 metres from the community hall, and descends steeply to the shore on rocks. There's a rope to keep you from falling, but be very careful if you use this informal access, especially in the winter when the rocks will be slippery.)

The easiest walking is on the fine shale at the high tide line. Ahead you can see Pylades Channel between Valdes Island on the left and Mudge, Link and De Courcy islands to your right. After about 1 kilometre you will see a large meadow behind the beach, where farmland runs right down to the shoreline.

Continue along the beach for another 500 metres. You will reach a steep, impassable cliff with interesting erosion patterns in the large sandstone rocks at its base. From here, return to your starting point by retracing your steps along the beach. You are now looking toward False Narrows, which runs between Gabriola and Mudge islands. Look for the stairs that will take you back to South Road. Turn right and return to the parking lot where you started.

If you wish to combine this hike with hike 10, stay on the beach and continue west toward False Narrows. After 500 metres look for the wide trail that comes down to the beach from the steep bank above; this is the start of the next hike.

## 10. FALSE NARROWS SHORELINE ★★

| | |
|---|---|
| Trail length | 3–4 kilometres |
| Time required | 1 hour |
| Description | A walk along a shale shore with views of Mudge, Link, De Courcy and Valdes islands, as well as the tidal action in False Narrows and herons feeding at low tide |
| Level | Easy, with the usual stone obstacles and slippery footing of the beaches |
| Access | A short, unmarked road access to the shore across from Stokes Road (off South Road about 9 kilometres east of the ferry), between a row of mailboxes and Gabriola's cemetery |
| Cautions | This walk should be done at low tide. |

*Note: This hike can be combined with hike 9.*

Take the wide trail to the shore and walk right (northwest) along the shore-line. The easiest walking is on the fine shale at the high tide line. After about 100 metres, turn around and look back at the beach-access trail you just descended; you will need to be able to find it again on your return. Then continue along the shoreline, with a view of downtown Nanaimo in the distance.

False Narrows runs like a river between Gabriola and Mudge islands. The tidal flow in the narrows is significant. It flows toward Nanaimo on an incoming tide; it flows in the reverse direction on an outgoing tide. At low tide a large sandbar is exposed, a favourite fishing spot for blue heron.

You will soon see a community boat launch and parking lot used by residents of Mudge Island, who leave their cars parked on the Gabriola side of the crossing. As you continue, the narrows opens into a wider bay. When you can no longer see residences, you have reached Brickyard Beach. You can still find remnants of the clay bricks made in a factory that once stood on the hill above.

At this point simply retrace your steps or take this short diversion: leave the shoreline and go up to South Road above the beach. Turn right and walk along the road until you reach El Verano Drive. Turn right (east) once more onto El Verano and walk along this residential road until you reach the boat launch access on your right. Take this access back to the shore, turn left (east) and follow the shoreline back to where you began.

## 11. ELDER CEDAR (S'UL-HWEEN X'PEY) NATURE RESERVE ★★★

| | |
|---|---|
| Trail length | 3–4 kilometres |
| Time required | 1 hour |
| Description | A walk through old-growth fir and cedar forest along a creek |
| Level | Easy |
| Access | A. On the north side of North Road just west of Degnen Road (Look for the large sign just inside the trees off the road.) |
| | B. From the end of Windecker Drive (off Seawind Drive off North Road) |
| Cautions | Be careful walking on the exposed roots and across the wet areas, especially where the trails border the creek. |

This 63.5-hectare nature reserve, an Islands Trust Fund property, contains many beautiful old-growth cedar and fir trees, rocky outcrops and a beautiful creek. The unsigned trails are easy to walk and to find if you follow these directions.

Start at access A and follow the trails clockwise. At the first junction take the trail to the left (you will return on the trail to your right). You will be walking parallel to the creek, which is fairly dry in the summer but very active in the wetter seasons. You may see another less-used trail going off to the left; it returns to another access on North Road. If you see this trail, ignore it and continue to the right. You will soon cross the creek using a bridge constructed by volunteers working for the Gabriola Land and Trails Trust (GaLTT).

At the next junction you can turn right and return to the trailhead to complete a half-hour walk. If you want a longer walk, take the trail to the left and continue to a grassy road, which crosses the adjacent piece of federal Crown land. Turn right on this road and follow it, keeping right when you see a house in the near distance where the road narrows back to a trail. Follow it around until you reach the end of Windecker Drive. From here, you can retrace your steps through the forest to the trailhead, taking left turns whenever you have the choice, or follow the roads (Windecker to Seawind to North) to where you began (about 3 kilometres in total).

## 12. 707 COMMUNITY PARK ★★

| | |
|---|---|
| Trail length | 5 kilometres |
| Time required | 60–90 minutes |
| Description | Unsigned logging roads and paths in recently logged forest |
| Level | Easy |
| Access | A. From the ends of Fisher Road, Mary Road, Ricki Road and Jeanette Avenue |
| | B. From a small community park on the north side of Coats Drive east of Aidan Road |
| | C. From North Road by a right-of-way through the federal Crown land (Stumps Block Trail) 8–9 kilometres from the ferry |
| Cautions | Be careful not to get lost on the unmarked trails in this huge community park, or to trespass on adjacent private land. |

This very large, undeveloped, 286-hectare (707-acre) community park was created in 2005. It contains a view ridge, a seasonal lake, some meadow and many alders filling in the land where the firs and cedars were logged. While many logging roads criss-cross the property, a trail system has been planned but not signed at time of writing. The Gabriola Land and Trails Trust (GaLTT) was not encouraging people to hike here, although they hoped to have the trails signed in a year or so. If you decide to walk here, take your compass and be sure you know how to use it, as many people have been lost in the large area (twice as large if you stray into the neighbouring federal Crown land). For up-to-date information on trails, consult the Regional District of Nanaimo website, www.rdn.bc.ca, or contact the Gabriola Visitor Centre (1-888-284-9332; 250-247-9332) or the GaLTT (information@galtt.ca).

# SHORT WALKS

## 13. EASTHOM ROAD

From the ferry, walk south along Easthom Road as far as Harrison Way. This quiet back road is very pretty, with views toward Nanaimo. On the way stop at the tiny (25-hectare) Coats Millstone Nature Reserve (owned by the Islands Trust Fund) to see the expansive view toward Nanaimo, as well as some of the grindstones once quarried on Gabriola and the intriguing holes (now pools of water covered with green algae) from which they were taken. (At time of writing these were closed to the public because the steep, rough approach to them was over dangerous, slippery rocks; the Islands Trust Fund indicated plans to build a proper trail to them.) You can retrace your steps at the end of Harrison Way. If you're feeling energetic, continue south along Easthom Road to Canso Drive and continue with walk 14. There are shore accesses on Harrison, Easthom and Canso, as well as a lookout about 500 metres along Canso from its junction with Easthom.

## 14. CANSO DRIVE TRAIL

Drive along Easthom Road (to your immediate right after leaving the ferry terminal) to the end of Canso Drive. Follow the old logging road south along the high sandstone cliffs. Make your way down to a beautiful flat rock that projects over the water. This shelf-like piece of sandstone is just large enough to shelter two people and a picnic lunch. It's particularly tranquil, as you are shielded from the views of Nanaimo and the Harmac pulp mill across the channel.

## 15. PETROGLYPHS BY THE CHURCH

There are a number of petroglyphs in an open area of provincially owned land on moss- and grass-covered sandstone behind the United Church on South Road, just east of Price Road. Look for the petroglyph sign behind the church and follow a trail beside a fence for about 5 minutes. Foot traffic and rubbings have eroded the petroglyphs. Treat them with care so that others may be able to enjoy them. Alternatively, you can see the copies of these and other petroglyphs at the Gabriola Museum. From the petroglyphs you can follow a community trail that ends at a road to the north called Petroglyph Way. You can then return the way you came or walk along roads (right to Crocker, left to Darby, right to Peterson and right at South) in a loop to return to the church. If you do all this, you will have walked about 6 kilometres and will have passed a pleasant 90 minutes.

## 16. COATS MARSH REGIONAL PARK

This 46-hectare park was purchased in 2008 by the Nature Trust of British Columbia and the Regional District of Nanaimo, which manages the property. The access to it is from Aidan Road (off Coats Drive off South Road). The park contains 10 hectares of wetland, as well as Douglas-fir forest, and has two creeks running through it. It is currently undeveloped and has no trail system. It has high value for birdwatching. While a corner of this park touches a corner of 707 Community Park, you cannot legally go from one to the other at time of writing without trespassing on private land. You should wear rubber boots if you decide to go birdwatching here.

# AND IF YOU PADDLE . . .

Gabriola is a paddler's delight—endless shore accesses from which to launch, kilometres of interesting shoreline and bays to explore and, aside from the strong currents in False Narrows and Gabriola Passage, generally placid waters to negotiate. As a rule of thumb, if the wind is from the southeast, the Gabriola Sands or Descanso Bay launch sites will provide calmer waters. If the wind is from the northwest, choose the Drumbeg Park or El Verano Drive launch sites. The following are a few of the many other shore accesses on Gabriola.

**Descanso Bay Road:** You can launch at the end of Descanso Bay Road (off Easthom Road, which is your first right off the ferry). From here you can paddle southeast into Northumberland Channel and, being very careful to check the current first, into False Narrows between Mudge and Gabriola islands. You might also paddle north to see the Malaspina Galleries from the water; in this case you'd want to be careful not to cross the ferry dock when the ferry is coming in or already docked and preparing to leave.

**Gabriola Sands Provincial Park:** The sheltered sandy bays here make for easy launch access. With this as a starting point, you can paddle the shoreline from Malaspina Galleries to Orlebar Point, where you'll have a good view of the Entrance Island lighthouse.

**Descanso Bay Regional Park:** The small cove at the beach parking lot is a good place to launch to see sunsets or to paddle north to view the Malaspina Galleries.

**From a short side road off El Verano Drive:** The El Verano boat launch (parking lot) gives you easy access to False Narrows and the northeastern shore of Mudge Island. Check your tide and current tables and be careful to pick your times carefully: the river-like current through False Narrows flows swiftly. This launch site is recommended only for experienced paddlers.

**Gray Road to Degnen Bay:** A shore access at the end of Gray Road puts you in Degnen Bay. From here, you can paddle out to explore Mudge, Link, De Courcy, Ruxton and Pylades islands, as well as the beautiful sandstone cliffs along the Valdes shore. The gently sloping sandstone at this shore access can have a coating of very slippery algae in winter, so use the access with caution. Be careful of the very swift tidal flow at the entrance to Degnen Bay.

**Drumbeg Provincial Park:** Put in at the sandy beach by the parking lot and explore the sandstone formations along the Drumbeg shoreline, the Flat Top Islands to the north and Silva Bay. Check your tide and current tables and keep away from the strong tidal flows through Gabriola Passage.

# Galiano

*L*ong, skinny Galiano is the second largest of the southern Gulf Islands, covering 57 square kilometres. Its approximately 1,260 residents enjoy a distinctly Mediterranean climate, with the lowest rainfall on the southern coast. Well-protected Montague Harbour is one of the most popular anchorages in the Gulf Islands and, along with Sturdies Bay, is home to most of the island's services. Galiano's mature forests and sandy beaches combined with its excellent hiking give credence to the locals' claim that it is the "gem" of the Gulf Islands. The views from Bodega Ridge and Mount Galiano alone are worth the trip.

## HISTORY

Long before the arrival of European explorers, the Penelakut people had summer camps on Galiano. The island was named after Spanish navy captain Dionisio Alcalá Galiano, who commanded the *Sutil* and explored the channels between Vancouver Island and the mainland in 1792.

One of the earliest white settlers was Henry Georgeson, who came from the Shetland Islands and built a cabin on what is now Georgeson Bay in 1863. Farming was never very successful on Galiano because of the lack of good land and the shortage of water. Most people also hunted deer, raised sheep and fished to support themselves. Herring was salted in five different places on Galiano, four run by Japanese and the fifth by Chinese. Settlement centred around Whaler, Sturdies and Georgeson bays—all areas where the majority of Galiano residents live today.

## GETTING THERE

BC Ferries has several ferry sailings each day from Swartz Bay (near Victoria) to Sturdies Bay on Galiano, two sailings from Tsawwassen (near Vancouver) and two sailings most days from Salt Spring Island. For details obtain a BC Ferries schedule or contact BC Ferries. Saltspring Air flies to Galiano from Vancouver and Vancouver airport; Seair Seaplanes flies to Galiano from the Vancouver airport (see page 320).

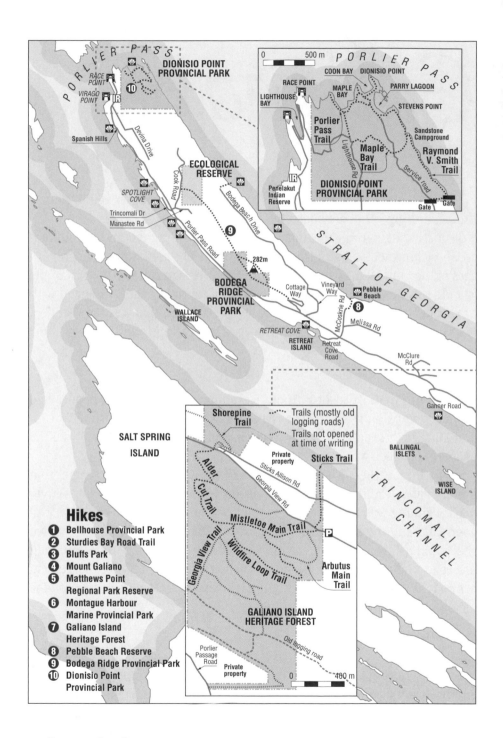

**Hikes**

1. Bellhouse Provincial Park
2. Sturdies Bay Road Trail
3. Bluffs Park
4. Mount Galiano
5. Matthews Point Regional Park Reserve
6. Montague Harbour Marine Provincial Park
7. Galiano Island Heritage Forest
8. Pebble Beach Reserve
9. Bodega Ridge Provincial Park
10. Dionisio Point Provincial Park

**Galiano Island**

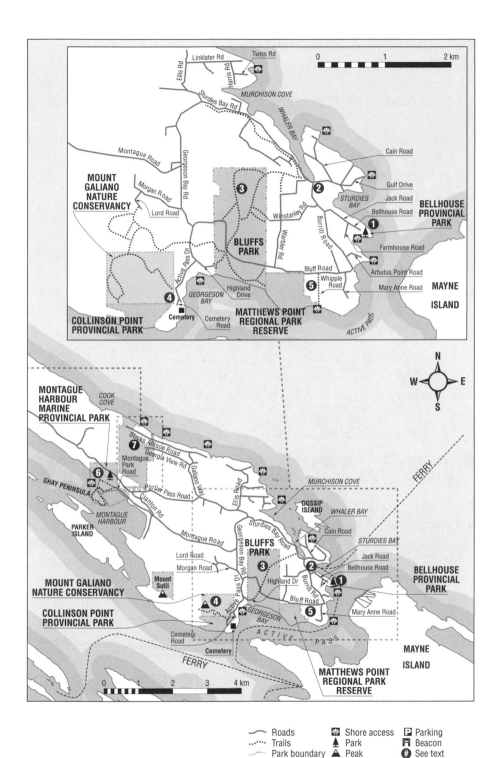

Roads
Trails
Park boundary

Shore access
Park
Peak

Parking
Beacon
See text

## SERVICES AND ACCOMMODATION

Most of Galiano's services are in the Sturdies Bay–Whaler Bay area near the ferry terminal, and include grocery stores, restaurants, a laundromat, bookstore and bakery, and ATM machines (at the pub and in the store), but no bank.

Accommodations are spread throughout the island and include bed and breakfasts, inns, lodges and cottages. There are two public campgrounds: Dionisio Point Provincial Park in the north (water access only) and Montague Harbour Marine Provincial Park in the south, with road access.

For more information, pick up a current visitors' guide at a store or on the ferry or visit www.galianoisland.com.

## ESPECIALLY FOR WALKERS

Galiano has several enchanting walks. If you are not interested in the more strenuous hikes, concentrate on the Shore and Road Walks listed at the end of this chapter, as well as the following:

- Bellhouse Provincial Park (see hike 1)
- Sturdies Bay Road Trail (see hike 2)
- Montague Harbour Marine Provincial Park (see hike 6)
- Galiano Island Heritage Forest (see hike 7)
- Pebble Beach Reserve (see hike 8)

## HIKES on GALIANO

If you want a day trip to Galiano without a car, consider walking from the ferry to Bellhouse Provincial Park and then continuing on to Bluffs Park and Mount Galiano. As you can combine the hikes here in a number of different ways, I suggest you read the following hike descriptions while consulting the maps carefully as you plan your itinerary.

When you hike on Galiano you may see signs for trails on private land, which are not described in detail in this book. While the signs seem to encourage public access to these trails, changes in land ownership could result in changes to public access. For this reason I have referred to these trails where relevant, but I have not included full descriptions of them. If you are interested in walking any of these trails, be sure that the property owner is still agreeable to allowing hikers access to the property before you begin.

## 1. BELLHOUSE PROVINCIAL PARK ★★★

Although this 2-hectare park on Burrill Point has only a 1-kilometre-long trail, it is one of the most scenic little paths in the Gulf Islands. The park is 2.5 kilometres from the ferry. Follow Sturdies Bay Road to Burrill Road. Turn left (south) and follow the signs to the end of Jack Road, where it becomes Bellhouse Road. The trail follows the bluffs around the point. At low tide you can descend to the sandstone that lines the shore in several places; from here it is possible to walk northeast toward Sturdies Bay along the rocks. While in the park please keep to the trails, as the mossy vegetation is very fragile. The sandstone formations are especially intricate. The park has picnic tables, benches and outhouses, but no overnight camping is allowed.

## 2. STURDIES BAY ROAD TRAIL ★

This commuter/neighbourhood trail starts on the south side of Sturdies Bay Road across from the old log staging area on Whaler Bay, about 1 kilometre from the ferry landing. The trail roughly follows Sturdies Bay Road for about 2 kilometres, returning to the road across from a popular local market centre, with food stores, a food stand and a pub. At one point the trail follows the road toward Galiano Island Community School and then continues northwest before returning to parallel Sturdies Bay Road.

## 3. BLUFFS PARK ★★★

| | |
|---|---|
| Trail length | 4 kilometres each way |
| Time required | 60 minutes |
| Description | This pleasant hike along a short ridge combines splendid views with beautiful forest. |
| Level | Easy |
| Elevation | About 168 metres |
| Access | From Bluff Road, 4.5 kilometres from the ferry via Burrill Road. Look for the small signed parking area in the woods on the edge of the bluffs. |

In 1948 Marion and Max Enke sold 15.4 hectares and gave another 37.2 hectares of land on the bluffs to the Galiano Island Development Association. The ownership of the land was turned over to the Galiano Club (a

*Tiny Bellhouse Provincial Park is a treasure trove of lovely seaside walks, spring wildflower meadows, sandstone formations and spectacular views across Active Pass.*

community association founded in 1924 to build a community hall) in trust and Bluffs Park opened in 1948.

From the parking area you can walk both ways along the ridge, with wonderful views across Active Pass and down Navy Channel between Mayne Island on the left and North Pender Island on the right.

If you follow the trail west along the bluffs for about 10 minutes, you'll find yourself at a turnaround off Bluff Road. A trail to the left leads to Highland Road (a 10–15 minute walk). From there you can either return the way you came or walk down Highland Drive and turn left onto Active Pass Drive, continuing south to the main trailhead for Mount Galiano. Other trails that you may see in this park invariably lead through private property and are often poorly signed, so they have not been described here.

## 4. MOUNT GALIANO ★★★★

| | |
|---|---|
| Trail length | Up to 3 kilometres each way, depending on route taken |
| Time required | About 2 hours return |
| Description | A pleasant hike through beautiful mixed forest in an 81-hectare park with a spectacular view at the top of the southern Gulf Islands and the San Juan Islands |
| Level | Moderate |
| Elevation | 341 metres |
| Access | You will find a parking lot and the signed trailhead near the end of Active Pass Drive on the west side of the road. This is the only public trail authorized by the Galiano Club, which owns the property. You may see other signed trails in other locations (e.g., Lord Park Trail, Grace Trail, Alistair Ross Trail) that connect with the Mount Galiano Trail; these all go through private property and have not been described here. |
| Cautions | Fire is a constant danger on Mount Galiano. Do not smoke or create any sparks in this very dry and unprotected area. This and other areas on Galiano are closed in times of extreme fire hazard. |

The trail climbs mainly north-northwest for about 10 minutes and then swings left (south) for a while. It climbs fairly steeply and in some places runs very close to the edge of the cliff. This trail is signed with unpainted metal arrows.

After you have hiked about 40 minutes, the trail merges with an old logging road. Turn left (south). From here it's a 15–20 minute climb to the top (south and then east). You'll find some offshoot trails, but the main one is easy to follow and marked with metal arrows.

At the top of the mountain you will encounter a stand of Garry oak and fantastic views of the southern Gulf Islands. Unfortunately, you can walk

*Views from the top of Mount Galiano include a large stand of Garry oaks, other Gulf Islands in the distance, and the San Juan Islands.*

only a short distance in either direction along the top of the mountain before the trail starts to head down the cliff. Be careful not to get too close to the edge, as the rock is eroding. When you have had enough of the splendid view, return the way you came. After about 1 kilometre (15 minutes), look for the trail to the right off the logging road. If you miss it you'll end up on trails through private property (the Lord Park Trail leading to Lord Road or the Grace Trail leading to Georgeson Bay Road).

### 5. MATTHEWS POINT REGIONAL PARK RESERVE ★★★

The Capital Regional District (CRD) established this 33.6-hectare park reserve in 1999. The park contains steep bluffs with spectacular views of Active Pass, stands of mature Douglas-fir and pockets of arbutus and Garry oak, a 400-metre-long sandy beach and many wildflowers in the spring.

A public beach access, improved by the Galiano Island Parks and Recreation Commission, can be found on the south side of Bluff Road, 400 metres west of Mary Ann Road (see the shore walk for Matthews Beach, page 107). The official park access is about 2 kilometres west of Mary Ann Road.

About two-thirds of the way to the beach on the public access, an unauthorized trail leads off to the right (west). It follows the bluff overlooking Active Pass and is both rough and dangerous (it is eroding badly in places). The trail eventually comes out on Bluff Road at the official park access. I don't recommend this trail because of its condition and because it may be partly on private property. Hopefully, the CRD will develop a better trail to connect the shore access to the east with the bluffs on the west, as well as a trail to connect this park with adjacent Bluffs Park.

## 6. MONTAGUE HARBOUR MARINE PROVINCIAL PARK ★★★★

| | |
|---|---|
| Trail length | About 3 kilometres return |
| Time required | 1 hour |
| Description | A very enjoyable trail following the shoreline of the park, around Gray Peninsula and along a lagoon. Other trails behind the campsites explore the woods on the park's north side. |
| Level | Easy |
| Access | From the end of Montague Park Road (a continuation of Montague Road) |

Known for its spectacular beauty, this 106-hectare park receives many visitors each year. In one place the trail parallels a white shell beach, one of six shell middens found here, estimated to be over 3,000 years old. Archeologists have found spearheads, stone carvings and arrows on this site. As with other archeological sites, care should be taken not to damage or disturb the area. Use the stairs provided to reach the beach, rather than climbing the bank.

You'll find excellent, though chilly, swimming here. Gray Peninsula was named after a Captain Gray, who planted an orchard here to supply fruit for the Victoria market.

The lagoon, a tidal salt marsh, contains reeds, sedges and glasswort. Although it is possible to walk around the lagoon past the walk-in campsites and the wharf until you reach a park road that will bring you back to your starting point, it is probably more interesting to turn around and return along the water.

| 7. GALIANO ISLAND HERITAGE FOREST ★★ | |
|---|---|
| Trail length | About 6 kilometres in total |
| Time required | 1–2 hours |
| Description | A network of trails on old logging roads through recently logged forest with views over Georgia Strait |
| Level | Easy |
| Access | The end of Georgia View Road (off Galiano Way) |
| Facilities | Signboard, outhouse |

This 126-hectare heritage forest was acquired by the Galiano Club in 2005 and, according to the management plan for the property, it is being "managed in a manner that maintains or enhances the integrity of ecosystems while contributing to the economic and social well-being of the Galiano community." The management plan stipulates that environmental values are to be protected while "local economic opportunities for small scale sustainable forestry" are to be encouraged.

Meanwhile, there is a 6-kilometre trail network partly developed, mostly on old logging roads. I walked the Mistletoe Main (650 metres), which climbs about 50 metres into the forest, and the Wildfire Loop (1.2 kilometres), which follows the perimeter of an area badly damaged during a fire in 2006. Wildfire Loop also has views of Vancouver across the Strait of Georgia. Of the other trails shown on the property's signboard, Alder Cut (1.3 kilometres) can be walked, but Shorepine Main (450 metres), Georgia View (1.2 kilometres) and Arbutus Main (600 metres) were not officially open at time of writing; they might not be well signed or even passable. Sticks Trail (500 metres) is a narrow, well-treed path descending to Sticks Allison Road through a community park. Across the road from this trail is the Gulfside shore access (see page 109).

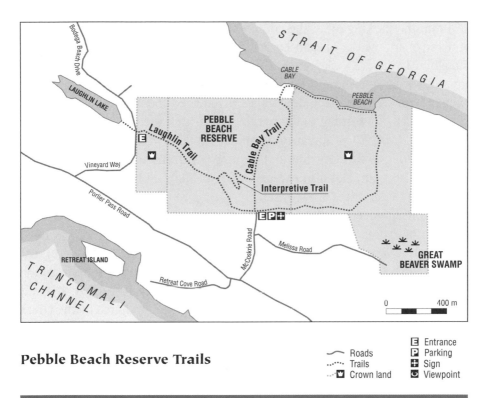

**Pebble Beach Reserve Trails**

| | |
|---|---|
| ⊟ | Entrance |
| ⌶ Roads | ⌿ Parking |
| ⋯⋯⋯ Trails | ✚ Sign |
| ⋯⋯◍ Crown land | ◍ Viewpoint |

## 8. PEBBLE BEACH RESERVE ★★★

| Trail length | 5–6 kilometres |
|---|---|
| Time required | 90 minutes |
| Description | A varied walk through young forest—which the Galiano Conservancy Association is restoring to a healthier state—to a small pond with water lilies and cattails, and then down to the ocean shore, returning through mature forest |
| Level | Easy |
| Access | A. A parking lot at the end of McCoskrie Road (east off Porlier Pass Road) |
| | B. On the north side of Vineyard Way, 550 metres north of Porlier Pass Road (parking available) |

This mixed bag of land and water is delightful. It consists of two pieces of Crown land and land owned by the Galiano Conservancy. It is expected that the Conservancy will ultimately manage all of this land.

From the parking lot at the end of McCoskrie Road you can walk these trails in many ways. I began by walking the trail through young forest to Laughlin Lake (1.25 kilometres). I then took a very short path through the grasses bordering Vineyard Way to the lakeside, where I watched a group of people who were studying dragonflies. I returned the way I'd come except that, instead of returning to the parking lot, I took the "restoration" or "interpretive" trail. A Conservancy pamphlet explains that it is trying "to convert the Douglas-fir monoculture to a forest with more diverse species and spaces." The pamphlet also explains each of the numbered points on this short (250-metre) trail.

The Interpretive Trail leads to the Cable Bay Trail (1 kilometre from the parking lot to the water). I followed this trail to the shoreline, where I stopped to enjoy the lovely beach. I then followed a trail (about 1 kilometre) just above the shoreline (at low tide this could be walked along the sandstone shore) through the Crown land to Pebble Beach. Finally, I returned on a trail through the Crown land to an old logging road, which took me by the Great Beaver Swamp to the parking lot (1.5 kilometres).

There are opportunities for excellent birdwatching and nature sightings at Laughlin Lake, and warm-water swimming at Cable Bay and Pebble Beach, thanks to the warming effect of fresh water from the Fraser River, which bathes the east shore of Galiano.

## 9. BODEGA RIDGE PROVINCIAL PARK ★★★★★

| | |
|---|---|
| Trail length | 6 kilometres each way |
| Time required | 70 minutes each way, but you'll want to spend longer in this beautiful park |
| Description | A ridge walk with constant views over Trincomali Channel, looking west to Salt Spring Island, Vancouver Island and the Strait of Georgia |
| Level | Moderate |
| Elevation | 282 metres |
| Access | The end of Cottage Way, which runs off Porlier Pass Road |

Bodega Ridge was named for Juan Francisco de la Bodega y Quadra, the Spanish commander of the *Nootka*, who explored the Strait of Georgia in 1792. The land was slated to be clear-cut until the Galiano Island Forest Trust bought a key section of it from the logger and then made payments on the mortgage while fundraising to buy the land. In 1995 the Nature Conservancy of Canada and the BC and federal governments contributed the remaining funds required to purchase the 233-hectare property.

One of the highlights of Bodega Ridge besides the great views is the manzanita that grows all along the edge of the ridge and blooms in April. Manzanita is particularly beautiful in spring when it flowers and then grows tiny, apple-like berries (the word *manzanita* means "little apples" in Spanish). The shrub's contorted reddish-brown branches flake and peel to reveal additional colours, as does the arbutus (madrone) tree.

From the end of Cottage Way you soon reach a sign indicating a trail for hikers to the left along the ridge, where the terrain is fragile, and an old logging road to the right for cyclists. It will take you up to 30 minutes to reach the ridge from the trailhead. (You're getting close when you walk through a thick patch of broom.) Once on the ridge you soon pass a natural rock bench with a spectacular view of nearby Wallace Island, other small islands and Salt Spring and Vancouver Island in the distance. The walk continues along the ridge with ever-increasing views toward the north.

*The fantastic views from Bodega Ridge include a group of small islands—Wallace, Jackscrew, South and North Secretary, Mowgli and Norway. Across Trincomali Channel is Salt Spring and to the north you can see Penelakut, Thetis, and even Chemainus and Ladysmith on Vancouver Island.*

You can continue past the BC Parks sign on the north end of the park and, after descending a bit, continue along the ridge edge. However, this trail is on private land and not nearly as beautiful as returning along the park trail to where you started.

| 10. DIONISIO POINT PROVINCIAL PARK ★★★★ | |
|---|---|
| Trail length | 7 kilometres in total |
| Time required | 2 hours, once you're there |
| Description | Sensational walks along the Porlier Pass and Georgia Strait shoreline and strolls through mature forest |
| Level | Easy |
| Access | People are expected to access the park by water, and there is no public land access. |
| Facilities | Benches, picnic tables, campsites, outhouses, signboards, water |
| Cautions | A. Porlier Pass between Galiano and Valdes islands is known for its strong currents, which run up to 9 knots at spring tides. These currents and the many exposed rocks have caused numerous shipwrecks over the years, making it one of the most respected stretches of water in the Gulf Islands. |
| | B. The land to the southwest is part of an Indian Reserve, which is home to members of the Penelakut First Nation. If you want to walk through this land to access the park, you must get permission from the band office (250-246-2321). If you walk through the reserve, be careful not to disturb the many middens. |
| | C. Numerous old roads connect the park with properties outside of it. These can be very confusing and can lead you onto private property. As well, some of the trails shown on the park's signboards are not being maintained. Stick to the trails shown on the map included here. |

Top: *Dionisio Point Provincial Park is the perfect place to watch the sun set over the Gulf Islands and the steady boat traffic navigating the swirling waters of Porlier Pass.* David Norget

*Above: Of special interest in Dionisio Point Provincial Park is this tombolo, a bar of sand connecting the tiny island bordering Coon Bay to Galiano.*

Perhaps the most interesting shore walks on Galiano are at Dionisio Point Provincial Park. This 142-hectare park, which includes most of the northern tip of the island around Coon Bay, was a gift to the community from MacMillan Bloedel when the logging company sold off most of its Galiano holdings. There are some trails through the woods, but the highlights are the shore walks.

Porlier Pass Trail connects the western edge of Maple Bay with the short trail to Dionisio Point. The Raymond V. Smith Interpretive Trail (1.3 kilometres) connects the tidal lagoon at Dionisio Point with the camping area on the park's east side and beyond. The Maple Bay Trail provides access from the shore to the mature forest in the park's interior.

You can walk along the sandstone formations of the shore at Dionisio in both directions, as well as along the shore of a small wooded peninsula that abuts Coon Bay. You can also walk almost indefinitely east and then south along Galiano's long, unsettled Strait of Georgia shore at low tide, with views of the Coast Mountains far away on the mainland. Or, if you walk west along the Porlier Pass Trail, you can walk from Coon Bay to Maple Bay, then past the light at Race Point and, finally, along a boardwalk for a total of about 1 kilometre.

## SHORE AND ROAD WALKS

### Shore Walks
The Galiano Island Parks and Recreation Commission manages more than 20 improved public shore accesses on Galiano and is working to improve more each year. Some accesses are simply a turnout on the road, whereas others have longer trails. The accesses are regularly monitored for public safety and are clearly signed, including access numbers at the trailhead and at the shore for emergency location purposes. Off-road or roadside parking is generally provided at each improved access. Once on the shore, at low tide you can often walk quite far. The following shore accesses are signed and easy to find. I've placed the reference numbers from the Galiano Island PRC's excellent website (www.crd.bc.ca/galianoparks/access.htm) in parentheses after each access name. The numbers are not sequential, because the website includes all possible shore accesses, not just those that have been improved (e.g., with signage, trails or steps).

Undoubtedly, by the time you read this there will be additional improved accesses to try. The accesses are listed in a clockwise direction around the island starting from just east of the ferry terminal.

**Cain Road (3):** From this access at the end of Cain Road, just off Sturdies Bay Road and less than 1 kilometre from the ferry, you can see Gossip Island and the Strait of Georgia. You can also clamber along the rocks on the beach for quite a distance.

**Gulf Drive (4):** Turn right on the first road you see after disembarking from the ferry. This short trail at the end of the road leads to a beautiful shoreline. Stone steps descend to a lovely tide pool area, driftwood and a pocket sand beach.

**Scorpion Point Road (10):** Off Farmhouse Road, this pretty 125-metre trail leads through a mixed wood of native and planted trees and shrubs to a lovely sand beach. Stone steps descend the rock retaining wall to the beach.

**Arbutus Road (11):** A short, gentle path at the end of the road next to 253 Arbutus Point Road leads to a scenic rocky shore with a fine view of Active Pass and Georgina Point lighthouse on Mayne Island. Wildflowers bloom here in profusion in the spring.

**Matthews Beach (Whipple Road) (15):** The access is opposite 556 Bluff Road, 400 metres west of Mary Ann Road. It takes 10 minutes to get down to the beach, which is exposed only at low tide. For the first 5 minutes the trail passes through lovely mixed forest alongside a fenced neighbouring property, before descending very steeply to the exquisite sandy beach below. There are ropes to hold as you descend about 40 metres. This challenging trail requires strength and good footwear. Be aware that the ferry wash and the currents in Active Pass can be dangerous. See the description of hike 5 for information on other trails here.

**Zuker Road (17):** In the past this access off Active Pass Drive was used both as a log skid and a trail. The 125-metre trail leads down several flights of stairs to a sandy beach that is especially pretty in morning light.

**Azure Road (27):** A 75-metre trail next to 192 Ganner Drive leads to a small, pretty pebble beach on Trincomali Channel, but it isn't possible to walk very far along it.

**Retreat Cove (Zilwood Road) (31):** Beside 13755 Porlier Pass Road, stone steps lead to a lovely beach beside the outflow of Greig Creek. Note that the private gazebo is on the public land.

**Lodge Road (33):** Across from Madrona Lodge (18715 Porlier Pass Road), a trail leads through the forest across a driveway to the rocky shoreline.

**Shaw's Landing (34):** This very short trail, opposite 19210 Porlier Pass Road, leads to a beautiful sand and shingle cove, a gurgling stream and some reed patches. This is a particularly easy place to launch a canoe or kayak and explore the shoreline.

**Trincomali Drive (37):** A short, steep trail at the end of Trincomali Drive leads to a rock shelf and a good swimming hole.

**Spotlight Cove (38):** At the end of Spotlight Cove Road. A rustic wooden bench overlooks a low bluff facing Trincomali Channel. Several stone steps lead to the rocks at the shoreline.

**Heather Shore (45):** Beside 21745 Porlier Pass Road, a few stone steps lead to a pleasant beach.

**Consiglio Trail (49):** Beside 4150 Bodega Beach Drive, 4 kilometres from Vineyard Way where Bodega Beach Drive becomes a gated private road leading to Dionisio Point. The 500-metre trail starts at the gate and follows a driveway for a short distance before descending to a shelving sandstone shore. There's parking just inside the driveway on the right. Be careful along the driveway, as the residents may not be able to see you as they drive toward you.

**Dewinetz Shore (50):** Beside 750 Bodega Beach Drive, 700 metres from Vineyard Way. A 450-metre dogleg trail descends 80 metres through Douglas-fir forest to a stony beach with long views to the mainland.

**Tricia Way (53):** On Sticks Allison Road, 300 metres west of its intersection with Galiano Way, this easy walk leads to a rocky shoreline lined with shore pines. There are community parks adjacent to the access. You can walk indefinitely along the sandstone shelf shoreline in either direction at low tide.

**Albion Lane (55):** This 125-metre path—100 metres east of the intersection of Sticks Allison Road and Galiano Way—doubles as the driveway for the property to the west and leads to a few steps that descend to the sandstone shoreline that runs along much of Galiano's north side.

**Ferris Road (Morning Beach) (59):** A lovely 350-metre trail from Ellis Road leads through mature forest to this pretty, sandy beach facing the Lion Islets. This was the first—and is still the most popular—shore access on Galiano. There is a portable toilet at the trailhead.

**Twiss Road (62):** A short path at the end of Twiss Road leads to a rock and driftwood shore. At low tide you can walk north to a sandy beach. This would be a good place to launch a canoe or kayak.

**Gulfside Shore (69):** At the west end of Sticks Allison Road and adjacent to the community park to the south, a trail leads down to the shelving sandstone shoreline. There are patches of wildflowers in the park in the spring. The trail through the park across the road leads to Galiano Island Heritage Forest (see hike 7).

There are also wonderful shore walks at Montague Harbour Marine Provincial Park (see hike 6) and Dionisio Point Provincial Park (see hike 10).

## Road Walks

Galiano also has some lovely road walks, made more enjoyable because of the light traffic. My favourite is the Georgeson Bay Road walk.

**Georgeson Bay Road:** Walk south along Georgeson Bay Road from Bluff Road and continue along Active Pass Drive. This is a little like walking along an old country lane—well-treed and green, with glimpses of the sea. Continue to Galiano's cemetery on Cemetery Road at the end of Active Pass Drive, where you will find headstones that bear the names of most of Galiano's early settlers. In 1928 George Georgeson deeded this land, originally a Native graveyard, to the Synod of the Anglican Diocese of British Columbia for use as a cemetery. The Georgeson family first settled on Galiano in 1863. On your way back consider walking along Highland Drive, which runs off Georgeson Bay Road just east of Active Pass Drive. Highland Drive climbs steeply and provides glimpses of Active Pass, so turn around and look behind you from time to time.

## AND IF YOU PADDLE . . .

Galiano's mainly unindented shoreline is not particularly interesting for paddling. Nevertheless, aside from Porlier Pass and Active Pass where there are very strong currents, paddling around Galiano is fairly safe, though kayakers should also be careful of the heavy boat traffic in Montague Harbour. In addition to the following suggestions, you can easily launch a canoe or a kayak at the shore accesses at Retreat Cove, Shaw's Landing and Heather Shore (see pages 107–8).

**Whaler Bay and Gossip Island:** Although most of the east side of the island is unprotected shoreline open to the Strait of Georgia, you might consider paddling in Whaler Bay and around Gossip Island. There's a government dock at the end of Whaler Road (off Cain Road).

**Twiss Road:** You can launch a canoe or kayak from this shore access to explore the northeast shore of Galiano, the Lion Islets and Gossip Island.

**Retreat Cove:** You can put in beside the old government dock on the west side of the island or from the shore access described on page 107. From there, paddle south to Montague Harbour (see hike 6) or out to Wallace Island where you will find numerous hiking trails (see pages 314–15). The rocks along the shore on the south side of Retreat Cove form a wonderful overhanging gallery and cave, which are best seen by kayak from the water.

**Spanish Hills:** A public dock at Spanish Hills gives boaters access to Trincomali Channel. There used to be a store here but it is now a private residence.

**Dionisio Point Provincial Park:** You can paddle to the park from the shore access at Spotlight Cove or the dock at Spanish Hills. Dionisio is in Porlier Pass, so either enter at slack tide or try to obtain permission from the Penelakut First Nation (250-246-2321) to land on their reserve just past the first light on Virago Point in Porlier Pass. This historic little inlet is connected with the provincial park by a beautiful trail that follows the rocky edge of the shore.

**Montague Harbour Marine Provincial Park:** This is a good place to put in. From here you can explore the harbour and nearby Parker, Charles and Wise islands. Do not disturb the wildlife in the Ballingall Islets Provincial Park, a provincial ecological reserve in which public access is not allowed.

*The 6-hectare Great Beaver Swamp was first mapped in 1888 by William Ralph. The beaver dam was breached in the mid-twentieth century so that the land could be used as pasture, but the beavers have returned to restore it, and the wetland is now protected by the Galiano Conservancy.* Christine Lester

# Hornby

*A*lthough farther from Vancouver Island than Denman, Hornby was settled first and continues to be the more popular of these sibling islands, hosting about 10,000 visitors each summer. Hornby's shoreline is punctuated with many bays, coves and spits. Its topography features the bluffs of Mount Geoffrey in the southwest and cliffs along cavernous Tribune Bay and into Helliwell Provincial Park in the east. Combine this with forest, sandy beaches and the warmest water in the Gulf Islands, and you have an unbeatable combination for an island of just over 30 square kilometres. Although it has only about 1,100 permanent residents, Hornby offers more services than some of the larger, more populated islands, including a credit union, gas bar, restaurants, bed and breakfasts, food store, pub and art galleries. With some of the most scenic hikes in the Gulf Islands, Hornby is well worth a visit.

## HISTORY

Hornby Island is named after Rear Admiral Phipps Hornby, commander-in-chief of the Pacific station from 1847 to 1851. The K'omoks First Nation camped and fished at Whaling Station Bay on the northeast side of the island long before Europeans gave it that name. Beginning in 1871 the bay was used as a base for the B.C. Whaling Company, until whales became too scarce a few years later. Two of Hornby's first settlers, George Ford and Horatio Maude, were friends from Devon, England. After arriving in the late 1860s they continued to receive incomes from abroad, and by 1885 owned about 40 percent of the island. Although the 1905 population was only 32 people, by then most of the island had been claimed. As on other Gulf Islands, the settlers supported themselves by farming, fishing and logging. Most of Hornby's original forest was logged between 1910 and 1920.

Hornby has a strong tradition of public involvement and community building. The Women's Institute and the Farmer's Institute were founded in 1921, the credit union in 1942 and the Hornby Island Co-operative Store in 1954. The Hornby Island Residents and Ratepayers Association currently helps administer a number of island facilities and services.

STRAIT OF GEORGIA

FLORA ISLET

CAPE GURNEY

Whaling Station Bay

ST. JOHN POINT

**1** HELLIWELL PROVINCIAL PARK

Anderson Road

TRALEE POINT

Fowler Road

St. John's Point Road

Shield's Rd

TRIBUNE BAY PROVINCIAL PARK

Spray Point

TRIBUNE BAY

LITTLE TRIBUNE BAY

**2**

DUNLOP POINT

Sandpiper Road

Sandpiper Beach

DOWNES POINT

Ostby Road

Slade Road

Seawright Road

Central Road

GRASSY POINT

Galleon Beach

Sollans Road

Fire Hall

Cemetery

Marylebone Rd

Strachan Road

Euston Road

**5**

NORMAN POINT

TOBY ISLAND

HERON ROCKS

Central Road

**3**

MOUNT GEOFFREY REGIONAL NATURE PARK

Mount Geoffrey △ 280 m

FORD'S COVE

Lea Smith Rd

**4**

Savoie Road

COLLISHAW POINT

Central Road

Mount Rd

**6**

**7**

SEE MOUNT GEOFFREY CLOSE-UP MAP

Shingle Spit Road

SHINGLE SPIT

MOUNT GEOFFREY ESCARPMENT PROVINCIAL PARK

PHIPPS POINT

LAMBERT CHANNEL

FERRY

DENMAN ISLAND

0      1      2 km

## Hikes

**1** Helliwell Provincial Park
**2** High Salal Ranch Trail
**3** Coltsfoot
**4** Cliff Trail from Lea Smith Road
**5** Cliff Trail from Strachan Road
**6** Bench Trail
**7** Ford's Cove–Shingle Spit Trail

〰 Roads
···· Trails
·▪·· Park boundary
⬛ See text
△ Peak
⊕ Crown land
🚻 Shore access
🛒 Shopping

## Hornby Island

# THE STORY OF YICK SHING

Yick Shing was a Chinese farmer who grew produce on his large farm for the Nanaimo market. Yick imported large amounts of rice from China, ostensibly to feed his Chinese workers, but in reality to make rice whiskey in a still that was camouflaged by hay in his barn near Heron Rocks. This was around 1920 during prohibition when whiskey was a very valuable product. The bottles of whiskey were packed in sauerkraut to hide them, placed in waterproof boxes and then shipped to Nanaimo under Yick's vegetables.

Eventually, Yick's "business" was discovered, and he was jailed for three years. But the story doesn't end there. Yick took advantage of the fact that his jailors could not tell Chinese men apart and managed to avoid serving his entire sentence by changing places with a cousin who came to visit him from time to time. When the guards weren't looking, Yick and his cousin would exchange clothes and identities, and after some time they would switch places again.

## GETTING THERE

To get to Hornby, you must first take the 10-minute ferry from Buckley Bay on Vancouver Island (about 20 kilometres south of Courtenay) to Denman Island, cross Denman Island (another 15 minutes) and then take the connecting 10-minute ferry to Hornby Island. For more information, obtain a copy of the BC Ferries schedule or contact BC Ferries (see page 320).

## SERVICES AND ACCOMMODATION

Most services are centred around the Hornby Island Co-op near Tribune Bay. The Co-op is a wonderful store that sells a wide variety of fresh and prepared foods at reasonable prices, as well as almost everything else, including liquor and gas. The Co-op also houses the post office and an ATM machine, and is surrounded by a couple of seasonal restaurants and several small stores. Another cluster of stores, including a pub and the credit union, is located at the Shingle Spit ferry dock. There is also a small general store, crafts shop, campground and marina at Ford's Cove. Store hours on Hornby vary with

*Hornby offers some of the most spectacular cliff walks in the Gulf Islands. This one in Helliwell Provincial Park is difficult to beat.* Mark Kaaremaa

the season. When I visited one March, no Hornby restaurant served dinner from Monday to Wednesday.

There are many bed and breakfasts on Hornby, as well as lodges and three or four private campgrounds. The three provincial parks are open for day use only. A combined visitor's guide to both Denman and Hornby, including a map of each island, is produced yearly and is available on the ferry and at other outlets. A great deal of tourist information is also provided on the Hornby websites, www.hornbyisland.com and www.realhornby.com. Hornby Island Outdoor Sports (1-877-977-2453; www.hornbyoutdoors.com), located by the Co-op, rents bicycles and kayaks, and also sells an excellent trail map of the island.

## ESPECIALLY FOR WALKERS
While hikers will enjoy climbing Mount Geoffrey, there are plenty of easy and beautiful walks for those less attracted to steep terrain. Here are a few suggestions:

- The trail at Helliwell Provincial Park (see hike 1) follows fairly level ground on a cliff edge with spectacular views over the Strait of Georgia. This is the premier walk on the island.
- The High Salal Ranch Trail (see hike 2) is almost as accessible as Helliwell and offers some of the views that Helliwell offers. But if you have to make a choice, choose Helliwell.

- The Spit Trail (see hike 7) follows the shoreline and has impressive views across Lambert Channel to Denman Island without the need for any strenuous climbing.
- Don't miss Tribune Bay Provincial Park (see page 125). At the very least, walk the park's spectacular beach.

Many easily accessible shore and road walks are outlined at the end of the chapter.

## HIKES on HORNBY

Hiking on Hornby is particularly good because of the large amount of public land. Three trails parallel each other at different heights along the southern slope of Mount Geoffrey (280 metres). These trails—the Ford's Cove–Shingle Spit Trail nearest the sea, the Bench Trail in the middle and the summit and ridge trails along the top of the bluffs of Mount Geoffrey—can be hiked individually, together or in combination with one of the innumerable other trails that interconnect with them and link them to other parts of the island. You might want to read about all these hikes (hikes 3–7) before deciding which you want to try. Additional suggestions for combinations are made in the descriptions that follow.

### 1. HELLIWELL PROVINCIAL PARK ★★★★★

| Trail length | 6-kilometre loop walk |
|---|---|
| Time required | 90-minute loop |
| Description | One of the finest walks in the Gulf Islands, through old-growth Douglas-fir forest and along weather-sculpted sandstone cliffs with glorious views of the mainland and Lasqueti and Texada islands. Consider visiting the park at low tide so that you can enjoy the tide pools. |
| Level | Easy |
| Access | The well-signed trailhead is at the parking lot toward the end of St. John's Point Road. |
| Cautions | No bicycles are allowed in the park. Dogs must be on leash. Stay on the trails. |

This 69-hectare park was a gift from John Helliwell to the people of BC in 1966. The best time to visit it is late April and early May, when wildflowers decorate the bluffs. A map at the trailhead illustrates the trail system.

After about 5 minutes from the trailhead, you reach a junction where you can choose either fork, the beginning of a loop trail. Turning left at the junction, you walk through forest containing old-growth fir, substantial red cedar, large maple and alder. The forest floor is covered with salal, Oregon grape, red huckleberry and leafy sword ferns.

In another 10 minutes you emerge from the forest at the edge of the water. Just offshore is Flora Islet, with its navigational light. Flora Islet is part of the park and accessible by canoe or kayak. In the spring, it's covered with wildflowers. It is also one of only two locations in the world where divers have seen the rare six-gill shark, which enjoys the relative shallows around the islet. Much farther east is Lasqueti Island, which is almost dwarfed by Texada behind it.

As you continue right along the shore, you will walk on the edge of spectacular cliffs worn by the wind and waves into sculptural shapes. At some point along here you will see a trail going off into the forest, which leads back to where you started. You can return this way if you're in a hurry, but I recommend continuing along the cliffs.

When you reach the park boundary on the southwest corner of the park, it's possible to continue along a marked public trail through the "Oak Grove" in the High Salal Ranch development and even as far as Tribune Bay (see hike 2). But you'll most likely want to turn back once this trail leaves the sea. As you return, you can take the trail back to the parking lot—a 5-minute walk through the forest—or, if you have the time and energy, retrace your steps along the water and see how different the views are when walking the other way.

*Cormorants pose on sandstone and conglomerate rocks that make up the Hornby shoreline.*

## 2. HIGH SALAL RANCH TRAIL
### (CONNECTING TO THE HELLIWELL PARK TRAIL) ★★★

| | |
|---|---|
| Trail length | 4 kilometres each way (from access A) |
| Time required | 50 minutes each way (from access A) |
| Description | A walk through the High Salal Ranch strata development on the west side of Helliwell Provincial Park that eventually follows bluffs overlooking the sea through a mixed forest of Garry oak, arbutus and Douglas-fir |
| Level | Easy |
| Access | A. Take St. John's Point Road to High Salal Ranch (1.7 kilometres from Central Road). You must park at the bottom of the strata's private road and walk along it to reach the trail. |
| | B. A trail from the east side of the outdoor education centre in Tribune Bay Provincial Park leads to the High Salal Ranch road. |
| Cautions | This trail is a public right-of-way through private land. It is important that hikers act responsibly and stay on the marked trail so this remains open to the public. No dogs, bicycles or horses are allowed in High Salal Ranch. |

High Salal Ranch Trail links Tribune Bay and Helliwell provincial parks and is clearly marked with signs for most of the way. Follow the strata road to lot 16 (25 minutes from St. John's Point Road), where the trail turns right toward the water and then left (east) along the bluffs from just beside a private house. The trail continues along the edge of the cliffs for a short distance through an undisturbed stand of Garry oak and soon joins the western boundary of Helliwell Provincial Park (see hike 1). Note that access B allows you to combine the two provincial parks in one hike.

If you are keen, here's a longer, more challenging hike: At low tide, walk along the shore from Tribune Bay to Helliwell Provincial Park. Hike the Helliwell loop trail and then return along the High Salal Trail to Tribune Bay.

## 3. COLTSFOOT ★★

| | |
|---|---|
| Trail length | 3 kilometres each way |
| Time required | 45 minutes each way |
| Description | Old logging roads connect Strachan Road with the fire hall on Central Road. |
| Level | Easy |
| Access | A. Behind and to the left of the fire hall off Central Road. See map on page 121. |
| | B. From the end of Strachan Road, about 2 kilometres from Central Road |
| | C. From the cemetery, just east of the fire hall |
| Cautions | In the winter and spring, parts of the trail may be washed out by Chasm and Beulah creeks. |

Coltsfoot is a former forestry road through a previously logged area that has filled in with alder and ferns. It passes by the rear of the Ministry of Highways yard near the fire hall. Innumerable trails connect the Crown land, Mount

*The Cliff Trail on Mount Geoffrey boasts unparalleled views of Denman Island on the far side of Lambert Channel and the peaks of Vancouver Island beyond.*

Geoffrey Regional Nature Park and Mount Geoffrey Escarpment Provincial Park. If you decide to combine Coltsfoot with some of the other trails, carry a compass and check the trail offshoots with those shown on the map to ensure that you end up where you want to be—or just enjoy the luck of the draw. Chances are if you end up some distance from your intended destination, someone will give you a ride to where you need to go. I found following Spasm Chasm (west off Coltsfoot) and then turning left (southwest) on Logging Railroad an enjoyable way to join Northwind (right) and then climb to Cliff Trail.

## 4. Cliff Trail from Lea Smith Road ★★★★★

| | |
|---|---|
| Trail length | About 4 kilometres each way, depending on how far you choose to hike along the bluffs |
| Time required | About 2 to 3 hours return |
| Description | Perhaps the most beautiful hike on Mount Geoffrey, this is a short, steep climb to spectacular western views. The trail leads into Mount Geoffrey Regional Nature Park. |
| Level | Moderate, except for a very steep beginning |
| Access | The trailhead is well marked at the end of Lea Smith Road (off Central Road). You'll also find a map showing all the trails in this area at the trailhead. See map on page 121. |
| Cautions | Take great care as you proceed along the bluffs, as the trail is badly eroded in many places. |

*Note: Much of this trail is the same as hike 5.*

This hike has everything going for it—lovely forest, spectacular views, rugged cliffs and rock faces. It also follows a real foot trail rather than an old logging road. The trail from the end of Lea Smith Road climbs very steeply, and you soon find yourself high above your starting place, still visible far below through the trees. The trail zigzags up the mountain, but is well established and clearly marked. Regional park signs identify almost every major trail that leaves Cliff Trail (but, unfortunately, not always correctly).

The trail climbs first through a pretty forest of fir, cedar, alder and some maple, with an understory of salal. In some more open parts of the trail you cross moss-covered rocks. After 15 minutes or so of climbing, you begin to see views west toward Denman and the mountains of Vancouver Island.

Picnic spots abound on the edge of the bluffs, with wide-angle views down to Shingle Spit by the ferry dock and out to Denman and Vancouver islands. You can continue along the edge of the bluffs for an hour or more. After that the trail goes deeper into the forest and begins to descend. You'll pass a short, unnamed trail marked by a large cairn that leads east to Mount Geoffrey's peak. It's not worth the effort to reach the peak, however; the views are obscured by the surrounding forest, and you'll have to retrace your steps to regain the main trail. Farther along, Cliff Trail merges with both Summit Trail and Ridge Trail. However, as Ridge Trail is less obvious, you will probably find yourself on Summit Trail, which leaves the ridge before joining Bench Trail (see hike 6). Nevertheless, both of these trails eventually merge with Bench Trail, allowing you to combine hikes 4 and 6.

| 5. CLIFF TRAIL FROM STRACHAN ROAD TO NORTHWIND TRAIL ★★★★★ | |
|---|---|
| Trail length | About 8 kilometres in total, depending on route chosen |
| Time required | 2.5 hours |
| Description | An uphill climb along an old logging road leads to gorgeous views west from a cliff edge. |
| Level | Moderate |
| Access | From Central Road proceed about 1.7 kilometres along Strachan Road until you see a regional park sign announcing the Northwind Trail entrance. Turn right and continue until you see the yellow steel posts placed to stop cars at the trailhead. The trail leads into the Mount Geoffrey Regional Nature Park. |

*Note: Much of this trail is the same as hike 4.*

The logging road trail climbs steadily to the northwest. This part of the hike is not very exciting. The forest here has been thoroughly logged and now contains a mixture of spindly alder and young fir. However, the well-packed trail, covered with fir needles and grass, is a pleasant enough place to stroll. Many other trails feed into it and are mostly identified should you want to take an alternative route to Cliff Trail. I took Cold Deck, which brought me

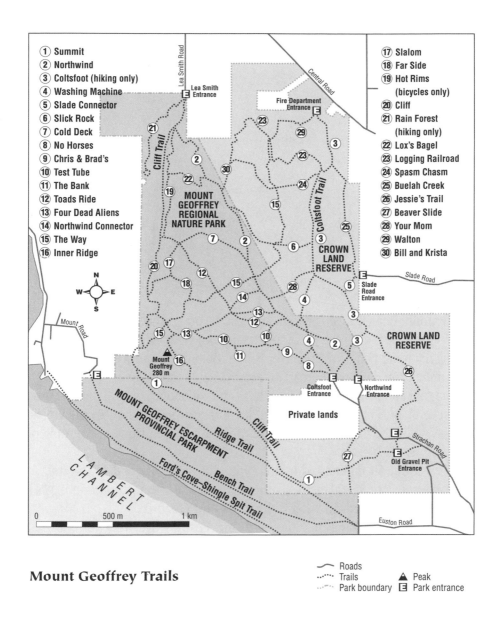

1. Summit
2. Northwind
3. Coltsfoot (hiking only)
4. Washing Machine
5. Slade Connector
6. Slick Rock
7. Cold Deck
8. No Horses
9. Chris & Brad's
10. Test Tube
11. The Bank
12. Toads Ride
13. Four Dead Aliens
14. Northwind Connector
15. The Way
16. Inner Ridge
17. Slalom
18. Far Side
19. Hot Rims (bicycles only)
20. Cliff
21. Rain Forest (hiking only)
22. Lox's Bagel
23. Logging Railroad
24. Spasm Chasm
25. Buelah Creek
26. Jessie's Trail
27. Beaver Slide
28. Your Mom
29. Walton
30. Bill and Krista

**Mount Geoffrey Trails**

Roads
Trails — Peak
Park boundary — Park entrance

about midway along Cliff Trail.

If you continue along Northwind, it will take you about an hour to reach the edge of the bluffs. You are now on Cliff Trail, which continues left (south) for quite some way and is very close to the edge of the bluffs in many places, so walk carefully. There are numerous offshoots along the way, so that you can vary your return to the trailhead if you like. For more information about Cliff Trail, see the description for hike 4.

## 6. BENCH TRAIL ★★★★

| Trail length | 3 kilometres each way |
|---|---|
| Time required | 1 hour each way |
| Description | This gently climbing trail through mixed forest provides superb views west to Denman and Vancouver islands. See map on page 121. |
| Level | Easy |
| Access | A. A sign marks the trailhead at the top end of Mount Road (1 kilometre from Shingle Spit Road).<br><br>B. From the end of Euston Road. This access is not suggested if you want to combine Bench and Shingle Spit trails to make a round trip. |

From Mount Road the trail heads southeast. It soon reaches the edge of a ridge and follows the bluffs east, providing wonderful views of Denman Island and the distant mountains on Vancouver Island. Below, you can see Shingle Spit to your immediate right and Ford's Cove to the left in the distance.

The trail climbs steeply in places, but is not difficult. You will pass arbutus and several large fir trees, as well as alder and a surprising number of maples. After a while the trail leaves the edge of the bluffs, returning at a couple of viewpoints.

After about 50 minutes of hiking, you will reach the end of the trail at Euston Road. About 200 metres before the end of the trail, another trail goes off to the left and leads to other trails on Mount Geoffrey.

If you are combining this hike with the Ford's Cove–Shingle Spit Trail (hike 7), a 4.3 kilometre road walk connects the two. Walk along Euston Road to Marylebone Road and then to Strachan—a distance of about 1.4 kilometres. Continue right (southeast) on Strachan to Central Road and then turn right again (southwest) down the hill. This last bit of road has views of rolling farmland edged by the sea and of Denman Island in the distance.

Before taking the Ford's Cove–Shingle Spit Trail portion of this hike, explore the wonderful sandstone shore around Ford's Cove (behind the shop). In Ford's Cove you can buy food and refreshments. To begin the Ford's Cove–Shingle Spit Trail, retrace your steps up Central Road for about 200 metres, where you'll find the trailhead on the left (west) side of the road. See the cautions in hike 7 before taking this trail.

## 7. FORD'S COVE–SHINGLE SPIT TRAIL ★★★

| | |
|---|---|
| Trail length | 2.5 kilometres each way |
| Time required | 45 minutes each way |
| Description | This picturesque, mainly forested trail runs between a spectacular conglomerate rock face on one side and bluffs overlooking the sea on the other. |
| Level | Easy |
| Access | A. Off Central Road about 200 metres from Ford's Cove Marina you'll see the narrow trail-head on the west side of the road.<br><br>B. The trail enters the woods to the east of the ferry dock. |
| Cautions | Several areas along this trail are subject to winter and spring washouts and can be difficult to cross. Until recently this was private land, and there's still a house to the south of the trail at its west end. Please respect the landowner's privacy. |

As mentioned above, this trail makes a good round trip with Bench Trail (hike 6). Starting from the Ford's Cove trailhead (access A), you'll pass through an area of short shrubs, as the trail follows a bluff overlooking the water.

Until the 1950s this hiking trail was a passable road. When it was washed out, the Ministry of Highways refused to rebuild it, thus cutting out a crucial link in a round-Hornby road.

Most of the trail passes through mixed young forest—alder, maple, cedar and fir, punctuated with the occasional grove of arbutus. To the north is the escarpment of Mount Geoffrey; to the south is the sea. Although the old roadbed can still be seen for much of the way, it has filled in with young trees in many places. Elsewhere large boulders of conglomerate have fallen onto the roadbed from the cliffs above. Don't miss the interesting rock formations along the shore that are visible from time to time through the trees. If you hike this trail during the wet months, you'll be treated to a gushing waterfall tumbling around moss-covered rocks down to the sea.

In less than an hour you emerge behind the pub and restaurant at Shingle Spit. This is a good spot to stop for an ice cream cone or something more substantial. The setting is so pleasant that you might make this your final hike of the day.

## SHORE AND ROAD WALKS

### Shore Walks

Hornby has many beautiful beach walks with ample access points. The following are listed clockwise as shown on the map on page 112.

**Shingle Beach:** From the ferry, you can walk north along sandy Shingle Beach for some distance at low tide. The oyster beds here are privately leased and the oysters should not be touched.

**Phipps Point:** Turn off Shingle Spit Road just where Central Road begins. (The beach-access road looks like a westerly extension of Central Road.) The view here is toward Denman Island. Look for the remains of Albert Savoie's ferry dock. Savoie ran a ferry service from here and from Shingle Spit beginning with a passenger service in 1929. He later built first a two- and then a six-car ferry.

**Collishaw Point:** Take Savoie Road (off Central Road about 3 kilometres north of the ferry) to its end. From here a trail descends to the rocky beach. You can walk right (northeast) as far as Collishaw Point. The oyster beds are privately leased and the oysters should not be touched.

**Galleon Beach:** Take Sollans Road (off Central Road) 1 kilometre to its end where you will find Hidden Beach Park. A short trail provides access to Galleon Beach. From here you can walk north to Grassy Point and another shore access and small park. It's possible to combine road and beach walks between these accesses.

**Tralee Point:** Take Ostby Road (off Central Road near Tribune Bay Provincial Park) to Fowler Road. At the end of Fowler Road a trail goes down to the beach. Herons nest in the nearby treetops, and if you're here in the spring, you'll hear their noisy chatter. At low tide you can walk along the beach for quite some way, much of it made up of sandstone boulders. There are petroglyphs visible on the rocks near Tralee Point to the north.

**Whaling Station Bay:** There are several shore accesses off St. John's Point Road. Summer cottages surround the soft, sandy beach here. This beach is said to have the warmest water around Hornby.

**Tribune Bay:** Off St. John's Point Road, 95-hectare Tribune Bay Provincial Park gives you access to perhaps the loveliest and longest sand beach in the Gulf Islands. At low tide you can walk far out into the bay to investigate tide pools, or you can scramble over the rugged sandstone boulders that line both sides of the bay and find rocks from which to launch yourself into the pleasantly warm water. While dogs are not allowed on the beach, they are allowed on leash on the short trails through the park's woods, one of which leads to an old lodge. The lodge was part of a resort that operated here from 1928 until the early 1970s. Since 1978, when the property became a park, the lodge has been used for the school district's outdoor education program. To the east of this building, a trail leads northwest to High Salal Ranch and ultimately to Helliwell Provincial Park (see hikes 1 and 2, pages 115–17). You can also access Tribune Bay by following Shields Road (beside the Co-op) to its end beside the Tribune Bay Campsite.

**Little Tribune Bay 1:** Take Seawright Road (off Central Road toward the south end of Little Tribune Beach). This access is a narrow, wooded path with houses on either side. There are rock steps down to the beach at the end of the path. (Watch out for the board joining the steps to the beach; it's quite slippery when wet.) At low tide you can walk along the beach all around Little Tribune Bay. The beach here is rocky, with great slabs of sandstone, so wear appropriate footwear. From here you can walk south to Dunlop Point and then along sandy Sandpiper Beach to Downes Point, where you will find another petroglyph. Caution: Be sure to check for a red-tide warning before eating any oysters or clams from this beach (1-866-431-3474 or www.pac. dfo-mpo.gc.ca/psp).

**Little Tribune Bay 2:** Take Little Tribune Road, a gravel road toward the middle of Little Tribune Bay. The road ends at an open area on the beach, which is very popular with skinny dippers. There's an outhouse located in this small community park area.

## Road Walks

**Seawright Road (near Little Tribune Bay):** You might use the shore access here to combine some beachcombing with a road walk.

**Whaling Station Bay (off St. John's Point Road in the northeast):** The roads here pass interesting homes, many of them summer retreats. Again, you can use one of the many shore accesses here to create a combined road-and-beach walk.

**Central Road from Strachan Road to Ford's Cove:** This route has been designated a "heritage road" in Hornby's official community plan. As you come down the hill toward Ford's Cove, you will enjoy excellent views of the beautiful farmland below and the sea beyond. From Ford's Cove you can continue along one of the loveliest sculptured sandstone shorelines in the Gulf Islands to Heron Rocks and Norman Point.

**Central Road from the bakery to the Co-op:** You can walk this 4-kilometre route mostly on a multi-use trail that parallels the road on one side or the other.

## AND IF YOU PADDLE . . .

If you bring your kayak, try to go out at high tide. If you don't, Hornby's shallow, rocky shoreline will force you to paddle quite far from shore. Here are three routes to try:

**Whaling Station Bay:** Put in here and paddle along Helliwell's rocky shoreline to the opening of Tribune Bay. On the way back stop at Flora Islet and enjoy the flowers for which it's named. In the spring the island is covered with blue-eyed Mary and sea blush. Be aware that there are no places to land along the Helliwell Provincial Park shoreline and that strong southeast winds can blow suddenly against these bluffs.

**Ford's Cove:** Start here and paddle to the mouth of Tribune Bay. If you're here in spring you'll likely have one or more sea lions for company. They frequent a rocky islet just offshore. The highlight of this paddle is Heron Rocks with their intricately weathered shapes.

**Phipps Point:** Launch here and paddle past Shingle Spit, the ferry terminal and, perhaps, as far as Ford's Cove. The logs on Shingle Spit are a good place to sit and have your lunch. There's lots of activity to watch, with the Beaufort Range on Vancouver Island as a backdrop. Give the ferry lots of space if you happen to arrive when it does.

# HERON ROCKS

South along the sandstone beach from Ford's Cove is the area known as Heron Rocks, where you'll find some of the most spectacular weathered sandstone formations in the Gulf Islands. At low tide you can walk for hours over the sandstone, examining the weird hoodoo-like formations and the tide pools.

Early morning is a wonderful time to be here, with the sun rising on the sea, eagles perched on the high points of the rock islands just offshore and, especially in the spring and fall, sea lions barking on the points below and many waterfowl swimming by. Continue walking to the small island off Norman Point, which is accessible at low tide. It has great views south to Vancouver Island.

On the way you pass the Heron Rocks Camping Co-op, owned by Hilary and Harrison Brown until 1967, when the Browns turned over the running of the campground to the campers.

*At low tide you can walk through the sandstone sculptures at Heron Rocks and closely examine the intricate formations nature has left behind.*

# Lasqueti

*E*ngaging Lasqueti Island lies midway between Vancouver Island and the mainland, and that's the way its approximately 370 permanent residents like it: alluring and almost out of reach. A magnet for draft dodgers in the 1960s, Lasqueti's artistic and close-knit community still enjoys an alternative lifestyle and is known for its self-reliance. Serviced by a private, passenger-only ferry from French Creek on Vancouver Island, all the cars on the island have been brought over by barge. By the residents' choice none of the homes are on the power grid, and as a result islanders have pioneered many ways of using alternative energy sources for power. Although Lasqueti is difficult to reach and has no public transportation, limited accommodation and no campgrounds, it's worth the trip. The islanders are friendly, the roads tranquil and in places the scenery is breathtaking. If you go, I suggest that you take a bicycle with you. Despite covering 66 square kilometres, Lasqueti has few public trails and is not a great place to hike. Nevertheless, its roads are good to walk or bicycle along and it's a great place to kayak. Everything from crafts to organic fruit can be purchased at businesses in False Bay.

## HISTORY

Lasqueti Island was named in 1791 by Spanish explorer José Maria Narvaez, master of the *Saturnina*, after naval officer Juan Maria Lasqueti. In times past the Pentlatch people summered on Lasqueti. The first non-Native settler arrived in 1860, but settlement proceeded very slowly. The first farmers raised sheep, which were taken to market in Nanaimo. Farmers tried to raise cattle in the 1960s, but had little success. Logging began in 1898 and reached its height in the 1950s. Around the same time, the Lasqueti Fishing Company, which still exists today, began to build and operate seiners. These days islanders support themselves through a variety of activities, including shellfish farming and growing produce. While Lasqueti's permanent population has not changed much since the 1980s, it attracts a large summer population, whose "view cottages" can be seen all around the island.

TEXADA ISLAND

JEDEDIAH ISLAND MARINE PROVINCIAL PARK

SQUITTY BAY MARINE PROVINCIAL PARK

SABINE CHANNEL

BULL ISLAND

BULL PASSAGE

PAUL ISLAND

BOHO ISLAND

JERVIS ISLAND

ANDERSON BAY

BOHO BAY

Gline and Fletcher Roads

Cemetery

Community Hall

Lake Road

ROUSE BAY

WINDY BAY

YOUNG POINT

SQUITTY BAY

SEAL REEF

Main Road

Good Rd

Grant Rd

Boat Cove Rd

BOAT COVE

OLD HOUSE BAY

RICHARDSON COVE

Mount Trematon 326 m

LAMBERT'S LAKE

OGDEN LAKE

Tucker Bay Road

TUCKER BAY

WELLS POINT

CONN BAY

WEST POINT

Mine and Lennie Roads

Main Road

Millicheap Road

Richardson Bay Road

MOUNT TREMATON NATURE RESERVE

JENKINS ISLAND

JENKINS COVE

SEA EGG ROCKS

JELINA ISLAND

LINDBERGH ISLAND

SCOTTIE BAY

MARINE ISLAND

MAPLE BAY

Oben Rd

HADLEY LAKE (KNOWN LOCALLY AS PETERSON OR PETE'S LAKE)

Weldon Road

McKINNEL LAGOON

BOOT POINT

Spring Bay Road

SPRING BAY

FEGEN ISLETS

FINNERTY ISLANDS

Laing Lane

Conn Road

ORCHARD BAY

FALSE BAY

PROWSE POINT

FERRY

N
E
S
W

0  1  2  3  4  5 km

Road
Crown land
Ecological reserve

Park
Peak
Shore access
Indian Reserve

## Lasqueti Island

# A TALE OF TWO SETTLEMENTS

There's little in Tucker Bay today to suggest what it looked like in the past. In the early part of the 20th century, Tucker Bay was the dominant community centre on Lasqueti. A dock was built here in 1913, and steamship service and mail delivery began. Up until then, the mailman had to row over 25 nautical miles (46 kilometres) to Nanaimo to pick up the mail and then deliver it personally to each recipient. A post office was built in Tucker Bay to receive the mail, and a school and store followed. But when a salmon cannery opened in False Bay in 1916, the population began to shift. Soon there weren't enough students to keep the Tucker Bay school open, and a new one opened in False Bay.

Tucker Bay's bad luck continued when, after a steamship hit a rock in Tucker Bay in 1923, the Union Steamship Company cancelled the service. Mail was then brought from Pender Harbour by small boat. However, the final blow for the community came in 1926 when the Tucker Bay store mysteriously burned down and the post office was moved to a private home. The next year False Bay acquired both steamship service and the mail contract. A new post office opened there, and with the school, store and steamship service, its position as the island's centre became permanent.

## GETTING THERE

Lasqueti's ferry leaves French Creek (3 kilometres north of Parksville) two or three times a day during the summer (except Tuesdays), and covers the 17-kilometre trip to False Bay in less than an hour. The ferry, currently the M.V. *Centurion VII* operated by Western Pacific Marine Ltd., takes no cars, but for an extra fee you can bring your bike, canoe, kayak or dog. The ferry crossing can be quite rough. For schedules, fees and further information check www. lasqueti.ca or www.wpm-1.com.

## SERVICES AND ACCOMMODATION

A small complex near the False Bay dock (where you will find a public telephone) includes a hotel, café, pub and gas pumps, all of which, if still functioning, have limited hours of operation. Across the road are a grocery store, which has take-out food, and a bakery, which serves pizza on Friday nights. Farther up Main Road you'll find the island's Free Store, an arts centre with an outhouse and a crafts shop. Of course, any of these could move or go out of business and new enterprises might start up at any time. Someone on the island usually offers a taxi service, often in a truck, and there may be other services available when you're there too. You can obtain up-to-date information on these on the notice board at the False Bay dock.

Lasqueti has only a couple of bed and breakfasts, and at time of writing, there was no public or private camping on the island, although residents did not object to people setting up tents on some of the beaches, such as those on Spring and Conn bays. There is no public washroom on Lasqueti, although there is a pit toilet and water pump at Squitty Bay Provincial Park and the outhouse behind the arts centre.

## BEACH AND ROAD WALKS on LASQUETI

Although much of Lasqueti is Crown land, little of it can be reached without trespassing on private land. The only parkland is Squitty Bay Provincial Park at the southeastern end of the island.

*Squitty Bay provides shelter for boats from the open strait at Lasqueti's eastern shore.*

With the permission of property owners, residents enjoy many trails that cross private land. If you wish to use these trails, find out who owns the land and request their permission. For visitors unwilling to go to this bother, walking on Lasqueti will be restricted to walking along the island's extensive and charming rural roads and the tough climb up Mount Trematon. With the exception of the road from the end of the dock at False Bay to the top of the hill (300 metres), none of the roads are paved, which makes them soft to the feet but dusty in the summer, and often muddy the rest of the year. The roads are also fairly hilly, so don't despair if you seem to be climbing a lot; you'll soon be walking downhill.

Main Road runs the length of the island, from the ferry terminal to Squitty Bay Provincial Park (18 kilometres). For convenience, the description of Main Road has been divided into three sections: Main Road from the ferry terminal to Conn Road (1.2 kilometres), Main Road from Conn Road to Tucker Bay Road (6.3 kilometres) and Main Road from Lake Road to Squitty Bay (10.5 kilometres). Worthwhile detours are also given, two of which are treated separately as they come up along the way: Conn Road to Spring Bay (5 kilometres) and Lake Road to Richardson Cove (4.5 kilometres).

*Conn Bay feels remote and isolated, snug in a corner of larger Tucker Bay and offering views of the little islands in Sabine Channel and hulking Texada beyond.*

It might be best to start with the road around False Bay and the closest detours, rather than the long hike to Squitty Bay. If you decide to come just for the day, try the walk along the beach from Boot Point to Spring Bay (see Conn Road to Spring Bay below), which can easily be done between ferries. Use this information to plan an outing that suits your energy level and the time you have available. You might also consider bringing a bicycle, as the roads are fairly quiet and bikes are the preferred means of transportation of many residents.

**Main Road from the ferry terminal to Conn Road (1.2 kilometres one way).** Main Road climbs steadily to its intersection with Conn Road. Just past the hotel you'll see Weldon Road on your right. It parallels the coast and provides views of McKinnel (a.k.a. Johnson) Lagoon, which stretches inland from the sea for some distance.

A bit farther down Main Road after Weldon Road you'll see the church parking lot on the left (the small church is hidden behind some trees at the end of the lot). Opposite the parking lot is the island's arts centre, with an outhouse behind it and a picnic table in front of it. No open fires or camping are allowed here. A farmers' market is held here every Saturday morning during the summer months. Not far from here is the island's tiny but still functioning post office.

Slightly less than 1 kilometre from the ferry is Laing Lane, on the left. Walk down this short road to a shore access that offers ocean views, a beach for swimming and the opportunity to collect clams and oysters from the large tidal flats, when it's safe to do so. For information on shellfish safety, call 1-866-431-3474 or go to www.pac.dfo-mpo.gc.ca/psp.

Next you'll see a gift shop, school, fire hall, recycling centre with its Free Store and, at Conn Road hidden behind some trees, the Teapot House. The building's name comes from the shape of its two chimneys: one looks like a teapot and the other like a sugar bowl (the sign of a bootlegger). However, it's difficult to see the building from the road through the thick foliage.

**Conn Road to Spring Bay (5 kilometres).** Conn Road heads north toward the sea. After a couple of kilometres, as it nears Scottie Bay, its name becomes Spring Bay Road.

At this point you'll see a cluster of signs where a roadway heads right. This road leads to the Lasqueti Fish Company on Scottie Bay. There is public access to the beach farther along and to the north of the boatyard. The dock is private, however, and you should ask permission if you want to use it.

Returning to Spring Bay Road and continuing north, you'll soon see a road heading off to the right, alongside some mailboxes. This short road leads to the beach along Maple Bay just north of Lindbergh Island. It's one of Lasqueti's few public shore accesses, and it's a good one. You can walk north along the beach toward Marine Island for some way.

Continuing along Spring Bay Road for a kilometre or so, you'll find another road going off to the right. It leads to Boot Point, where there is another public shore access. From here at low tide you can walk all the way left (northwest) to Spring Bay.

The next road off Spring Bay Road is called Nichols Road. It leads to Spring Bay beach, where you can beachcomb, swim, enjoy the views of Texada Island, picnic and examine rock formations left over from the ice age. From here you can return to Main Road the way you came, or at low tide walk around Spring Bay Point to Boot Point, where you can regain Spring Bay Road.

**Main Road from Conn Road to Tucker Bay Road (6.3 kilometres one way).** About a kilometre from the Teapot House you'll pass Hadley Lake (known locally as Peterson or Pete's Lake), which is the source of False Bay's water supply. Half a kilometre farther is Oben Road on the right (south). I don't recommend that you take this forested road.

After 1 kilometre or so you'll see a sign for Mine and Lennie roads heading off on the left (north). This is another detour that is not worth taking. Somewhat over 2 kilometres farther down Main Road, however, Millicheap Road goes off to the left (north) for about 1 kilometre and takes you down to a public shore access on Conn Bay. Here the trail leads onto a peninsula consisting of moss-covered rocks and windswept arbutus trees. This rugged peninsula is a very pretty place to walk and perhaps picnic. The trails here are probably sheep trails, and you could meet some of the island's feral sheep as I did.

Back on Main Road, the next road on the left (north) is Tucker Bay Road. It descends less than 1 kilometre to Tucker Bay. On the way to the bay you'll pass a covered steam donkey left over from an old logging operation. At the end of the road there is public access to the water near an old house. The coast is quite rugged here. If you walk out to the point at the mouth of the bay, you will have good views of Texada and Jervis islands, and it's possible to swim here.

**Lake Road to Richardson Cove (4.5 kilometres, one way).** Lake Road runs right (south) off Main Road, just beyond Tucker Bay Road. This narrow country road rises past farms that look as though they've been here for generations. The road passes moss-covered rock outcroppings, as well as Lambert's Lake and Ogden Lake. There is no public access to either lake, but near Ogden Lake you get a good view of Mount Trematon, a rugged landform named after Trematon Castle in Cornwall, England.

At 326 metres, Mount Trematon is the highest point on Lasqueti and offers panoramic views of the Strait of Georgia from Campbell River in the north to Vancouver in the south. The summit of Mount Trematon is within the Mount Trematon Nature Reserve, 57 hectares of land that was donated by the Gordon family to the Islands Trust Fund (ITF). The ITF's management plan for this reserve states that "the ITF will accept, but in no way promote, informal use of the nature reserve by hikers." The management plan outlines three ways to access the summit:

1. Legal access via Lake Road, which partly crosses private property (the owners of this property keep monkeys as pets, so dogs should be leashed);
2. Via an old logging road near the intersection of Lake and Richardson Bay roads, which runs roughly northwest through private land and which the owners have permitted public access to in the past; and
3. Through Crown land via Forbes Road and the Lasqueti landfill site. The latter access is an unmarked route through hazardous terrain.

Note that the routes for the final access to the summit in all cases are rough, unimproved and unmaintained.

When I climbed Mount Trematon the trails were mostly marked with pink surveyor tape. The approximately 100-metre climb is steep but not exceptionally challenging until you reach the "chimney" or "chute," a narrow channel in the rocky face of the mountain that you have to climb very carefully. At time of writing a rope was in place to help you ascend and descend the mountain, but this part of the trail was definitely not for the faint-hearted. The views from the top are quite spectacular, especially looking east to Ogden Lake and the islands off Lasqueti's northern shore. En route you might see spotted grouse or some of the feral sheep that still live here.

Richardson Bay Road descends steeply for 1 kilometre, past a large farm to the very small bay, surrounded by sheer cliffs. There is public access to the beach, but little walking. When you're through exploring, you must return to Main Road the same way you've come. (Note that the official marine charts identify Richardson Bay as Richardson Cove.)

**Main Road from Lake Road to Squitty Bay (10.5 kilometres one way).**
Continuing east along Main Road from Lake Road, you almost immediately
pass a seasonal waterfall on your right and, soon after, the island's community hall.

Lasqueti's cemetery is on Main Road about 2 kilometres from Lake Road,
just past Gline and Fletcher roads. The land for the cemetery was donated,
and the two donors are buried here along with about 50 others.

Boat Cove Road goes off to the right after another 500 metres. Take the
5-minute walk down the road to a lovely cove, where you can dig clams at
low tide along an extensive beach. The access is at the end of the road, just
left of the Bergen farm. The swimming here is good, and there's a fine view
of Vancouver Island. Please do not disturb the creek that empties into Boat
Cove: as part of a salmon enhancement program conducted since 1952, it is
a spawning stream for coho and chum.

Continuing along Main Road you will pass several side roads over the
final 7 kilometres to Squitty Bay. None of these roads has access to the
water.

Squitty Bay Road runs off Main Road into the provincial park. With a
purchase of adjacent land in 2007, the park now covers over 51 hectares
and has almost 1 kilometre of shoreline, a heritage orchard, sheltered bays
and beaches, windswept coastal bluffs and a salmon-bearing creek. There
is a pump for drinking water at the head of the bay and picnic tables and an
outhouse near the government dock. Nearby is a 5.7-hectare piece of land
obtained by the Nature Trust of British Columbia in 1987, which contains
Rocky Mountain juniper and is fenced to protect the natural flora from
animals. Walk through it to its outer point, which provides a magnificent
270-degree view of Texada Island and Sabine Channel on the left, of Thor-
manby Island to Mount Baker on the mainland straight ahead and of Vancouver Island on the right. There are a couple of short trails in the park, as
well as a pleasant rocky area overlooking Little Squitty Bay to your right as
you enter the park.

If you wish to explore farther, you can continue walking beyond the park
along Main Road, which winds away from the shoreline. The road descends
into a relatively new subdivision and finally ends a couple of kilometres from
Squitty Bay, some distance from the water.

# AND IF YOU PADDLE . . .

Lasqueti's indented shoreline is ideal for paddling. You can bring your canoe or kayak with you on the passenger ferry and put it into the water as soon as you disembark. You can then explore Lasqueti's shoreline, as well as some of the nearby islands. Be aware that except for False Bay and Bull Passage, Lasqueti is quite exposed and subject to strong winds, and Sabine Channel has quite strong currents that create steep seas. Check the marine forecast before leaving and consult your tide and current tables. Novice paddlers should not venture outside of Bull Passage or False Bay without a guide.

Here are some suggestions:

• Tour Jedediah Island Marine Provincial Park (see pages 302–4).

• Circumnavigate Lasqueti, using the many pieces of Crown land to rest, including the Finnerty Islets, Jervis Island and the islets to its west, and Paul Island. (Much of the Crown land on Lasqueti's own shore is cliff and inappropriate for camping.) Stop at one of Lasqueti's shore accesses or government docks—at Spring Bay, Scottie Bay, Tucker Bay, Anderson Bay, Rouse Bay, Windy Bay, Squitty Bay, Boat Cove and Richardson Cove—and explore some of the nearby roads on foot.

*In addition to providing a venue for the island's artists, Lasqueti's arts centre accommodates a Saturday market in the summer and functions as a picnic site.*

# Mayne

*A*t 21 square kilometres Mayne is one of the smaller islands described in this book, but its scenic country roads, sandy beaches and numerous bays and coves make it a major attraction. The majority of Mayne's approximately 1,100 residents are retired and have time to enjoy the island's quiet pace, bucolic landscape and mild weather. For an island of its size, Mayne has a surprising number of stores and services, including galleries, cafés and a pub. Although there are settlements near Bennett Bay, Georgina Point, Dinner Bay, Horton Bay and Gallagher Bay, most businesses are concentrated around Miners Bay. Mayne has fewer parks and hiking trails than most of its neighbours but has some pleasant and worthwhile walks. Wildflower enthusiasts will be enthralled by the profusion of blooms in the spring and early summer and birdwatchers by the great variety of birds that visit or live on the island.

## HISTORY

Mayne Island was named by English captain (later admiral) George Henry Richards in 1791 after Lieutenant Richard Charles Mayne, who served on Richards' vessel *Plumper*. Archeological evidence shows that First Nations people had a presence on Mayne more than 5,000 years ago. In 1794 Captain George Vancouver's crew camped on Georgina Point, leaving a coin and knife that would be discovered by settlers more than 100 years later.

The large bay at the northwest corner of the island became known as Miners Bay following the 1858 gold rush, when prospectors heading from Victoria to the mainland would frequently stop and camp along its protected shores. A couple of years later a community developed in Miners Bay. Historic buildings from the 1890s still stand in this area, including the Springwater Lodge, the original jail (now a museum) and the Church of St. Mary Magdalene.

Good agricultural land attracted settlers, and by the 1890s several farms were thriving. There were many orchards on the island at the time, and the

*Miners Bay Pub is the perfect place to relax after a long day's hike and watch the sun set over the boat traffic in Active Pass.*

Mayne Island King apple was one of the first varieties developed in BC. In the 1930s a third of the island's residents were Japanese, who collectively grew 50 tonnes of tomatoes each year. These settlers were displaced during the internment of Japanese Canadians during World War II, but their contribution to the island's heritage is now honoured with an exquisite memorial Japanese garden at Dinner Bay (see sidebar, page 148).

## GETTING THERE

There are daily sailings to Mayne from the Swartz Bay terminal (near Victoria) and two sailings from Tsawwassen (near Vancouver). There is also almost daily service between Mayne and Galiano, North Pender, Salt Spring and Saturna islands. For further information obtain a BC ferries schedule or contact BC Ferries. Saltspring Air flies to Mayne from Vancouver and the Vancouver airport; Seair Seaplanes flies to Mayne from the Vancouver airport (see page 320).

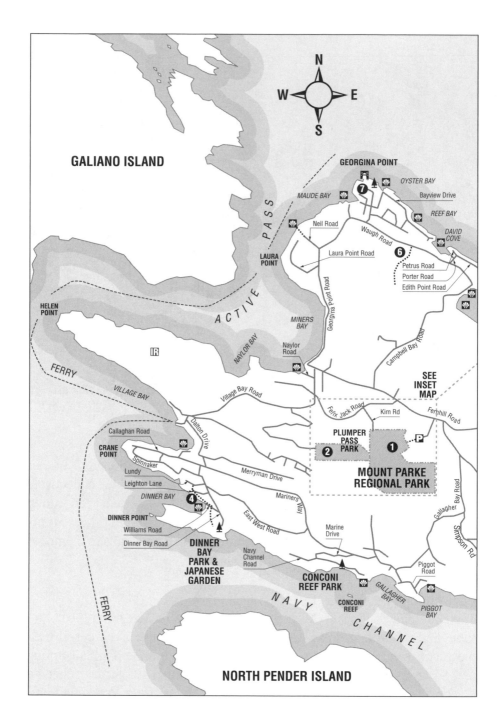

**Mayne Island**

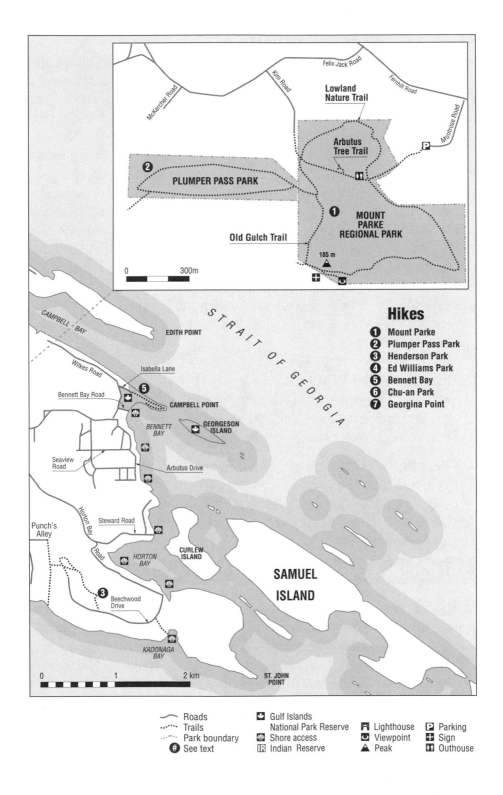

### Hikes

1. Mount Parke
2. Plumper Pass Park
3. Henderson Park
4. Ed Williams Park
5. Bennett Bay
6. Chu-an Park
7. Georgina Point

**Roads**
**Trails**
**Park boundary**
1 **See text**

Gulf Islands
National Park Reserve
Shore access
Indian Reserve

Lighthouse
Viewpoint
Peak

Parking
Sign
Outhouse

## SERVICES AND ACCOMMODATION

Most of Mayne's stores and services are located on Fernhill and Village Bay roads in Miners Bay. Mayne has no bank, but there is an ATM at the general store in Miners Bay. There are bed and breakfasts, lodges, inns and resorts, as well as a few restaurants and cafés. At time of writing only limited private camping was available. The island also has a health centre.

The Mayne Island Community Chamber of Commerce (www.mayneislandchamber.ca) provides a tourist information brochure, including a good map of the island and lists of accommodation and services. You can pick up a copy of the map on the ferry or from stores and tourist outlets. The Mayne Island Parks and Recreation Commission (MIPRC) also puts out its own *Hiking and Walking Trail Map*, which is available at many trailheads and information racks on the island. You may also be able to obtain information on hiking and local natural history from the Mayne Island Naturalists Club, the MIPRC, from www.mayneisland.com and from Parks Canada/Gulf Islands National Park Reserve (1-866-944-1744, 1-250-654-4000 or www.parkscanada.gc.ca/gulf).

## ESPECIALLY FOR WALKERS

Mayne Island's gentle terrain offers numerous places for easy walking, many of them in stunning locations along the shore. In addition to the many shore and road walks suggested below, try the following:

- Bennett Bay Trails—part of the Gulf Islands National Park Reserve (GINPR); see hike 5
- Georgina Point—part of GINPR; see hike 7
- Japanese Garden, Dinner Bay Community Park (see page 153)

## HIKES on MAYNE

Most land on Mayne is privately owned. The island has one regional park, a few community parks, and Bennett Bay and Georgina Point form part of GINPR. However, Mayne has no provincial parks or Crown land. The island has a growing number of short trails and small parks established by the volunteer-run parks and recreation commission. The MIPRC trails are usually marked with brick-red diamonds (tilted squares).

## 1. MOUNT PARKE REGIONAL PARK ★★★★

| | |
|---|---|
| Trail length | About 5 kilometres in total |
| Time required | 90 minutes to 2 hours for all the trails |
| Description | A woodland loop trail and a second, steeper trail lead to a ridge with panoramic views |
| Level | Easy to moderate |
| Elevation | 185 metres at the Halliday Lookout (The summit of Mount Parke is 255 metres, but is on private land.) |
| Access | The parking area at the end of Montrose Road (off Fernhill Road) |
| Cautions | Stay on the trails at all times, as the moss and lichen are very fragile and slow to recover from any disruption. |

The trails in this 47-hectare regional park have something for everyone. From the parking lot a 300-metre trail leads to a junction where three trails lead deeper into the park. There's also an outhouse at this junction and a plaque commemorating Mary Jeffery, who bequeathed much of this land to the island in 1992.

The trail to the left leads to a splendid viewpoint. The first half of the trail is relatively flat, but then it climbs steeply through an arbutus and Douglas-fir forest. Near the top you will see signs for the Halliday Lookout, named after one of Mayne Island's first parks and recreation commissioners. On a clear day you will have terrific views of Saturna Island to the southeast, Navy Channel and the Pender islands to the south, Vancouver Island to the southwest and Prevost and Salt Spring islands to the west. In the spring wildflowers adorn the edge of the bluff. From here you can return the way you came or continue along the 600-metre Old Gulch Trail, which hooks up with the lower loop trail.

The other paths that start near the outhouse form a 1.3-kilometre loop called the Lowland Nature Trail. Starting on the right-hand trail, you pass through first a mature cedar forest with an understory of sword fern and step moss and then through arbutus and Douglas-fir. Just before the end of the trail a side trail takes you to a very large arbutus, which is definitely worth the detour. The loop takes about half an hour.

*This is the excellent view of Navy Channel from the end of the short trail in Conconi Reef Community Park.*

## 2. PLUMPER PASS PARK ★★

| | |
|---|---|
| Trail length | Over 2 kilometres |
| Time required | An hour or more |
| Description | A loop trail through mature, second-growth forest on the north slope of Mount Parke and parallel to the summit ridge. A short trail leads to a viewpoint with a view corridor looking out over Village Bay and the Strait of Georgia. |
| Level | Moderate |
| Access | From the end of Kim Road (south off Felix Jack Road) an access trail heads south for 270 metres to the loop trail. |
| Cautions | The trail is steep in parts, with an elevation gain of 135 metres. |

The access trail from Kim Road goes through heavy underbrush for about 100 metres and then heads south on an old skid road for another 170 metres to the beginning of the loop trail. Going left, you proceed up a steep switch-back for 150 metres, and then traverse the Mount Parke slope for 500 metres, still gaining in elevation.

At the southernmost point on the loop trail, a short, 90-metre linking trail going south (uphill) takes you to Mount Parke Road, a private road that goes to the strata development to the west and to the summit transmission towers to the east. Crossing Mount Parke Road, you may continue on uphill on another short (170-metre) trail to a viewpoint with a bench and a glimpse of Miners Bay, Active Pass and the Strait of Georgia.

After you return to the loop trail from the viewpoint, around the halfway point of the loop, the trail veers suddenly to the east and follows a berm. At the foot of the berm is a large, beautiful seasonal pond. The last 300 metres of the loop trail take you on an old logging road.

## 3. HENDERSON PARK ★★

| | |
|---|---|
| Trail length | About 3 kilometres in total |
| Time required | 90 minutes round trip |
| Description | 1,100-metre loop trail to a viewpoint over Navy Channel, with a connecting trail to a 700-metre trail through recently logged forest to a steep descent to a driftwood-littered beach |
| Elevation | 200 metres |
| Level | Moderate to difficult |
| Access | A. From the parking area 200 metres beyond the cul-de-sac at the end of Beechwood Drive, you can take either the trail to the west, which links to the Doreen McLeod Beach Access trail, or the Vulture Ridge Viewpoint Trail to the east, which climbs to the viewpoint and then loops back to Beechwood Drive. |
| | B. The Vulture Ridge Viewpoint Trail can be started or completed from access points at the east end of the trail on the pedestrian right-of-way, 240 metres into the Henderson Hill |

| | |
|---|---|
| | subdivision on Beechwood Drive, or from the west end adjacent to the second yellow gate inside the park and about 200 metres from the "Visitor Park" sign by the cul-de-sac at the end of Beechwood Drive. Park your vehicle at the parking lot by the picnic area. Do not block the road as it is used for emergency vehicle access to the park and to the private lands surrounding the park.<br><br>C. The 700-metre Doreen McLeod Beach Access trail can be started from the east end of Punch's Alley, a development road that is gated at its start from Simpson Road (off Gallagher Bay Road). |
| Facilities | Picnic table, outhouse, signboards |

Henderson Park (10.4 hectares) really encompasses two distinct trails connected by a short link trail across a field. The link trail connects the access to the Vulture Ridge Viewpoint Trail to the middle of the Doreen McLeod Beach Access. In case you're wondering, Doreen McLeod was one of the first Mayne Island parks and recreation commissioners.

If you start the Doreen McLeod Beach Access trail from the trailhead on Punch's Alley, you will first pass through a short section of very large and beautiful trees before reaching the recently logged area near Beechwood Drive. From there you descend to the beach on Navy Channel along a lightly treed but shady corridor. A solid and storm tide-proof "stone cradle" staircase has been built from the foreshore to the beach. At time of writing an observation platform above the stairs was planned, along with other trail improvements.

The 1,100-metre Vulture Ridge Viewpoint Trail can be accessed from Beechwood Drive or from beyond the cul-de-sac at the end of Beechwood Drive, so that you can climb from one access and loop back to the other. From access A you soon have a choice of taking the steep route up or the 268-metre Don Herbert Memorial Trail, which is a less difficult ascent. The two trails merge about halfway up to the viewpoint, which is about 200 metres above sea level. Note that the summit of Henderson Hill is on private property.

While the climb to the viewpoint is steep and difficult in places, the view at the top makes the ascent worthwhile. From the customary bench at the end of the trail, you can see Hope Bay on Pender Island across the channel and Fane Island in between. To complete the loop, continue on the trail from the viewpoint, which descends steeply down to Beechwood Drive. An intricate system of cables has been devised to help you keep your footing as you descend the rocky, slippery trail. It is then a quick walk west back to the parking area along Beechwood Drive.

## 4. ED WILLIAMS MEMORIAL TRAIL ★★

| | |
|---|---|
| Trail length | 600 metres each way |
| Time required | 15 minutes |
| Description | Pleasant walk through woods to Dinner Bay Park, a shore access and the Japanese Garden |
| Level | Easy |
| Access | From Leighton Lane at the corner of Dinner Bay Road or from the Japanese Garden in Dinner Bay Community Park |

This trail is an enjoyable alternative to taking the road to Dinner Bay Park. Ed Williams was an early Mayne Island Parks and Recreation commissioner.

## 5. BENNETT BAY TRAILS (GULF ISLANDS NATIONAL PARK RESERVE) ★★★

| | |
|---|---|
| Trail length | 3 kilometres in total |
| Time required | About an hour, although you'll want to linger here |
| Description | Wide, relatively flat trail to Campbell Point with a return along a lower trail along the cliff edge that ultimately accesses stairs to the beach or returns to the main trail |
| Level | Easy |
| Access | From the parking lot near the beginning of Wilkes Road or from the end of Isabella Lane (east off Wilkes Road) |
| Facilities | Signboards, picnic tables, outhouse |

# JAPANESE GARDEN

*Mayne's Japanese Garden has it all, beautiful shrubs and flowers, ponds, Zenlike rock formations and gently curving paths leading to wonderful places for picnics, reading or meditating on the splendours of the Gulf Islands.*

The Japanese Garden at Dinner Bay Community Park is a must-see. To commemorate the Japanese settlers who were integral to Mayne's development, locals created this beautiful garden on 2 hectares of land that once belonged to a Japanese Canadian family. The garden has a waterfall, ponds, Japanese lanterns, a great variety of plants, including traditional Japanese cherry trees, and a reconstructed charcoal kiln.

Although the idea for the garden dates back to the 1980s, it wasn't until 1999 that the construction of the garden really began. It was dedicated by Lieutenant-Governor Iona Campagnola on May 29, 2002.

The construction of the garden and the ongoing maintenance is the work of volunteers, and many of the plants were gifts. A donation box has been installed to help cover expenses. There are many trails through the garden, as well as lovely spots to sit, contemplate the exquisite surroundings or meditate.

*The beautiful, sandy beach at Bennett Bay is very popular among Mayne Islanders both for swimming and for launching kayaks.*

Part of the Gulf Islands National Park Reserve (GINPR), this land consists of 9.4 hectares on the Campbell Point peninsula and along Bennett Bay. The beach at Bennett Bay is perhaps Mayne's finest beach and one of the most popular swimming and kayak launching sites on the island. Nearby Georgeson Island can be seen from the trail, but it is a Zone 1 Special Preservation Area in the park and access is only permitted with prior written authorization from the park superintendent.

Campbell Point contains arbutus and Douglas-fir. The terrain is relatively flat, and there are views of Edith Point to the north and Georgeson Island offshore to the east. Rocky Mountain juniper thrives on the outside edge of the peninsula. The main trail proceeds down the centre of the peninsula to the point (about 15 minutes). On your return you can access a secondary trail that parallels the main trail but follows the edge of the cliff above the shore. At its end you can descend a staircase to the beautiful beach (a great place for swimming), cross a field to return to the main trail near the parking lot or return to the main trail by another link trail.

## 6. CHU-AN PARK AND VIEWPOINT ★★

| | |
|---|---|
| Trail length | 1.2 kilometres in total (600 metres each way) |
| Time required | 30 minutes round trip |
| Description | A short, steep walk to a viewpoint with a great view of the Strait of Georgia |
| Level | Moderate |
| Access | Opposite 537 Waugh Road, 600 metres east of Georgina Point Road |
| Cautions | The trail is steep, climbing about 150 metres in a short distance, so don't try it if you don't like climbs. |

*Chu-an* means "looking out over the sea" in the Coast Salish language, and this is possible from the viewpoint at the top of this 0.6-hectare local park. This trail is contained in a 3-metre strip of land provided by a developer and ends up at a gravel viewpoint that is barely 2 metres wide, although the park allows room for expansion. From here you can see Roberts Bank on the mainland.

## 7. GEORGINA POINT (GINPR) ★★★

| | |
|---|---|
| Trail length | 1 kilometre in total |
| Time required | 10–30 minutes, depending on how relaxed you are |
| Description | Shore access, picnic area and grasslands along the seashore |
| Level | Easy |
| Access | The end of Georgina Point Road |
| Facilities | Washroom facilities, picnic tables |

There is good walking on the rocks in front of the lighthouse and through the grounds. This is a great spot to watch ocean traffic negotiating the turbulent opening to Active Pass. You can see right across to the mainland, and at low tide you can walk east along the beach for quite some distance. It is also an excellent place for viewing wildlife, including seals, orcas (if you're lucky) and seabirds. The site is open from dawn to dusk and is an excellent picnic spot.

# SHORE AND ROAD WALKS

**Shore Accesses** (listed clockwise on the map on pages 140–141)

**Active Pass:** You can access the fascinating Active Pass shoreline at Miners Bay in a community park at the end of Naylor Road (across from the Mayne Street Mall). The beach walk is short, but provides a perfect location to use your binoculars to examine the distant Galiano shore, check the prowess of the anglers mooching for salmon or watch the constant boat traffic through one of the busiest bits of water on the West Coast.

The narrowest place in the channel is at Helen Point, where the tidal flow can sweep through the narrow passageway north toward Georgina Point at up to 8 knots, creating a problem for navigation. When this fast-moving water meets wind coming from the opposite direction, dangerous rip tides result. The combination of the swirling water and the heavy boat traffic has resulted in many serious mishaps in Active Pass over the years.

A highlight of being in Active Pass, especially in the spring, is the wildlife viewing. Seals, sea lions, porpoises and, occasionally, killer whales visit the waters of this narrow channel. At different times of the year there are high concentrations of bald eagles, gulls, cormorants, loons and many varieties of duck. For this reason this area has been designated the Active Pass IBA (Important Bird Area; see www.activepassiba.ca). Pacific loons and Brandt's cormorants winter here, and Bonaparte's gulls frequent Active Pass during the fall and spring migration. In all, about 40 species of marine and marine-related birds regularly use Active Pass at some time in their annual life cycle.

**Neil Road Seaview:** An 80-metre, steep, rocky trail leads from the end of Neil Road (off Georgina Point Road) to a pretty viewpoint of Active Pass and the Strait of Georgia. When I walked here the trail was new and rough, and only agile hikers should attempt it with great care. Hold on carefully to the rope provided on the descent. There is parking provided for two cars at the end of Neil Road and additional parking at the side of Georgina Point Road. A bench at the viewpoint and perhaps the largest yew tree on Mayne Island add to the pleasure of this spot, where you can also observe the Active Pass IBA.

**Georgina Point:** See hike 7.

**Oyster Bay:** The small beach on the north tip of the island at the end of Bayview Drive has beautiful rock formations and terrific driftwood.

**David Cove:** This attractive beach at the end of Petrus Road (left off Porter Road from Waugh Road) is too small to afford much walking.

**Campbell Bay:** By far the deepest bay on Mayne. At low tide you can walk along the beach for a long way. Although the peninsula leading to Edith Point is private land, you are free to explore the foreshore. You can access this beach by a narrow, tunnel-like path through the trees off Campbell Bay Road. To find this access, follow the fence of the large farm opposite 327 Campbell Bay Road.

**Bennett Bay:** The longest beach walk on Mayne is along this sandy beach, where you can easily spend an hour or more beachcombing and swimming. The easiest public access point is from Wilkes Road at the end of Bennett Bay Road. From the beach you have good views of Georgeson Island and part of Curlew Island just offshore.

**Seaview Drive:** This access at the end of Seaview (off Arbutus, which runs off the end of Bennett Bay Road) provides views of Georgeson and Curlew islands and the open sea in between. You can relax and picnic here, or possibly launch your kayak or canoe.

**Arbutus Drive:** At the south end of Arbutus Drive, stairs lead to a rocky beach opposite Georgeson Island.

**Curlew View Drive:** This boat launch looks like it's at the end of Steward Drive (off Horton Bay Road) on the map, although Steward continues north at this point and this stub acquires a new name. You can walk along the beach here for quite some distance both south into Horton Bay and north toward Bennett Bay. This access faces Curlew Island.

**Anson Road:** This road access off Horton Bay Road, which doubles as a driveway for 694 Horton Bay Road, leads 100 metres down to a canoe and kayak launch, picnic table and viewpoint. A flight of stairs descends to the rocky shore.

**Kadonaga Bay:** A 300-metre trail on Deer Lane (500 metres south of Horton Bay Road on Beechwood Drive) leads to a pristine, secluded, rocky beach on Navy Channel. It is a perfect spot to meditate and watch wildlife, but not to walk on the rough rocky beach. The trail descends very steeply for its last 50 metres and depends on a series of intricate cables to give you something to hold onto as you work your way down to the shore. Note that the MIPRC warns that the trail requires "a reasonable level of physical fitness."

**Piggot Bay:** This driftwood-littered sand beach on Piggot Bay (Plumper Sound) can be walked for some distance (20 minutes or so at high tide but much more at low tide). The access is at the east end of Piggot Road (off Gallagher Bay Road). A path from a second access on the west end of Piggot (at its intersection with Gallagher Bay Road) offers more limited walking, but nice views toward Hope Bay on North Pender Island.

**Conconi Reef Community Park:** Off Navy Channel Road, 600 metres east of its intersection with Marine Drive. A 100-metre trail on the south side of the road leads down to a sandy beach on Navy Channel. Although the walking here is somewhat limited, this sandy beach is a peaceful spot, with views of the Pender Islands and the navigational beacon on the nearby reef. A steep, rough, 110-metre trail on the north side of the road leads to a 35-metre-high viewpoint of Navy Channel.

**Dinner Bay:** You can access the beach at Dinner Bay Community Park at the end of Williams Road using steps that begin just beyond the washrooms. Although the beaches do not provide much space for walking, you can walk to the nearby 600-metre trail that connects the corner of Dinner Bay Road and Leighton Lane with the Japanese Garden. The trail goes through woods and along the shoreline at Dinner Bay Park before reaching the stunning Japanese Garden.

**Village Bay:** You can access this bay using a trail that begins where Merryman Drive intersects with Dalton Drive. There are two trails: the one on the right side leads to a beach on Village Bay, which is also at the end of Callaghan Road (off Mariners Way); the left-hand trail leads to Mariners Way. This pocket community park has an outhouse, picnic tables and a boat launch.

## Road Walks

The road walks on Mayne are pleasant but unspectacular. You might try Edith Point Road (right off Porter Road from Waugh Road) and the roads around the Georgina Point lighthouse. Georgina Point Road from Miners Bay follows the shore for some distance, is very pretty and offers great views of the entire length of Active Pass.

Near the south end of Georgina Point Road you'll find the Church of St. Mary Magdalene, one of the prettiest churches in the Gulf Islands. St. Mary's was consecrated in 1898 and its wooden steeple is a familiar sight to boats travelling through Active Pass. You will enjoy walking its pleasant grounds and having a look at its charming interior. The 180-kilogram sandstone baptismal font was brought from Saturna Island by rowboat.

## AND IF YOU PADDLE . . .

Mayne Island has more bays than many of the larger islands, and many of these are suitable for beginners. Only experienced paddlers, however, should even consider going into Active Pass or in the passages between Mayne and Saturna islands without a guide, and then only at slack tide after consulting tide and current tables. Ferry traffic is quite heavy to Mayne Island, so watch for these large ships and their wash if paddling in or near Village Bay.

**Georgina Point:** On a calm day you can explore the Strait of Georgia shoreline. From here you can paddle as far as Edith Point and around into cavernous Campbell Bay.

**Horton Bay:** Put in from the dock or the accessible shoreline at the end of Horton Bay Road. From here you can explore Curlew Island and continue north along the Mayne shoreline to Bennett Bay, Campbell Point and Georgeson Island (Gulf Islands National Park Reserve). The south shore of Georgeson Island has fantastic sandstone formations, but as there is virtually nowhere to land, you're best to restrict your visit to the water. An alternative launch site is at the end of Stewart Road (known locally as Spud Point), where you can paddle either north to Bennett Bay or south along the shore of Curlew Island and into Horton Bay.

**Village Bay:** The access is at the end of Callaghan Road (off Mariners Way). From here you can paddle south to Dinner Bay. Be careful to avoid the ferries in Village Bay. Always clearly point your boat away from them so that they cannot mistake your intention.

*St. Mary Magdalene Church in Miners Bay dates from 1897.*

# North and South Pender

*L*ocated just west of Saturna and east of Salt Spring, "the Penders" cover 36 square kilometres. A bridge connects the more rugged south island to the gentler north island. Just 236 of the Penders' 2,232 year-round residents live on South Pender, and the majority of the islands' services, including pubs, restaurants and a grocery store are on North Pender. With beautiful bays and coves, and more public shore accesses for their size than any other Gulf Island, boaters and hikers alike enjoy these islands. Although there are only a couple of lengthy (half-day or longer) hikes on the Penders, their parks, roads and shores provide plenty of opportunities for pleasant walking and exploration.

## HISTORY

North and South Pender islands were named by English captain (later admiral) George Henry Richards in 1791 after naval officer Daniel Pender, who served on surveying ships on the BC coast. Until 1902, when the federal government dredged a canal between them, the

*The rocky terrain, beautiful vegetation and expansive views at the top of Castle Rock make the tough climb worthwhile.*

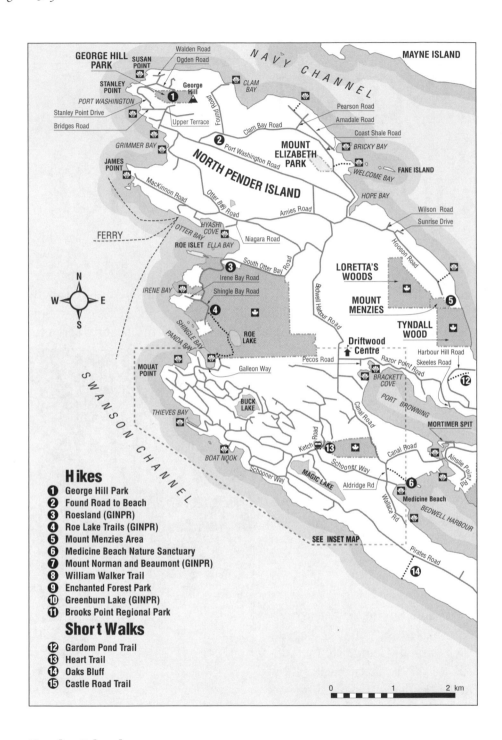

**Hikes**

1. George Hill Park
2. Found Road to Beach
3. Roesland (GINPR)
4. Roe Lake Trails (GINPR)
5. Mount Menzies Area
6. Medicine Beach Nature Sanctuary
7. Mount Norman and Beaumont (GINPR)
8. William Walker Trail
9. Enchanted Forest Park
10. Greenburn Lake (GINPR)
11. Brooks Point Regional Park

**Short Walks**

12. Gardom Pond Trail
13. Heart Trail
14. Oaks Bluff
15. Castle Road Trail

**Pender Islands**

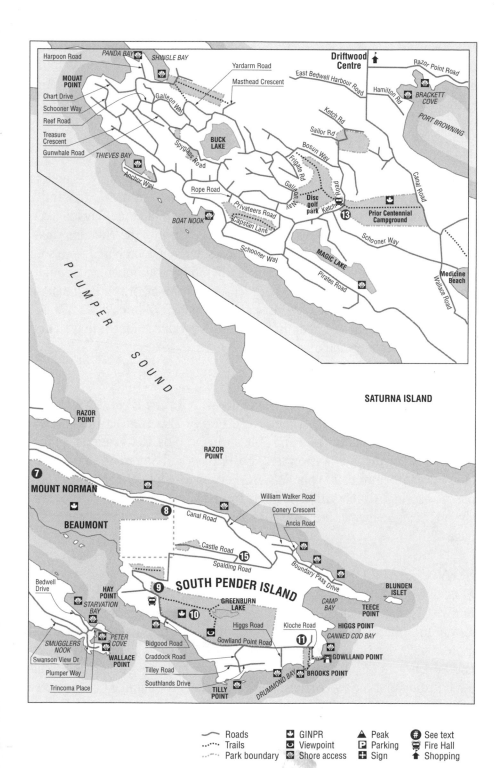

Legend:

Roads
Trails
Park boundary

GINPR
Viewpoint
Shore access

Peak
Parking
Sign

See text
Fire Hall
Shopping

Penders were a single island joined by a narrow isthmus. Prior to the creation of the waterway, residents used to drag their boats across the narrow bit of land separating Port Browning and Bedwell Harbour to avoid the long, and at times dangerous, trip around the south island. It wasn't until 1955 that a bridge was built to span the canal. In the mid-1980s, the largest archeological excavation in the Gulf Islands took place here, and artifacts dating back 5,000 years were found in the midden.

Until steamship service began at the turn of the 20th century, islanders transported all their goods by sailing sloop. The first wharf on North Pender was built at Port Washington in 1891; a second wharf in Hope Bay followed this some years later. Early settlers sold their produce in the Nanaimo market and the products of North Pender's farms and apple orchards were sold in Victoria. Logging was an important early industry, although other enterprises such as the herring saltery and fish-processing plant run by Japanese residents at Hyashi Cove in Otter Bay and a commercial brickyard at Bricky Bay were also lucrative. A plant in Shingle Bay produced lubricating oil and fertilizer from herring and dogfish.

## GETTING THERE
Ferries connect Otter Bay on North Pender with Swartz Bay (near Victoria) and with Tsawwassen (near Vancouver). Ferries also connect the Penders with Mayne, Saturna, Galiano and Salt Spring islands. Reservations are recommended for the Tsawwassen ferry on Fridays and Saturdays in the summer. For more information obtain a BC Ferries schedule or contact BC Ferries. Saltspring Air flies to the Penders from Vancouver and the Vancouver airport; Seair Seaplanes flies to the Penders from the Vancouver airport (see page 320).

## SERVICES AND ACCOMMODATION
Most of North Pender's businesses can be found in the Driftwood Centre on Bedwell Harbour Road. These include a bakery, grocery store, gas station, restaurant, pharmacy, laundromat, post office, bookstore, liquor store and more. You'll also find pubs in the marinas at Poets Cove (Bedwell Harbour) and Port Browning. Other restaurants and many bed and breakfasts are scattered throughout the two islands. The Pender Island Chamber of Commerce publishes an annual visitors' guide and map, both of which are available on the ferries and in many of the local shops. You can also get information on the Penders from the chamber website, www.penderislandchamber.com. A

good map of the islands, also available on the ferries and in island stores, is produced by Pender Island Realty, www.penderislandrealty.com. Camping is available in the Gulf Islands National Park Reserve's (GINPR) Prior Centennial Campground from mid-May to the end of October and at Beaumont campsites (water access or walk-in sites) from mid-May to the end of September. The national park has information posted at its field office at Hope Bay.

## ESPECIALLY FOR WALKERS

The Penders, especially North Pender, are excellent for walking. At time of writing the Pender Islands Parks and Recreation Commission (PIPRC) listed about 70 parks and ocean accesses. Most of these are shown on the map and described below. Many of these parks are so small that exploring them takes only a few minutes. Information on many of them is included in the Road and Short Off-road Walks section near the end of this chapter.

In addition to these walks, don't miss:

• Roesland and Roe Islet (see hike 3)
• Enchanted Forest Park (see hike 9) with its interpretive signs
• Brooks Point Regional Park (see hike 11)

## HIKES on NORTH & SOUTH PENDER

The PIPRC produces a *Community Parks and Trails Map* that identifies all the parks and their location on the islands. You can obtain copies of it from the Islands Trust office in the Driftwood Centre. The trailheads of all the local parks and trails are clearly identified by vertical posts with the name of the trail or park engraved in white paint.

There is a walking/hiking club on the island that meets at 9:30 a.m. Mondays and Fridays at St. Peter's Anglican Church. For more information ask at local stores, consult the monthly *Pender Post* or check the PIPRC's website, www.crd.bc.ca/penderparks. Biking is not permitted on the islands' trails.

## 1. GEORGE HILL PARK ★★★

| | |
|---|---|
| Trail length | 2 kilometres each way |
| Time required | About 60 minutes round trip |
| Description | A steep but beautiful walk through mixed forest to spectacular views |
| Elevation | 183 metres |
| Level | Moderate to strenuous |
| Access | The trailhead is on the south corner of Walden Road and Ogden Road |

This well-constructed, steep trail climbs 130 metres to 180-degree views. Benches are provided at the two viewpoints. The climb to this remarkable spot is well worth the effort.

## 2. FOUND ROAD TO BEACH ★★★

| | |
|---|---|
| Trail length | 1.5 kilometres each way |
| Time required | 30 minutes each way, including some time to explore the shoreline |
| Description | An up-and-down hike through mixed forest to a rocky beach that you can walk for some distance |
| Level | Moderate |
| Access | Off Clam Bay Road, 500 metres northeast of Port Washington Road. The trailhead sign is between the western boundary of Clam Bay Farm and the private property at 2218 Clam Bay Road. Parking is on the road; do not block the neighbouring driveways. |

This beautiful trail descends, ascends and finally descends again about 70 metres to the water. According to the parks commission, you pass through five ecological zones on the way down to the shoreline. Once on the beach, you can walk southeast all the way to Bricky Bay during summertime low tides.

## 3. ROESLAND (GINPR) ★★★

| | |
|---|---|
| Trail length | 600 metres |
| Time required | About 30 minutes, but you could easily spend a relaxing day here |
| Description | A short walk through a former seaside resort, part of which is on a beautiful islet. At time of writing access to the islet was by two sets of stairs (check tide tables as the stairs are not accessible at high tides). |
| Level | Easy |
| Access | On the west side of South Otter Bay Road, 1.6 kilometres from its intersection with Otter Bay Road (about 3.5 kilometres from the ferry terminal) |
| Facilities | Signboard, outhouse, parking lot, Pender Island museum located in the historic Roe house (open from 10:00 a.m. to 4:00 p.m. on weekends in July and August), picnic tables, benches |
| Cautions | This property contains a very sensitive ecosystem, so be sure to stay on the trails. |

This former resort was popular from the 1920s until the 1970s, finally closing in 1991. Only a few of the old cottages still stand, but they provide a hint of the busy resort that was once here. The original Roe family house, on the left as you walk toward the water, has been restored by the Pender Island Museum Society and houses its office, archives and exhibits. For me, the highlight of this site is Roe Islet, a real gem with its old-growth Douglas-fir, spring wildflowers, beautiful moss-covered rock and lovely path.

## 4. ROE LAKE TRAILS (GINPR) ★★★

| | |
|---|---|
| Trail length | 6 kilometres or more, depending on route taken |
| Time required | 75 minutes to circle the lake and return to the trailhead, but more hiking on other trails is possible |
| Description | A trail through second-growth forest and around a lily-filled lake |

| Level | Easy, with one steep area on the south side of the lake. At time of writing the trail around the lake was not an official park trail and was not maintained. |
|---|---|
| Access | 300 metres along Shingle Bay Road (off South Otter Bay Road) on left (east) side. This is the official Parks Canada access and is marked with a signboard and map. |
| Cautions | Watch for ticks, especially near the south end of the lake. |

You will reach the lake in about 5–10 minutes from the trailhead. There are many old logging roads in this area, and it is possible to walk around the lake, although it is not an official park trail and it is easy to get lost here with so many of these old roads to choose from. The official park trail on the west side of the lake descends steeply to the end of Galleon Way (near Shingle Bay).

## 5. MOUNT MENZIES AREA TRAIL ★★★

| Trail length | 2 kilometres or more, depending on trails taken |
|---|---|
| Time required | 30 minutes to complete the short local park trail |
| Description | The trail climbs 80 metres to a ridge with a bench but no view |
| Elevation | 195 metres |
| Level | Moderate |
| Access | On the southwest side at the end of Hooson Road |
| Cautions | This area is ecologically sensitive, so stay on the trails. When I last walked the trail in early morning in August, there were a lot of mosquitoes. |

The loop trail through the local park affords a pleasant walk through mature forest rising about 80 metres to a ridge. Stop at the bench, as this is the boundary of the local park. Be sure to admire the lovely large trees in this park.

The local park lies between two parcels of land that are part of GINPR—the 40-hectare Loretta's Wood property to the northwest and 28-hectare Tyndall Wood property to the southeast. When you walk in the local park, you may notice unmarked trails that lead into these areas as well as to pieces of private land. Although there were no official park trails on either GINPR property at time of writing, there was a well-used trail from the southeast end of the Hooson Road cul-de-sac through Tyndall Wood that leads east to spectacular views to Saturna Island. Part of the trail is very steep, as are the cliffs by the viewpoint. Use caution if you follow any of these unmarked trails, as it's easy to get lost in here.

## 6. Medicine Beach Nature Sanctuary ★★★

| | |
|---|---|
| Trail length | Up to 4 kilometres, depending on trails taken |
| Time required | 30 minutes to 1 hour |
| Description | A trail through mixed forest above an expansive beach and beside a marsh |
| Level | Moderate |
| Access | A. From a short cul-de-sac off Wallace Road just south of Aldridge Road |
| | B. On the east side of Aldridge Road about 200 metres north of Schooner Way |

Note: There is no trail through the marsh, which is fenced off.

Medicine Beach is a special, 8.5-hectare property comprising about 200 metres of beach; a 76-metre-long, 23-metre-high bluff, behind which is mixed forest of western Douglas-fir, western red cedar and grand fir; an undisturbed brackish marsh, which is unusual in the Gulf Islands; and rare and endangered plant species. While the marsh is fenced off, it can easily be viewed from the beach and from the higher ground on Wallace Road behind it. In addition to its ecological values, this land has had spiritual value to aboriginal peoples for millennia. For all these reasons a fundraising campaign raised over half a million dollars to purchase it in 1995. It is currently owned and managed by the Islands Trust Fund.

Steps climb the bluff to the north of the property and a trail follows the top of the bluff with wonderful views over Bedwell Harbour, which can be enjoyed from two benches you'll find on the trail. Two side trails—starting from each of the benches—connect with an interior trail parallel to the bluff trail, which leads to the second access point on Aldridge Road. From there you can loop back by road to your starting place near the beach. Don't forget to walk the beach and look for birdlife in the marsh.

## 7. MOUNT NORMAN AND BEAUMONT (GINPR) ★★★★

| | |
|---|---|
| Trail length | Up to 6 kilometres, depending on route taken |
| Time required | Up to 2 hours return if climbing to the summit and descending to the beach |
| Description | A hike up to a viewpoint with panoramic views, followed by a descent through Douglas-fir and western red cedar forest to a campground near the beach |
| Elevation | 244 metres |
| Level | Moderate |
| Access | A. The main access and parking area for Mount Norman–Beaumont is off Canal Road on the right, 2.5 kilometres past the Pender Islands bridge. |
| | B. An alternate access is located off Ainslie Point Road. After crossing the bridge immediately turn right onto Ainslie Point Road. The trailhead is about 500 metres from the bridge on the left side of the road. |
| Facilities | Outhouses at both trailheads and at Beaumont |
| Cautions | From access B follow an easement across private property into the park. Respect the owner's rights and stick to the trail. |

*Note: From access A the trail for hike 8 heads southwest from the parking lot near the outhouses. If you have the energy, you may wish to combine these hikes.*

It's a 30-minute, 1.5-kilometre steep climb to the summit from access B. A grassy roadway leads to the park boundary, marked by an outhouse. Soon after, the trail to Beaumont branches off to the right and descends steeply 1.5 kilometres (about 30 minutes) to the campground. To reach the summit continue straight ahead until you see a signed, second trail. Turn right into it.

The summit trail ends at a well-constructed viewing platform. The view from the top makes the whole climb worthwhile. Here you can sit on a bench,

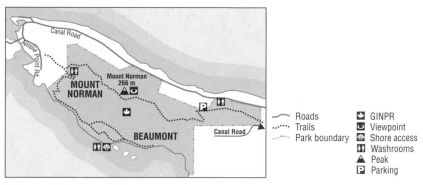

**Mount Norman/Beaumont**

enjoy a drink or a picnic lunch and get a panoramic view of the nearby Gulf Islands, the San Juan Islands in the distance and, on a clear day, the Olympic Mountains in Washington and the Sooke Hills on Vancouver Island.

It's a longer (3 kilometres) but more interesting hike from access A through open second-growth forest and heavy salal to the top of Mount Norman. From the summit you can continue down toward Ainslie Point Road and then take the trail that descends to Beaumont.

The trail to the campground descends steeply but takes you to what is arguably the loveliest part of the Penders and then continues along the trail above the rocky shoreline to the campground, with views of Bedwell Harbour, Trincomali and Poets Cove Resort.

## 8. WILLIAM WALKER TRAIL ★★

| | |
|---|---|
| Trail length | 5 kilometres |
| Time required | One hour each way |
| Description | The trail crosses a managed-forest woodlot and includes a short loop along the beach using two shore accesses. |
| Level | Moderate |
| Access | A. From the GINPR parking lot off Canal Road (2.5 kilometres from the bridge)<br><br>B. From the trailhead along Canal Road (4 kilometres east of the bridge) |

*Note: You can combine this hike with hike 7.*

*Beaumont (GINPR) is one of the most beautiful, tranquil spots to camp. While it's close to a nearby mega-resort, it retains its rustic ambience.*

From access A, the trail heads southeast. It passes an osprey's nest and offers some glimpses of the sea before heading into the woodlot, where it parallels logging roads. This is mature forest and there is at least one huge old-growth fir to admire; however, the trail is otherwise not very interesting until it comes out at Canal Road. Here you cross the road to a shore access (see the William Walker shore access, page 175). Continue left (west) along the beach about 1 kilometre to another shore access, where you return to the road, passing the historic Walker house. At this point you can loop back to the William Walker Trailhead 1 kilometre left (east) along the road or you can walk right (west) along the road 3.5 kilometres to the GINPR parking area, where you started.

## 9. Enchanted Forest Park ★★★

| | |
|---|---|
| Trail length | 2 kilometres each way |
| Time required | 40 minutes if you return by the road |
| Description | Trail containing interpretive signs through forest and marsh |
| Level | Easy |

| Access | There are three accesses on the right side of Spalding Road as you follow it down-island. The first is just past 9832 Spalding Road; the second is 275 metres farther along Spalding Road; and the third is another 225 metres from the second, or 500 metres from 9832 Spalding Road. The third access is on the right side of a private driveway; another trail on the left side of the driveway leads to a seasonal waterfall. |
|---|---|
| Facilities | Benches, bike rack, interpretive signs |

This interpretive trail identifies aboriginal uses for plants such as electrified cat's tail moss, goose-necked moss, slough sedge, Menzies tree moss, sword fern, wild rose, stinging nettle and vanilla leaf. The trail meanders through this 4-hectare park, passing through wetland and ending at a seasonal waterfall. You can either return the way you came, or turn south and take a shortcut along the road.

## 10. GREENBURN LAKE (GINPR) ★★★

| Trail length | 1 kilometre to reach the lake and then several kilometres of unmarked trails |
|---|---|
| Time required | 10 minutes to reach the lake |
| Description | An old access road, logging roads and trails leading to the lake and to viewpoints over Boundary Pass to Stuart Island and Turn Point |
| Level | Easy |
| Access | On the north side of Gowlland Point Road just north of the fire hall |

A gravel road heads north from the Parks Canada "Welcome to Greenburn Lake" sign on Gowlland Point Road. It takes about 10 minutes to reach the lake. By skirting along the berm at the west (lower) end of the lake and following the trail/old logging road, you can either turn sharply to the right (south) on a well-used trail climbing to a bluff with views south to the San Juan Islands, or you can continue to the east end of the lake. None of these trails were signed or maintained at time of writing, as Parks Canada had no official trails in this part of the park.

## 11. BROOKS POINT REGIONAL PARK ★★★

| | |
|---|---|
| Trail length | About 2 kilometres return for both trails |
| Time required | 40 minutes |
| Description | Trails through rocky coastal bluffs and grassy meadows with views of the sea and many beautiful flowers in the spring |
| Level | Easy |
| Access | Trail A: The right (south) side of Gowlland Point Road just before Jennens Road, which runs off the north side of Gowlland Point Road |
| | Trail B: East off the end of Kloche Road (off the south side of Gowlland Point Road just beyond the access to Trail A) |

This little (less than 6 hectares) park is a real treasure with a wonderful display of wildflowers in the spring, including many chocolate lilies. For this reason the Capital Regional District (CRD) has classified Brooks Point as a Regional Conservation Area, its most protected category of park. Please stay on the designated trails and enjoy the flowers and sea views from there.

In 2010 the CRD and The Land Conservancy of BC (TLC) purchased a private piece of land to connect the two pieces that were already part of the park. By the time you visit the park, a new trail may connect the two trails that now exist. Meanwhile, trail A through the western part of the park features wildflowers in the spring and views south and west over Swanson Channel. Trail B to the east follows a road access to the property and then proceeds east to a navigational beacon on Gowlland Point with views to the south and west over Boundary Pass. There are excellent views of the San Juan Islands from both trails and of Mount Baker (in clear weather) from Trail B (see photo on page 7).

## ROAD WALKS AND SHORT OFF-ROAD WALKS

There are many quiet, pleasant roads on the Penders. The areas around Hope Bay and Port Washington in the north are particularly scenic and historic. The area around Gowlland Point in the south is also an enjoyable place to walk. Here are some off-road walk suggestions, none of which should take more than 30 minutes.

**12. Gardom Pond Trail:** Park near the end of Harbour Hill Road and walk up the paved road in the subdivision. The trail, marked with a signboard containing a map, goes off to the left (east). It ends at a viewpoint above Gardom Pond. If you turn right at the sign, another trail leads to a bench and a view over Port Browning.

**13. Heart Trail/Heart Trail Extension:** The access to this trail is on the east side of Ketch Road just north of the fire hall. This trail connects the Magic Lake area with Prior Centennial Campground (part of GINPR). The Pender Island Parks and Recreation Commission (PIPRC) built the trail with the help of the First Open Heart Society of BC, in appreciation of continuing community support. A link trail connects the Heart Trail with Disc Park.

**14. Oaks Bluffs:** The access to this trail is on the south side of Pirates Road about halfway to Wallace Point. This steep, 20-minute trail in a 5-hectare park starts from Pirates Road and continues to the bluffs. It offers two spectacular views: the first of the Bedwell Harbour marina and the second of Swanson Channel and the Sooke Hills on Vancouver Island in the distance. The strategically placed benches are perfect for enjoying the magnificent views.

**15. Castle Road Trail:** This steep trail off the north side of Castle Road (off Spalding Road) leads to Spalding Hill in South Pender. Allow about an hour to climb the hill, enjoy the fine views and beautiful rock faces, and return to the trailhead. This is one of the best sites in the Gulf Islands for viewing turkey vultures and bald eagles, and how they interact. This trail can be very hot in the summer.

In addition to these walks, there are a number of short strolls you can take on the Penders. Most of the following trails will take only about 5 minutes round trip, though a few will take up to 15–20 minutes. Most of the trails in the Magic Lake area, and some of the others listed here, are short community link trails. There is a picnic area and a swimming spot at Magic Lake that you may want to visit. Most walks with a viewpoint require some climbing. The numbers in parentheses after the names of the parks are the numbers used by the PIPRC on its *Community Parks and Trails Map*.

## North Pender

I gave Magic Lake Estates its own subsection below to distinguish the large number of parks in that area from other North Pender parks.

## Magic Lake Estates

**Shingle Bay (1):** This park, near the end of Galleon Way, gives you access to North Pender's western shoreline (see Irene Bay description on page 177).

**Ursula Poepel Park (79):** Opposite 1610 Chart Drive or 1615 Schooner Way. This short trail leads uphill from Chart Drive to a bench on the left and a trail to Schooner Drive on the right. The bench overlooks Shingle Bay. This trail could form a loop with the following park (10).

**Schooner Way to Chart Drive (10):** You will find this trail at the end of Chart Drive. It connects Chart Drive to Schooner Way.

**Schooner Way at Reef Road (65):** There's a bench at this viewpoint.

**Yardarm Road to Shingle Bay (60):** This steep trail links the middle of Yardarm Road with Shingle Bay Park.

**Masthead Crescent to Shingle Bay Park (61):** This trail at the end of Masthead Crescent leads to Shingle Bay Park and crosses Galleon Way in the process. If you take Galleon Way to its end, you will find a trail leading up to Roe Lake in the Gulf Islands National Park Reserve (GINPR). This is a favourite walk with locals.

**Sandy Sievert Park (52):** This 175-metre shady, heavily wooded trail connects two access points near 2621 Spyglass Road and 2640 Gunwhale Road (close to the Galleon Way–Gunwhale Road intersection).

**Buck Lake Link Trail (63 and 69):** This trail, which links Spyglass Road to Privateers Road and Privateers Road to Schooner Way, takes about 15 minutes to walk. The trail passes two small waterfalls.

**J.M. Abbott Park (4):** This trail, off the west side of Spyglass Road, returns farther along the road. The steep, rough trail with rock faces was named for surveyor Mel Abbott who developed Magic Lake Estates, which was completed in 1974. There are benches and a picnic table along the trail.

**Thieves Bay (2):** Two trails lead from Anchor Way to the sandy beach at Thieves Bay.

**Compass Crescent/Starboard Crescent/Tiller Crescent (8 and 66):** Two short, steep trails leading to Buck Lake.

**Capstan Lane Park (3 and 29):** Access the trails off Capstan Lane or Rope Road. Two trails link both roads and pass through a fine wetland area.

**Galleon Way to Disc Golf Park (6 and 67):** Trails at the east end of Galleon Way lead to Disc Golf Park and connect with other trails leading to the fire hall and Prior Centennial Park (now part of GINPR).

**Bosun Way–Galleon Way Trail (11):** Access this trail from Bosun Way, Galleon Way or Schooner Way. It will take you about 20 minutes to complete.

**Lively Peak Park (7):** This steep trail near Sailor Road leads off to the left of a skid road to a viewpoint, and benches on which to enjoy it. You will need about 15 minutes to complete this trail.

## Other North Pender Parks

**Plumper Way Viewpoint (59):** The viewpoint is at the end of Plumper Way (at the southeast point of North Pender). There's no shore access (it's very steep), but there is a bench at this excellent viewpoint looking toward Turn Point on Stuart Island.

**Von Road Viewpoint (68):** This 5-minute path off MacKinnon Road (just west of its intersection with Otter Bay Road) leads to a picnic table with a view of the Otter Bay Marina. The path is within walking distance of the ferry, if you have time to spare while you wait.

**Shorecliff Viewpoint (70):** Between 1317 and 1321 MacKinnon, this viewpoint is also within walking distance of the ferry if you have time to spare. A 5-minute trail leads to a rocky shore with a bench to sit on while you enjoy the views south to the Olympic Mountains.

**Ogden Road Viewpoint (71):** At the end of Ogden Road (off Walden Road at North Pender's most northern point), a 5-minute trail leads to a bench at a viewpoint overlooking the south end of Navy Channel and Galiano to the west.

**Grover Sergeant Cairn (12):** The boardwalk to the cairn is on Clam Bay Road, just west of Pearson Road (north of Hope Bay). Walk on a wheelchair-accessible boardwalk to a memorial to Grover Sergeant, who crashed his plane on this site while training during World War II.

**Mount Elizabeth Park (17):** This 350-metre trail (20 minutes return) is off Clam Bay Road just north of Hope Bay. The walk was named after Elizabeth Auchterlonie, a member of one of North Pender's pioneer families. The park is a good example of a pristine sword fern environment. The PIPRC provided a nature guide at time of writing.

**Wilson Road Viewpoint (33):** Park at the corner of Hooson Road (just south of Hope Bay) and walk down Wilson Road to the trail, which leads to a viewpoint looking north over Plumper Sound and little islets. It's possible to reach the rocky beach here, but be careful not to trespass on the adjacent private property.

**Lock Road Viewpoint (72):** At the end of Sunrise Drive (off Hooson Road), a short path leads to a bench and a more limited viewpoint than the following.

**Seawest Trail Viewpoint (51):** This trail begins 1.5 kilometres from the end of Hooson Road on the left (north) side. The trail climbs to a viewpoint 75 metres above the shoreline, where you have good views of Mayne Island, the Coast Mountains and Saturna Island.

**Skeeles Road Viewpoint (19):** Skeeles Road is a gravel lane off Razor Point Road that leads to a single house. The trail parallels the road and ends at a viewpoint above a beach (no shore access) complete with a bench for enjoying it. The view is south over Port Browning to Mortimer Spit.

**Mumford Road Viewpoint (62):** This appealing trail leads down to the shoreline of Pender Canal, providing good views of Mortimer Spit and the Penders' bridge. This is a great place to see river otters. Mumford Road runs off Canal Road.

## South Pender

**Bridge Park Viewpoint (41):** Access this trail off Ainslie Point Road. The trail, which is near the mailboxes, leads to a viewpoint overlooking the canal area and the bridge. There is no shore access.

**Ainslie Point Viewpoint (75):** From the bench at the end of this short loop trail (at the end of Ainslie Point Road just past the Pender Islands bridge) you can look southeast down Bedwell Harbour.

**Saturna View (76):** Just south of 8840 Canal Road, this rustic loop trail descends gradually to a bench overlooking a magnificent view of Plumper Sound looking north to Razor Point on North Pender Island, Mayne Island beyond and Boat Passage and Saturna Island to the right.

**Ellena Road (77):** Just south of 8850 Canal Road. This loop trail leads to a bench with a partial view of Saturna Island across Plumper Sound.

**Lilias Spalding Heritage Park (39):** The public access is by foot up the fire road off Spalding Road past the Castle Road turnoff. There is no access off Castle Road. Stroll through history at this homestead site of one of South Pender's pioneer families. Lilias MacKay and Arthur Spalding married in 1889, and Lilias continued to live here until about 1938, six years after Arthur's death. This 4-hectare park contains many heritage trees and shrubs, as well as the ruins of a farm building. The park has an outhouse.

**Southlands Drive–Tilley Road Viewpoint (53):** The trail, which is at the intersection of Southlands Drive and Tilley Road, leads to a bench and a somewhat obscured view over Tilley Point.

**Craddock Drive–Gowlland Point Road (58):** This loop trail, which connects Gowlland Point Road and Craddock Road, passes through prickly gorse thickets.

## SHORE ACCESSES

There are also a number of places on the Penders where you can reach the shore. The Parks Commission has provided a bench and other amenities at most of the following shore accesses. On most beaches you can walk only a short distance.

## North Pender

**Magic Lake Estates** (see the map on page 157)

**Panda Bay (25):** End of Harpoon Road (off Galleon Way). A short trail leads to stairs to a mixed sand and gravel beach.

**Shingle Bay:** Off Galleon Way. This short trail leading to stairs to a sandy beach is part of the Masthead Crescent Trail.

**Thieves Bay (2):** This community park off Anchor Way Road has a lovely beach, picnic tables and an outhouse.

**Boat Nook (26):** Off Schooner Way, just west of Capstan Lane.

**Magic Lake Swim Hole Park (13):** Off Pirates Road at the south end of Magic Lake. Pender Islands' official swimming place boasts a diving float and an outhouse.

### Other North Pender Island Accessess

These accesses are listed clockwise around North Pender starting from its southeast point. See pages 156–57.

**Bedwell Drive (74):** This access is near the end of Bedwell Drive (off Plumper Way). There's a bench overlooking Bedwell Harbour with a beautiful view of Poets Cove and Mount Norman on South Pender, and stairs leading down to a rocky beach.

**Starvation Bay (27):** End of Bedwell Drive. Take steps to a sand, shell and gravel beach.

**Peter Cove North (18):** At end of Trincoma Place. Steps lead down to a sandy beach.

**Peter Cove South (28):** Beside 7946 Plumper Way, a narrow roadway leads to a sandy beach where you could easily launch a canoe or kayak.

**Niagara Road (34):** Opposite Pender Lions Info Centre (2332 Otter Bay Road). Walk to the end of narrow Niagara Road, where steep stairs descend to the best sand beach on the Penders. Park on Otter Bay Road and do not block neighbours' driveways.

**MacKinnon Road (24):** End of MacKinnon Road. Stairs lead to a small, ecologically sensitive beach.

**Grimmer Bay (32):** Percival Cove, just south of Port Washington, north of 1211 Otter Bay Road. Low-tide access only.

**Percival Cove (Zolob Road) (31):** Off Otter Bay Road, at the corner of Port Washington Road. A short trail leads through thorny Blackberry Lane (local name), which is habitat for quail, to stairs to a sandy beach with good views of Port Washington.

**Bridges Road (23):** 200 metres west of Stanley Point Drive. Steps lead to a shell and sand beach.

**Walden Road (35):** Just past Stanley Point Road. A short trail leads to stairs to a pebble beach.

**Found Road (off Clam Bay Road) (50):** See hike 2.

**Tracy Road (55):** East off Armadale Road, northwest of Pearson Road. Tracy Road is no more than a lane to a house. The 10-minute trail leads to stairs to a rocky beach on Navy Channel. At low tide you can walk from here south to the Bricky Bay access and north to the access at Found Road.

**Bricky Bay (22):** At the south end of Armadale Road. Steps lead down to a rocky beach on Navy Channel that can be walked, at very low tide, as far as the Found Road access.

**Welcome Bay (56):** Just north of Hope Bay, off Clam Bay Road. Walk 5 minutes to stairs down to a beautiful pebble beach.

**Pecos Road (73):** End of Pecos Road (off Razor Point Road). A short path leads to a beach with a view of Port Browning marina.

**Pender Island Portage:** On the east side of the North Pender side of the bridge over the Pender Canal. This short trail to the water follows the route Native people followed when they portaged their canoes across the narrow isthmus that was cleared away to construct the Pender Canal. There's a plaque commemorating the history of this trail at the trailhead.

**Wallace Road (54):** Off Wallace Road, just north of Schooner Way. Steep steps and a ramp provide access to the corner of Medicine Beach on Bedwell Harbour, which has a short loop trail (see hike 6).

## South Pender

These accesses are listed clockwise from the Penders' bridge (see map on pages 156–57).

**Fawn Creek Park (36):** Off Ainslie Point Road, south of the Bridge Trail (Bridge Park Viewpoint on page 172). A 10-minute loop trail passes through beautiful mature forest (large cedars and firs) and gives access to a shady, muddy beach.

**Mortimer Spit Park (38):** Near the bridge on Canal Road. This gravel road allows easy car access to the beach and mud flats, and the site is a favourite launch site for kayakers. There's also an outhouse here.

**Canal Road (48):** Between 9858 and 9864 Canal Road, about 3 kilometres east of the bridge. A rope handrail at the end of this steep descent will help you reach the flat, rocky shore, which can be walked for some distance at low tide. You might walk as far as the following shore access, passing the William Walker heritage house as you do.

**William Walker Road (43):** Opposite William Walker Trail, leading to the Gulf Islands National Parks Reserve (GINPR) parking area for accessing

Mount Norman, about 4 kilometres east of the bridge. Steps lead down to this sand and rock beach.

**Ancia Road (45):** Off Conery Crescent. A wide path leads to two long flights of very steep stairs to a rocky beach with a beautiful view across Plumper Sound to Mount Warburton Pike on Saturna Island.

**Mirada Road (78):** Beside 9953 Boundary Pass Drive, 200 metres from Conery Crescent. A short, ferny path leads: (a) down to a bench (on the left) overlooking Plumper Pass and Saturna Island opposite; and (b) to stairs (on the right) that descend to a rocky beach. On a clear day you'll have a good view of Mount Baker to the east from the beach.

**Boundary Pass (44):** Opposite 9930 Boundary Pass Drive (near the end of the road). A short trail leads to a bench and then stairs descending to the beach. At low tide you can walk to a small rocky islet with tide pools.

**Gowlland Point (46):** End of Gowlland Point Road. Stairs lead to a pebble and sand beach.

**Drummond Bay (64):** End of Higgs Road. You can access the beach here at low tide. Bring your picnic lunch. It's possible to launch a canoe or kayak here.

**Craddock Road (47):** End of Craddock Road. Stairs lead to a sizable pebble beach east of Tilly Point with a grand view of Mount Baker to the left (east).

**Bidgood Road (57):** Off Gowlland Point Road. A steep, 5-minute trail leads to steps and a handrail that permit access to this small but beautiful pebble beach.

## AND IF YOU PADDLE . . .

The Penders are well endowed with deep bays that provide interesting exploration. You can launch from the marinas in Hyashi Cove, Port Browning or Bedwell Harbour. You can also launch from government docks at Port Washington in Grimmer Bay and at Hope Bay, both of which are worth visiting to see a bit of historic North Pender. Be aware that there are strong currents in many places around the islands and watch for turbulence around the points on South Pender and around Blunden Islet. Watch for ferries and their wash if paddling around Otter Bay, in Navy Channel or in Swanson Channel, and for afternoon winds in the summer. Overall, Bedwell Harbour and Port Browning are probably the safest places to explore. You can launch from the following shore accesses:

**MacKinnon Road:** Near the end of MacKinnon Road, stairs lead down to the beach on the west side of the road. From here you can paddle north or south along North Pender's fascinating western shoreline.

**Irene Bay:** End of Irene Bay Road, 3 kilometres down South Otter Bay Road from its intersection with Otter Bay Road. A short path leads to an easy launch site on the beach. Paddle north, avoiding ferries and pleasure boats, to explore Otter Bay, Grimmer Bay and Port Washington, or south to Shingle and Thieves bays. This is very appealing shoreline.

**Shingle Bay Park:** This park near the end of Galleon Way gives you access to North Pender's western shoreline. See the previous description for Irene Bay.

**Thieves Bay:** You can launch your canoe or kayak from the park off Anchor Way Road. From here you can easily access North Pender's western shoreline. The most interesting shoreline is to the north, where you'll find Shingle Bay, Irene Bay, Ella Bay, Otter Bay and Grimmer Bay.

**Hamilton Beach:** Just past the Port Browning Marina Resort on Hamilton Road. From this access you can paddle south and under the bridge to explore both shorelines of Bedwell Harbour.

**Mortimer Spit:** It's possible to drive down to this beach to launch. From here you can explore Port Browning or go under the bridge into Bedwell Harbour.

**Medicine Beach:** There's a parking area right behind the beach, at the end of a signed driveway off Wallace Road. Launching at this beach will give you easy access to the fascinating Bedwell Harbour shoreline.

**Drummond Bay:** End of Higgs Road (southwest corner of South Pender). This is a good access for exploring the eastern end of South Pender.

**Peter Cove:** A lane at the end of Plumper Way leads northeast to a great spot where you can launch your canoe or kayak on the south side of Peter Cove. From here you can explore the southern shore of Bedwell Harbour or the outside southern shore of North Pender. There's a parking space at the top of the lane.

**Gowlland Point Road:** Launch at the end of Gowlland Point Road and paddle around the beautiful eastern shore of South Pender, north to Teece Point and Blunden Islet, and south to Tilly Point and the entrance to Bedwell Harbour.

# Quadra

*C*onsidered a Discovery Island as well as a Gulf Island, Quadra is the most northern island described in this book and the second largest (310 square kilometres). Quadra straddles climatic and geological zones, creating a diverse environment that is rich in hiking possibilities. Most of the island's approximately 2,700 residents live on the narrow southern half of the island, where you will find shops, restaurants, accommodation and other services. The north end of the island is mostly Crown land, managed by the Ministry of Forests or forestry companies. In addition to the usual Gulf Island animals—blacktail deer, raccoons, Douglas squirrels, otters, harbour seals and sea lions—Quadra has wolves and cougars. Quadra's mountainous terrain, many lakes, numerous anchorages and long beaches make it a popular destination for outdoor enthusiasts.

## HISTORY

Quadra Island was named by the Geographic Board of Canada in 1903 in honour of Spanish naval officer Juan Francisco de la Bodega y Quadra. The We Wai Kai First Nation have lived at Cape Mudge since the early 1800s, when they overcame and replaced the northern Coast Salish people, who had established a large village there. Geographers in the 19th century thought Quadra and neighbouring Maurelle and Sonora islands were all one island, which they called Valdes. This caused confusion when another Gulf Island was given the same name in 1859. The matter was clarified when the three islands were correctly mapped, and Quadra was renamed.

Splendid stands of timber and the promise of gold drew loggers and miners to the island in the 1880s. The Lucky Jim Mine, which opened in 1903, yielded tonnes of gold and copper ore. By 1904 Quadra had two post offices, a public school, a hotel, lumber camps and mills, twice-weekly steamer connections, a Methodist mission and a large salmon cannery at Quathiaski Cove. Logging is still an important economic activity, but land development and tourism are now more significant to the island.

## GETTING THERE

There are hourly 10-minute ferry sailings from Campbell River to Quathiaski Cove on Quadra Island from early morning to late night. For more information obtain a BC Ferries schedule or contact BC Ferries (see page 320).

## SERVICES AND ACCOMMODATION

All of Quadra's services are on the narrow southern end of the island. Most are within a short distance of Quathiaski Cove, mainly in two strip malls: one on Harper Road and another on West Road near Heriot Bay. Quadra has a 24-hour taxi service.

A good range of accommodation is available on Quadra, from several very comfortable resorts to more basic bed and breakfasts. Camping is available at the We Wai Kai Campground and the Heriot Bay Inn RV Park.

A free map of the island that notes features, accommodation and services is available at most stores. An invaluable resource for hikers is the island trails map produced by the Trails Committee of the Quadra Island Recreation Society.

For more information on Quadra, check www.quadraisland.ca, www.quadraisland.com and www.discoveryislands.ca. You can also contact the Trails Committee of the Quadra Island Recreation Society (QIRS), 970 West Road, PO Box 10, Quathiaski Cove, BC V0P 1N0; 250-285-3243; www.quadrarec.bc.ca.

## ESPECIALLY FOR WALKERS

Although there are many challenging hikes on Quadra, there are also some relatively easy trails. In addition to the Shore and Road Walks described later in this chapter, try one or more of the following:

- Rebecca Spit (see hike 9)
- Community Centre Trails (see hike 10)

*The trail linking Small Inlet and Waiatt Bay is lush and cool.*

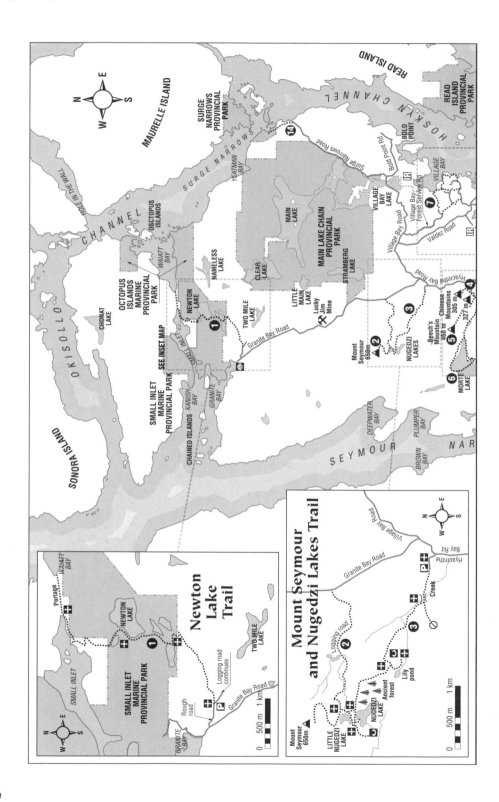

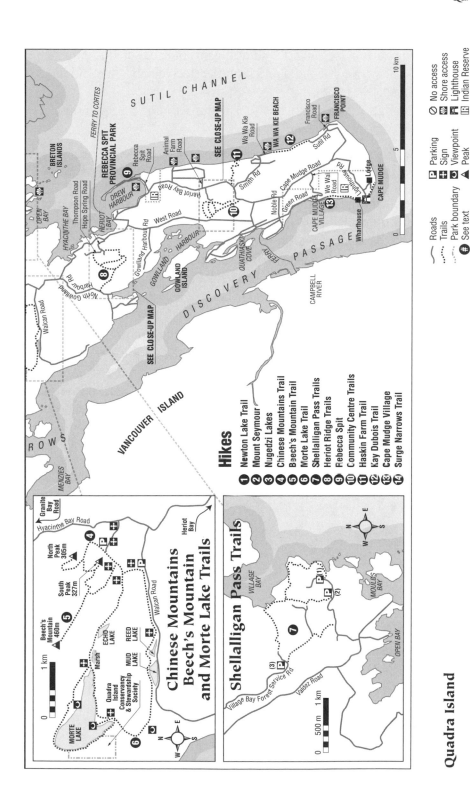

## Hikes

1. Newton Lake Trail
2. Mount Seymour
3. Nugedzi Lakes
4. Chinese Mountains Trail
5. Beech's Mountain Trail
6. Morte Lake Trail
7. Shellalligan Pass Trails
8. Heriot Ridge Trails
9. Rebecca Spit
10. Community Centre Trails
11. Haskin Farm Trail
12. Kay Dubois Trail
13. Cape Mudge Village
14. Surge Narrows Trail

**Chinese Mountains, Beech's Mountain and Morte Lake Trails**

**Shellalligan Pass Trails**

Legend:
- Roads
- Trails
- Park boundary
- See text
- # See text
- Parking
- Sign
- Viewpoint
- Peak
- No access
- Shore access
- Lighthouse
- Indian Reserve

## Quadra Island

- Kay Dubois Trail (see hike 12). If doing this one, be sure to start from the end of Wa Wa Kie Road and omit the steep climb at the end to Sutil Road.
- Cape Mudge Village (see hike 13). The trails around the lighthouse at Cape Mudge are particularly scenic.

# HIKES on QUADRA

Hiking on Quadra can be strenuous and tricky. There are countless trails, including many unmarked trails on old logging roads. Many of these trails are threatened by the tremendous amount of logging activity that is taking place, or is slated to take place, on Crown land. Because of the dangers of hiking in areas where there is active logging or poorly marked trails, I have restricted the hikes in this chapter to well-established trails maintained by the Trails Committee of the Quadra Island Recreation Society, whose volunteers have signed the trails beautifully, spending time and money to make the trails accessible to the public. Some of the hikes and walks in this chapter can be grouped together to make a longer day out, as indicated in the text.

These trails may be quite wet from fall to spring, particularly the areas around Waiatt Bay (hike 1) and the Nugedzi Lakes (hike 3). If you decide to try roads and hikes that aren't outlined below, check with locals before setting out.

| 1. NEWTON LAKE ★★★/ NEWTON LAKE TO WAIATT BAY ★★★★ | |
|---|---|
| Trail length | 6.4 kilometres to Newton Lake return; 12.8 kilometres to Waiatt Bay return |
| Time required | 2 hours to Newton Lake return; 4.5 hours to Small Inlet and Waiatt Bay return |
| Description | A pleasant hike to a pretty lake. If continuing on to Waiatt Bay, you will descend steeply through mature forest. |
| Level | Moderate |
| Access | From Heriot Bay it's about 20 kilometres to the trailhead. Take Hyacinthe Bay Road and turn left at Granite Bay Road. Continue for about 10 kilometres to within 200 metres of Granite Bay. Just after you cross a one-lane bridge, take the unsigned road on the right and drive carefully |

| | |
|---|---|
| | (it's rough) for about 600 metres to the sign indicating the trailhead. |
| Cautions | The hike from Newton Lake to Waiatt Bay is on private land owned by the Merrill and Ring logging company. Permission to hike in this area has been granted informally and could be rescinded if the land is not respected. Stay on the trail, light no fires, do not camp and do nothing to disturb the land or the midden at Waiatt Bay. The descent to Small Inlet is very steep in places. |

**Newton Lake:** The hike to Newton Lake heads first east and then north along an old, often rocky, logging road. In spring the ground along the first part of the hike is often quite wet. The trail soon crosses a little wooden bridge over a stream, which parallels the logging road for a while. You hike steadily uphill for about 1 kilometre through alder and small, feathery hemlock. After about 1.6 kilometres (15–20 minutes), you pass the first of three small lakes and the hike becomes more interesting.

After about 2.5 kilometres, you reach Newton Lake, touted locally for its emerald colour. The rest of the trail follows the west shore of the lake, ending at a rocky knoll that is a great swimming spot. At this point you will have walked 3.2 kilometres. From here you can return or continue another 3.2 kilometres to Waiatt Bay.

**To Waiatt Bay via Small Inlet:** A faded sign just past the Newton Lake knoll points you right (east) to a trail leading across a creek (over a jumble of logs) and then down (north) to Small Inlet. (A side trail to the east takes you to another fine picnic rock on Newton Lake.) The first part of the trail is difficult to find, but once you're on it, you'll find it flagged here and there with red survey tape.

The trail follows the east side of the creek, which tumbles down through the canyon to meet the sea below. About 10 minutes after leaving Newton Lake, you will see a seasonal waterfall. You walk through lovely open rain forest, past the charred stumps of old-growth trees that were logged many years ago. The trail winds its way right down to the bottom and ends 1.6 kilometres (45 minutes) from Newton Lake at the aptly named Small Inlet.

From a rocky knoll jutting out into the water you can look at the small islets in front of you and beyond them through the mouth of the inlet to the mountains on Vancouver Island. The trail continues another 600 metres (10 minutes) through the boggy terrain to a small, spring-fed pool of water behind the head of the inlet. This area, lush with ferns, still contains some large trees. From the pool the trail doubles as a portage to Waiatt Bay, another 800 metres (10 minutes) away.

This part of the trail passes old-growth stumps with the springboard notches carved by the hand loggers who felled them still visible. At Waiatt Bay there is a view of the Octopus Islands and Maurelle Island behind them.

Waiatt Bay was the site of a large aboriginal summer settlement. You can see the shell midden in the badly eroding banks. Great care should be taken here as the site is deteriorating. Do not dig into the bank or camp on it.

## 2. MOUNT SEYMOUR ★★★★★

| | |
|---|---|
| Trail length | 10 kilometres return; up to 15 kilometres if combined with hike 3 |
| Time required | Up to 3 hours; up to 6 hours if combined with hike 3 |
| Description | The first two-thirds of this hike follows an old logging road that climbs the mountain. The last third is on a trail with expansive views and lovely vegetation. |
| Level | Strenuous |
| Elevation | 650 metres; elevation gain 475 metres |
| Access | A. On the left (west) side of Granite Bay Road, about 2 kilometres from its junction with Village Bay Road (see map on pages 180–81). Just beyond the entrance to the trail (an old logging road), there's a small parking space on the shoulder of Granite Bay Road. |
| | B. From the Nugedzi Lakes trails on the east side of Little Nugedzi Lake (see hike 3) |
| Cautions | Even though the last part of this trail is well marked with cairns, red flagging and occasional red metal diamonds, it crosses mossy rocks and is easy to lose. Try to keep a cairn or trail marker in view ahead of you at all times. |

From access A you climb quickly and soon link up with a rocky logging road, which heads alternately south and west, is occasionally marked with flagging tape and is easy to follow. The trail forks after 25 minutes and again after 45 minutes; go left both times, following the wooden trail signs.

After about 50 minutes of walking up the logging road, you reach the junction of the Nugedzi Lakes trails (left) and the trail to the summit of Mount Seymour (right). If you are planning to combine the two hikes I suggest you see the summit first and then continue with the Nugedzi Lakes trails on the way back. The climb to the summit takes only about 30 minutes but it is complicated, changing directions repeatedly. Fortunately it is well marked and you can usually spot a cairn or a flag ahead of you.

After about 10 minutes on the summit trail you'll have a view over Nugedzi Lake. Soon you will see Brown Bay and other points on Vancouver Island. When you emerge on the summit, note where you came from so that you won't have trouble finding your way back. The view from the summit looks northeast to Bute Inlet and Estero Peak. You can also see Cortes Island to the east.

## 3. NUGEDZI LAKES ★★★★★

| | |
|---|---|
| Trail length | 10 kilometres return, including side trips; up to 15 kilometres if combined with Mount Seymour |
| Time required | 4 hours; 6 hours if combined with Mount Seymour |
| Description | From access B (the main access), it's a hard, boring climb up a stony logging road for about 2 kilometres, followed by a delightful hike through some old-growth forest and around two lovely lakes with good viewpoints. From access A, it may be a little less arduous but it's still a slog. |
| Level | Strenuous |
| Elevation | 510 metres |
| Access | A. On the left (west) side of Granite Bay Road about 2 kilometres from its junction with Village Bay Road (see map on pages 180–81). Just beyond the entrance to the trail (an old logging road), there's a small parking space on the shoulder of |

| | |
|---|---|
| | Granite Bay Road. The trail meets the nicest part of the Nugedzi Lakes trails at the east end of the boardwalk at Little Nugedzi Lake. |
| | B. The parking area is 100 metres up the Old Plumper Bay Road, a rough gravel road running left (west) off Hyacinthe Bay Road, 3.1 kilometres north of Walcan Road (a.k.a. Missing Links Road). Look for the sign "Nugedzi Lakes." |
| Cautions | Fires prohibited |

*Note: If you want to hike to the Nugedzi Lakes only, I recommend you start at access B (described below). If you plan to combine this outing with hike 2, I recommend you start at access A, climb Mount Seymour, follow the Nugedzi Lakes trails and end your hike at access B. From there it's 3 kilometres along Hyacinthe Bay Road and Granite Bay Road back to your starting point.*

The Nugedzi Lakes—Nugedzi Lake and Little Nugedzi Lake—were named in 1992 to honour Billy Assu (1867–1965), chief of the Cape Mudge We Wai Kai First Nation for many years. Nugedzi means "big mountain" in the Kwakwala language. The well-marked trail was developed co-operatively by the Quadra Island Recreation Society and Fletcher Challenge (now TimberWest).

*Glimpsed from the trail to Mount Seymour, Nugedzi Lake reflects the surrounding forest in its calm waters.*

Using access B, walk 700 metres past the designated parking area on the gravel road. After crossing a bridge over a creek bed, turn right onto another old logging road. This part of the hike takes you up a steep, stony gully. Don't be put off, as the last part of the hike is magnificent and makes the slog worthwhile.

You will see a cairn on your left about 2 kilometres from the parking area. At this point the logging road ends and an excellent foot trail heads off to the left (south). The hike is very pleasant from here.

About 5 minutes farther, at a small bridge, you'll find signposts directing you south to a lily pond and a viewpoint. It's worth doing the 20-minute detour to see the pond and view, but leave the Chinese Mountains for another day. It takes about 5 minutes to reach the pond, and from here a sign will direct you another 5 minutes to the spot overlooking the Breton Islands, Read Island and Rebecca Spit.

Return to the bridge and continue toward Nugedzi Lake. The trail now passes through an ancient forest that includes about half a dozen old-growth giants, as well as diverse vegetation that includes several varieties of wild mushrooms.

About 1.5 kilometres (20 minutes) from the bridge, you'll see a sign for Nugedzi Lake, Little Nugedzi Lake and Seymour Narrows Lookover. Be sure to visit them all.

Nugedzi Lake is very pretty. There's a huge rock on the lake's edge that's perfect for a picnic, and swimmers will find the water irresistible—if the weather and time of year are right. I once braved it in October and it was, well, quite refreshing.

Another 15 minutes takes you to the viewpoint looking southwest toward Seymour Narrows. You can descend to a second, lower viewpoint that offers a good view of Brown Bay on Vancouver Island.

When you've had enough of the viewpoints, return the way you came and take the turnoff for Little Nugedzi Lake. Much of the trail to the lake is on a boardwalk over marshy ground. Despite the wetness there are many small pine trees and quite a lot of kinnikinnick. The lake is exquisite, like something constructed for a Japanese garden, with little grassy islands dotting the surface. It will take you only 15 minutes to walk this part of the trail, but you'll probably want to linger here.

If you're going to access A or decide from here that you want to combine this hike with Mount Seymour, you'll find the trail at the south end of the boardwalk at Little Nugedzi Lake. Otherwise retrace your route to access B.

## 4. CHINESE MOUNTAINS ★★★★

| | |
|---|---|
| Trail length | Up to 5 kilometres, depending on routes chosen; 16 kilometres if combined with Morte Lake trails; 7 kilometres if combined with Beech's Mountain Trail |
| Time required | 2–3 hours; 5–6 hours if combined with the Morte Lake trails; 4 hours if combined with Beech's Mountain Trail |
| Description | A fairly steep climb along ridges and over rocky knolls to two separate peaks offering excellent views |
| Level | Strenuous |
| Elevation | South peak 327 metres; north peak 305 metres |
| Access | A. From a parking area on a road that goes left (west) off Hyacinthe Bay Road 600 metres north of Walcan Road (a.k.a. Missing Links Road) |
| | B. From a short connector trail that intercepts the Morte Lake Trail (see hike 6) shortly past its trailhead. This is not recommended unless you are combining this hike with a circumambulation of Morte Lake. |
| Cautions | The trail is very steep and rugged in parts. In many places it crosses mossy, rocky knolls, where the route may not be easy to discern. Cairns mark the trail but it is still easy to get lost. Take a compass, do not hike alone and make sure to leave yourself lots of time. |

*Note: The trails to the north and south peaks of the Chinese Mountains (sometimes called China Mountain) are linked, and you can hike them following a somewhat circular route.*

Since the South Chinese Mountain Trail and Beech's Mountain Trail (see hike 5) share the same path for some distance, you may wish to combine these hikes.

Take the South Chinese Mountain Trail on the left (southwest) side of the parking lot at access A. This lovely hike passes first through hemlock and fir forest and then along moss-covered rock bluffs. The trail heads south and west and soon opens up with views of mountains and Rebecca Spit to the southeast. For a while the trail follows a stream bed. It will take you about 35 minutes to reach the well-signed junction of Beech's Mountain Trail and the South Chinese Mountain Trail. If you are combining the hikes, I recommend taking the Beech's Mountain Trail first (see hike 5) and then returning to hike the Chinese Mountains.

From this junction it's at least 25 minutes to the south peak (3 kilometres from the parking lot). Here there are panoramic views of Read and Cortes islands and the Coast Mountains to the east, and of Campbell River and the Vancouver Island ranges to the southwest.

You can descend by a second trail, leading northwest, which branches off from the trail just below the south peak. You will have walked about 1 kilometre (about 15 minutes) by the time you reach the junction with the trail to the north peak. From here it's another 500 metres (20 minutes) of climbing to the north peak, which I recommend you skip. The views are not as good as those from the south peak and the trail is a bit tricky to find in places, especially on the way back. The parking lot is about 1 kilometre (15 minutes) from the junction of the trails to the two peaks.

## 5. BEECH'S MOUNTAIN TRAIL ★★★★

| | |
|---|---|
| Trail length | 3–4 kilometres each way; 7 kilometres if combined with hike 4 |
| Time required | 2 hours return; 4 hours if combined with hike 4 |
| Description | A climb through beautiful forest and over mossy rock bluffs to a spectacular 180-degree view |
| Level | Strenuous |
| Elevation | 460 metres; elevation gain 345 metres |
| Access | Follow the trail on the southwest side of the Chinese Mountains parking area (see hike 3) to the signed junction of Beech's Mountain Trail. |
| Cautions | Even though the trail is marked with cairns and flagging, it crosses rocky bluffs and is easy to lose. Try to keep a cairn or flag in view ahead of you at all times. |

This lovely hike passes first through hemlock and fir forest and then along moss-covered bluffs. The trail heads south and west and soon opens up with views of mountains to the south and Rebecca Spit to the east. For a while the trail follows a stream bed. It will take about 35 minutes to reach the well-signed junction of the Beech's Mountain Trail and the South Chinese Mountain Trail. Turn left.

More views soon open up—west to Brown Bay on Vancouver Island and south to snow-capped mountains. The hike is a steady uphill climb until the last 60 metres, which are dramatic and fast. The spectacular 180-degree view to the east is worth the effort. Turkey vultures soar on the updrafts above, below is Rebecca Spit and, in the distance, are the Breton Islands and Cortes Island.

On your way back you can hike the Chinese Mountains (hike 4) before returning to the parking area.

*From the top of Beech's Mountain, hikers get a splendid view of Quadra Island and the maze of waterways that surround it and other nearby islands.*

## 6. MORTE LAKE ★★

| | |
|---|---|
| Trail length | 10.5 kilometres including all trails; 16 kilometres if combined with hike 4 |
| Time required | 3 hours; 5–6 hours if combined with hike 4 |
| Description | A rocky trail that crosses streams, passes lakes and follows a ridge with several fine viewpoints above Morte Lake |
| Level | Moderate |
| Access | On the right, 800 metres along Walcan Road (a.k.a. Missing Links Road). Walcan Road runs left (west) off Hyacinthe Bay Road (watch for the Walcan Seafood sign). |
| Cautions | Much of this trail follows a humdrum, rocky logging road that is not very pleasant to walk along. In places the trail crosses rocky outcrops, where cairns mark the trail. |

After about 5 minutes, you reach the signed junction for the Chinese Mountains Trail (on the right). Another 10 minutes or so farther along is Little Morte Lake (a.k.a. Echo Lake), with a great echo that's well worth trying. Fifteen minutes past this lake is a signed junction that gives you a choice of circling Morte Lake (3.6 kilometres) clockwise or counter-clockwise. I recommend continuing straight ahead and walking counter-clockwise around the lake. This route will take you up some steep slopes as it follows the north and west sides of the lake, but then it ambles nicely along the south shore of the lake back to the junction. There are several pretty spots along here to picnic and swim.

*Quadra's trails sport beautiful, clear trail markers like these on the new Surge Narrows Trail.*

Although the trail map shows an alternative trail back to Walcan Road that passes a couple of small lakes, I recommend that you stick with circling Morte Lake and retrace your route to the parking area.

| 7. Shellalligan Pass Trails ★★★ | |
|---|---|
| Trail length | Up to 15 kilometres of trails (including 9 kilometres on logging roads), depending on route taken |
| Time required | Up to 4–5 hours, depending on your speed, how long you might want to spend on the beaches and how much of the trail system you want to hike |
| Description | Two loop trails through ferny woods, descending to the sea, where you scramble up and down over the rocky shoreline |
| Level | Moderate to strenuous |
| Access | A. Follow Village Bay Road 2.3 kilometres east from Granite Bay Road to Valdez Road. Turn right (south) and continue 4 kilometres to the signed trail turnoff (on the left). From here drive 1.5 kilometres to parking area 2 or 1.8 kilometres to parking area 1.

B. Take Village Bay Road to Village Bay Forest Service Road (500 metres beyond Valdez Road). Turn right. You'll see the sign for the trail 2.4 kilometres along this road. Park here (parking area 3) and walk the remaining 200 metres to the trailhead. |

These trails are well flagged and "You Are Here" maps are provided at the trailheads at the three parking areas and at the junction of the two loops. You could do either loop or both.

From parking area 1 (access A) the trail descends quickly to the nearby beach, where it follows the rocky terrain above the shore. Be aware that the trail can be slippery and strenuous in places. Leaving the beach, you will climb steeply inland (about 60 metres) for another 10–15 minutes, eventually reaching a junction of the two loop trails. If you want to complete the first loop, turn left and head to parking area 2 (about 15 minutes away). From here it's another 5 minutes to parking area 1. This last bit of trail passes ferny woods and then goes through a recently replanted woodlot. This loop would take you about an hour to walk, but allow more to enjoy the beaches and views.

I suggest continuing straight ahead on the second loop. The trail descends quickly (about 40 metres) to a bay where there is an oyster farm. It continues along the shore for about 5 minutes and then heads up and inland, climbing through beautiful ferny woods beside a seasonal stream and then through a logged area before reaching parking area 3 (just off the Village Bay Forest Service Road). Turn left on the forest service road and walk about 200 metres to where you'll see a signed trail beginning on the right. This will take you back to the woodlot logging road, where you turn left to return to the parking area.

### 8. Heriot Ridge Trails (Hope Spring Trail, Heriot Ridge Trail, Thompson Trail, Gowlland Harbour Trail) ★★★

| | |
|---|---|
| Trail length | 12 kilometres, depending on route taken |
| Time required | 2-3 hours |
| Description | A beautiful trail that crosses a variety of terrains and ecosystems—wetland, fern- and moss-covered rocky outcrops, and mixed forest, including old-growth trees |
| Level | Moderate |
| Access | A. The end of Hope Spring Road. The signed access is just inside and on the right-hand side of the driveway to 855 Hope Spring Road.<br><br>B. The signed access is on the left near the end of Thompson Road, which runs off Hope Spring Road (see map on page 194). |

These trails were built by the Quadra Island Trails Committee, volunteers and Katimavik students. They offer viewpoints and pass by old-growth Douglas-fir. The trails are well signed and flagged whenever there is any possibility that you might miss a step.

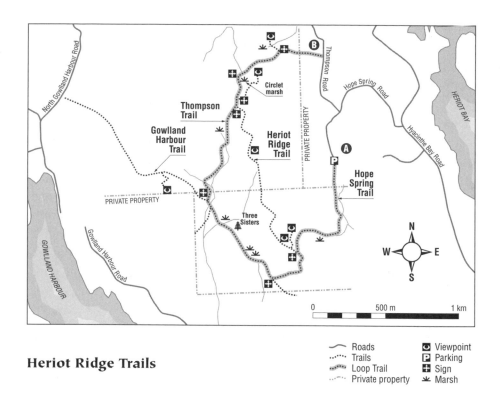

**Heriot Ridge Trails**

| | |
|---|---|
| ⌢ Roads | ◔ Viewpoint |
| ⋯ Trails | Ｐ Parking |
| ⌒ Loop Trail | ✚ Sign |
| ⋯ Private property | ⚱ Marsh |

Beginning at the Hope Spring Road trailhead, the Hope Spring Trail follows a stream and passes lovely moss- and fern-covered rock outcrops. After 15 minutes of walking, you reach the first two viewpoints (elevation about 250 metres) and the junction of the Heriot Ridge Route (see the description below). Ignore this trail for now (you can follow it back here later if you want) and allow yourself time to enjoy the views. One looks east to Rebecca Spit and the Breton Islands and southwest to Campbell River on Vancouver Island.

From here the Hope Spring Trail passes through a wet area containing skunk cabbage and becomes the Gowlland Harbour Trail. Look for a stand of old-growth Douglas-fir with three huge, fire-blackened trees called the Three Sisters to the right of the trail.

A short distance from the Three Sisters, the Gowlland Harbour Trail heads off left (northwest) and the main trail (right) becomes the Thompson Trail. If you want, you can follow the Gowlland Harbour Trail for another 2 kilometres (25 minutes) to where it meets North Gowlland Harbour Road, but you will want to retrace your steps to the main trail to get back to where you parked. (Otherwise you will have to walk 5.6 kilometres along North Gowlland Road, Hyacinthe Road and Hope Spring Road to return to your vehicle.)

Continuing on the Thompson Trail you will soon come to another junction, this time with the Heriot Ridge Route (the other end of which you passed near the two viewpoints at the beginning of the hike). You can elect to take this route back (see description below) or continue another 2 kilometres on the Thompson Trail to Thompson Road, from where it's 800 metres back to the trailhead on Hope Spring Road.

If you elect to stay on the Thompson Trail, you should give yourself an additional 40 minutes to see the two remaining viewpoints (see map). The trail to the first viewpoint (on the right) rises steeply to about 240 metres above sea level. The view from a rocky ridge is east to Drew Harbour and Rebecca Spit on the right, and Read Island on the left. Take time to explore the ridge, as the view opens up as you walk farther along it. This detour will take at least 20 minutes. The next viewpoint (on the left) is somewhat lower (about 200 metres), and you have to climb a steep rock outcropping to reach it. The view here is northeast to the Breton Islands and Read Island.

Heriot Ridge Route: If you prefer not to walk along the roads, you might try this rugged route. Although well marked, the trail can be a bit of an adventure, passing over a moss-covered ridge and through thick salal. As the vegetation can easily obscure the trail, to avoid getting lost retrace your steps if you do not see a flag or cairn ahead of you. If all goes well, it will take you about half an hour to return to the two viewpoints near the beginning of the hike.

## 9. REBECCA SPIT MARINE PROVINCIAL PARK ★★★★

| | |
|---|---|
| Trail length | 2–4 kilometres return, depending on whether you use the park entrance or the parking lot as your start and end point |
| Time required | 30–60 minutes, but you'll want to stay longer |
| Description | This idyllic spot has great beachcombing, lovely views west across Drew Harbour and east toward Cortes and the snow-topped mainland mountains beyond, and pleasant trails through mature second-growth forest. |
| Level | Easy |
| Access | The park entrance is just past the We Wai Kai Campground on Rebecca Spit Road, which is off Heriot Bay Road (see map on pages 180-81). |

# A BRIEF HISTORY OF REBECCA SPIT

Archeologists believe that in the late 18th century a major battle was fought at Rebecca Spit between the Coast Salish and the Kwakwaka'wakw (Kwagiulth). A few grass-covered trenches are all that remain of the extensive Coast Salish fortifications.

The spit was named in about 1864 after a British trading schooner. It was a We Wai Kai First Nation reserve until the government traded nearby land for it during World War I so that the spit could be used for military purposes. For many years after the war the land belonged to the Clandening family, whose members allowed Quadra islanders to use it. In 1946 an earthquake reduced the total area of the spit by more than a third. The land was eventually obtained by the province and made into a park in 1959.

*The trail at Rebecca Spit parallels the shoreline of Drew Harbour to the light on the point and then returns along the open water of Sutil Passage.*

The spit is just over 2 kilometres long. You can hike from the park entrance down the centre of the spit or drive to a parking/picnic area partway along the spit. Here you will find an easy path that follows the inner Drew Harbour shore and then continues around the outer Sutil Channel shore. For a short stretch at the spit's narrowest point, the two paths combine. You can also walk around the spit along the beach.

Rebecca Spit is a magical place. The sounds of grebes, ducks, scoters, mergansers, herons, gulls and other waterfowl are often the only thing you'll hear. In the summer pleasure boats bob at anchor in expansive Drew Harbour, and fishing boats head out or return. The light is particularly pleasant here, as the spit is narrow and well separated from the land around it. Whether you wind in and out of the second-growth forest or beachcomb along the shore, you will inevitably spend much longer than the hour or so it takes to walk all the trails.

## 10. COMMUNITY CENTRE TRAILS (BLENKIN MEMORIAL PARK) ★

| | |
|---|---|
| Trail length | Over 10 kilometres |
| Time required | 2 hours or more |
| Description | Hikers share these short trails with equestrians and cyclists. |
| Level | Easy |
| Access | These trails start from the Community Centre on West Road and link with Heriot Bay Road at Animal Farm Road (at Smokey's Bike Shop) and again just west of Smith Road. The trails also have accesses on West Road. |

Note: This hike can be combined with the Haskin Farm Trail (hike 11).

Blenkin Memorial Park was established in 1962 after islanders raised the money to acquire these 16 hectares in memory of John and Mary Blenkin and their two daughters, who were killed in a car crash. The park is on the original homestead of "Black Jack" Bryant and his family.

The park has several trails, with the longest being the Homestead Trail and the Community Centre Trail. The original Bryant home was near the junction of these trails (reportedly in the vicinity of a large maple tree growing here today), and the marsh here was once drained to make way for the family's garden.

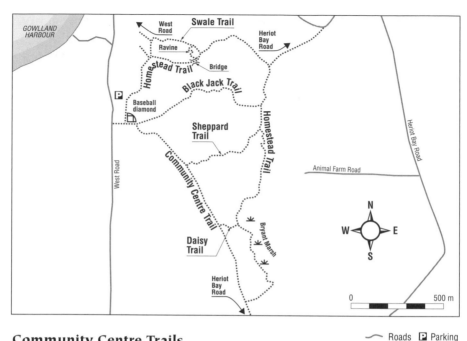

**Community Centre Trails**

Roads   P Parking
······ Trails   ⛌ Marsh

The woodsy trails are pleasant and serve an important community function. I found some sections quite soggy, especially on the southeast side. There are picnic tables in a couple of spots and a number of bridges over the seasonal creeks that cross the property.

- The Homestead Trail starts northeast of the Community Centre and loops around the property until it merges with the Community Centre Trail at the southern part of its loop. Several trails run off it. Of these, I found the Swale Trail (at the north end of the park) particularly enjoyable with its mixed forest and old stumps sprouting little gardens.
- The Community Centre Trail runs southeast from the Community Centre and joins with Heriot Bay Road.
- Two trails link the Homestead Trail with West Road: an unnamed trail comes out across the street from 1015 West Road, while one end of the Swale Trail comes out opposite 1033 West Road.

- The Black Jack Trail starts at the ballpark and heads northeast to meet the Homestead Trail.
- The Sheppard Trail (named after Mary Sheppard, Black Jack's wife) and the Daisy Trail (named after their daughter) run roughly east-west, linking the Homestead Trail with the Community Centre Trail.

## 11. HASKIN FARM TRAIL ★

| | |
|---|---|
| Trail length | 1.5 kilometres each way |
| Time required | About 30 minutes each way |
| Description | This trail follows bridle paths down to a beach. |
| Level | Easy |
| Access | The signed trailhead is on the northeast side of Heriot Bay Road at the intersection of Smith Road. (There is also an unsigned linking trail from the end of Fir Drive.) |
| Cautions | The trail is very easy for its first two-thirds but then drops steeply to the ocean for the final 10 minutes. |

Note: This hike can be combined with the Community Centre Trails (hike 10) and the Kay Dubois Trail (hike 12).

This well-established trail proceeds east from Heriot Bay Road down to the beach. After about 500 metres the trail branches off in several directions but the paths all seem to merge again farther on. The trail then narrows and crosses a grassy meadow before entering into the forest again. After crossing an old logging road the trail snakes its way down an escarpment to the beach.

From the beach there is a beautiful view of Marina and Cortes islands to the east and the mountains on the mainland behind them. You can return the way you came or walk for about 1 kilometre south along the beach until you reach the access off Wa Wa Kie Road. From here you can continue walking south down Wa Wa Kie Road and take the Kay Dubois Trail (see hike 12) or you can follow nearby Smith Road back up to Heriot Bay Road.

## 12. KAY DUBOIS TRAIL ★★★

| | |
|---|---|
| Trail length | 2 kilometres each way |
| Time required | 40 minutes each way |
| Description | This beautiful path through mature rain forest connects Wa Wa Kie Road to Sutil Road. |
| Level | Easy |
| Access | A. At the end of Wa Wa Kie Road |
| | B. At the end of Sutil Road |
| Cautions | The trail descends steeply from Sutil Road. |

*Note: This hike can be combined with the Haskin Farm Trail (hike 11) and Francisco Point (hike 13).*

The trail is named to honour the memory of a popular long-time resident of Wa Wa Kie Road. For most of its length it follows the southeast coast. As you walk through this splendid second-growth forest, you'll see huge stumps left over from early logging days. The path through the alder and fir trees is a rich, soft bed of humus covered by fir needles, with only a few exposed roots to trip you up. Along the way are glimpses through the trees of the sea, which is only a few short steps away at any time.

If you want to extend this hike, you can walk south along Sutil Road to Francisco Road and then follow the rocky beach to Francisco Point.

## 13. CAPE MUDGE VILLAGE–LIGHTHOUSE–FRANCISCO POINT ★★★

| | |
|---|---|
| Trail length | About 6 kilometres each way (2.5 kilometres if you go only as far as Tsa-Kwa-Luten Lodge) |
| Time required | 2 hours each way |
| Description | A pleasant walk along a trail, past a lighthouse and local lodge, and along a rocky beach |
| Level | Easy |
| Access | To the right of the hydrant at the southern end of Green Road in Cape Mudge Village |
| Cautions | Much of this hike is on land owned by the We Wai Kai First Nation. Official permission to use these trails should be obtained from the Cape Mudge Band Council (1-877-915-5533). Watch your footing on the rocky beach between the lodge and Francisco Point. |

Walk for 1 kilometre along the trail until you reach the Tsa-Kwa-Luten Wharf House. Another 500 metres along a driveway takes you to the Cape Mudge lighthouse. The trail then winds around behind the lighthouse and follows the shore for another 1 kilometre to the Tsa-Kwa-Luten Lodge. You may choose to return from this point or continue past the lodge and down to the rocky beach, where you can continue on to Francisco Point.

Cormorants, gulls, ducks and herons can be viewed around the offshore rocks. Past the lodge are impressive sand cliffs above the beach. You will enjoy expansive views south and west to Campbell River and the Vancouver Island mountains beyond.

## 14. SURGE NARROWS TRAIL ★★★

| | |
|---|---|
| Trail length | 7 kilometres return |
| Time required | 1.5 hours round trip, plus time to view the rapids |
| Description | A moderate hike along the shore of Surge Narrows, with wonderful views of the rapids that form between Quadra and Maurelle islands |
| Level | Moderate; some steep sections |
| Access | The end of Surge Narrows Road (6 kilometres beyond the bridge on Village Bay Road). Two parking lots serve the Hoskyn Channel Landing community dock to the outer Islands; park in the upper parking lot and walk down the very steep road to the second parking lot. The trailhead is located in the northwest corner of the lower parking lot. |

The fern-lined trail leads to the Quadra Island section of Surge Narrows Provincial Park. The first part of the trail is through young forest and crosses four bridges over four small creeks, only the first of which had water in it when I was there in October. The trail is up and down, climbing about 60 metres above the water at its highest point. It will take you about 30 minutes to reach the border of the provincial park and another 5 minutes to get to where you can see the rapids in Surge Narrows. Try to come when the current is running swiftly for the best show (check a current table for the day you visit to see when the flood or ebb tide is at its peak). The Quadra Island Trails Committee is planning to build a lower trail along the shoreline to create a loop back to the trailhead. Watch for these changes to the trail in the future.

You may notice what looks like a trail continuing west from the viewpoint. Avoid it unless you feel particularly adventuresome and have nothing better to do; this is a route rather than a trail. I followed the steep, narrow, often rocky and sometimes treacherous route up and down (in one especially steep place a rope has been provided to help you) for about 15 minutes until I reached a small bay on the narrows opposite the rocky islets in the middle of the channel. From here the route seemed to head inland and I gave up on it.

## SHORE AND ROAD WALKS

It is possible to walk all around the southern end of Quadra by a combination of trail and beach. The total distance from Cape Mudge Village (on the west side of the island) to just north of Wa Wa Kie beach (on the east side) is about 15 kilometres, but you might choose to do only one or more sections of it. This walk would include hikes 11 to 13, using beach and roads as connections. Be very careful to walk beaches only at low tide.

**Green Road:** Just south of the Quathiaski Cove ferry dock down to Cape Mudge Village is a very pleasant walk. The road offers glimpses of the ocean through large trees and the village is picturesque. While in the village you might visit the United Church, Quadra's first church (dedicated in 1932), as well as the rich Nuyumbalees Cultural Centre (open from June to September). The cultural centre's museum contains an intriguing potlatch collection, including some of the artifacts taken by the federal government in 1922, when it enforced its law banning the potlatch. There are also a number of petroglyphs in the grounds around the museum that were taken from Cape Mudge beaches. For more information contact the Nuyumbalees Cultural Centre, PO Box 8, Quathiaski Cove, Quadra Island, BC V0P 1N0; 250-285-3733; www.nuyumbalees.com.

**Wa Wa Kie Road (at the foot of Smith Road):** The houses along this pleasant road are interesting and distinctive, and you can glimpse the sea between them all along the walk. This walk can be combined with the walk along the beach north of Wa Wa Kie Road, with the Haskin Farm Trail (hike 11) or with the Kay Dubois Trail (hike 12).

**Granite Bay:** The quiet roads in this area are interesting to explore. You can drive or walk down to the dock to look at the boats—some of which are quite old—by turning into the road opposite the access to the Newton Lake trail (hike 1).

*The cool promise of Morte Lake is a strong draw for hikers following the trail around it in the summer.*

## AND IF YOU PADDLE . . .

Quadra has the finest lakes in the Gulf Islands. If you hike many of the trails described in this chapter, you will see several of these lakes; however, you will miss some of the loveliest. The lakes in Main Lake Chain Provincial Park (off Village Bay Road)—Village Bay, Main and Little Main lakes—together with Mine, Stramberg and Clear lakes, form the largest freshwater lake system on the Gulf Islands.

I strongly recommend spending a day or two exploring these lakes by canoe or kayak. There are a number of excellent places for picnics and several campsites. If the weather is fine, you might like to swim at one of the beaches or off a rocky ledge. And if you're feeling ambitious, try the 2.6-kilometre, water-access-only hike along the Yeatman Portage, a steep, old logging road that links the northeast corner of Main Lake with Yeatman Bay.

If you want to paddle in the ocean, keep in mind that Quadra is surrounded by some of the most treacherous passages on the West Coast, with strong currents affecting most of its coastline. In some channels, these currents reach between 11 and 16 knots, and during tide changes, there are whirlpools and rapids in Seymour Narrows, Hoskyn Channel, Surge (a.k.a. Beazley) Narrows and parts of Okisollo Channel. In addition, winds and waves can pound the southeast side of the island. Except in protected harbours, novice and intermediate kayakers would be wise to head out with a guide. Here are a few of the more benign paddles:

**Rebecca Spit:** Launch at the boat ramp and paddle around Drew Harbour or along the Quadra shoreline. When it's calm the Breton Islands east of Open Bay are fun to paddle around. If you have a few days you might like to venture up the coast through Surge Narrows (at slack current only) to the gorgeous Octopus Islands at the mouth of Waiatt Bay. This is one of the most beautiful places I've ever camped.

**Granite Bay:** Put in here and paddle out to the Chained Islands. When you reach the last one you'll see the turbulent water in Seymour Narrows. On the way back to Granite Bay you might like to paddle into Small Inlet. At the head of the inlet you can take the portage trail, with or without your boat, from Small Inlet to Waiatt Bay and continue on to Newton Lake (see hike 1).

**Valdez Road:** You can easily launch your boat from the rocky beach at the end of this road. You can then paddle south around Open Bay to Hyacinthe Bay, Heriot Bay and, finally, Drew Harbour and Rebecca Spit. Alternatively, you can paddle out to the Breton Islands offshore or north to Village Bay and Bold Point at the south end of Hoskyn Channel between Quadra and Read islands.

*The Cusheon Cove museum in Salt Spring's Ruckle Park contains many artifacts from the days when there was a large mill here.*

# Salt Spring

$S$alt Spring has everything you could want in a Gulf Island: mountains, lakes, old-growth forest, arbutus and Garry oak groves, farmland, beaches, protected bays and lots of great hiking trails. Most of its shops, eateries and galleries are in Ganges. At 193.5 square kilometres, it is the third largest Gulf Island, but with about 10,000 full-time residents, it has more than twice the population of Gabriola, the second most-populous island.

Salt Spring islanders are an eclectic bunch. Many are artists whose music, writing, films or performances have worldwide audiences. A highlight for many visitors is the extensive crafts and farmers' market that takes place every Saturday in Ganges from April to mid-October. As well, local and visiting musicians and artists perform and display their work at ArtSpring, the island's beautiful arts centre.

*With about 7 km of waterfront, moss-covered rocks, and some of the biggest Douglas-firs on the island, Ruckle Park is Salt Spring's crown jewel. Irish immigrant Henry Ruckle homesteaded here in 1872, and about 100 years later his grandson Gordon sold the land to the provincial government.*

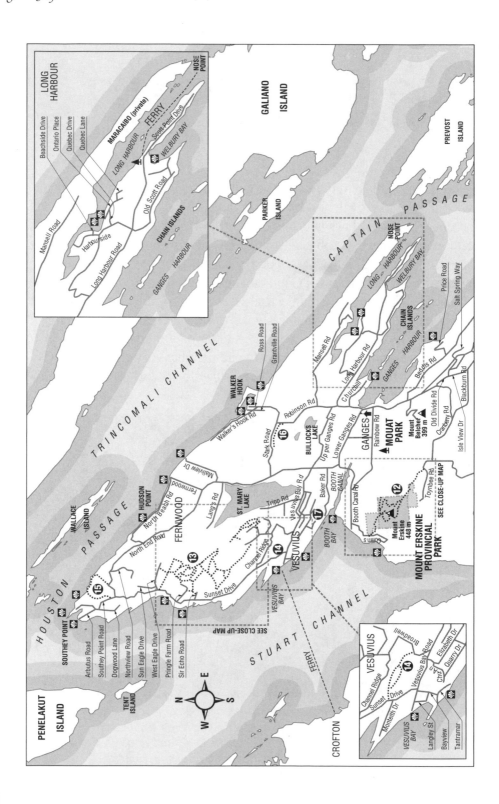

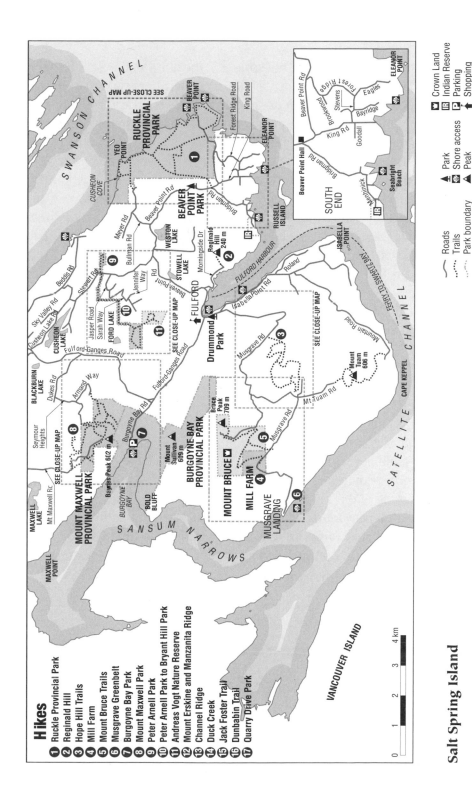

## Hikes

1. Ruckle Provincial Park
2. Reginald Hill
3. Hope Hill Trails
4. Mill Farm
5. Mount Bruce Trails
6. Musgrave Greenbelt
7. Burgoyne Bay Park
8. Mount Maxwell Park
9. Peter Arnell Park
10. Peter Arnell Park to Bryant Hill Park
11. Andreas Vogt Nature Reserve
12. Mount Erskine and Manzanita Ridge
13. Channel Ridge
14. Duck Creek
15. Jack Foster Trail
16. Dunbabin Trail
17. Quarry Drive Park

## Salt Spring Island

**Legend:**
- Crown Land
- Indian Reserve
- Parking
- Shopping
- Park
- Shore access
- Peak
- Roads
- Trails
- Park boundary

SOUTH END

VANCOUVER ISLAND

## HISTORY

Salt Spring was named after the salt springs in the north of the island, which Governor James Douglas considered "of the greatest importance" and a future source of wealth. The Tsawout people lived for centuries on Salt Spring and today maintain a small, unpopulated reserve on the south coast of the island. Among the first non-aboriginal residents were blacks who fled California and its oppressive laws, as well as some of the would-be prospectors who arrived from all over the world to join the 1858 Fraser River gold rush, failed to get rich and ended up on Salt Spring a year later. All the early arrivals acquired unsurveyed land on the island for virtually no money. Most of them established farms—often with large orchards—and sold what they produced in Vancouver Island markets.

In the years that followed Salt Spring boasted a multicultural population, with immigrants from areas as disparate as the British Isles, Portugal, Scandinavia, Japan and Hawaii. The hospitable climate, fertile soil in some parts of the island and abundant seafood sustained the newcomers. By 1900 Salt Spring was famous for its large harvests of fruit. Fruit growing was later replaced by dairying (especially butter) and poultry and sheep farming in importance, and the island's lamb is still considered a delicacy.

By the 1930s vacationers discovered the island, and resorts opened to welcome them. Cottagers from Vancouver and Victoria grew in number from the 1950s, and islanders began subdividing land to take advantage of this interest. A spiral of growth began, with increased services and infrastructure attracting more people, and vice versa. Artists and craftspeople began arriving on the island in the 1960s, and today their signs dot island roads. These studios are a popular tourist attraction, and the seasonal Saturday market supports many of the island's artisans all on its own. The largest areas of employment continue to be in such service industries as tourism, construction, real estate and retail business, although electronic media allow others to live and work on Salt Spring.

## GETTING THERE

Salt Spring has three ferry routes: one travels almost hourly between Vesuvius Bay (near the north end of the island) and Crofton (an hour south of Nanaimo); a second connects Fulford Harbour (at the south end of the island) and Swartz Bay (near Victoria) every two hours; and the third makes the trip between Long Harbour (5.5 kilometres from Ganges) and Tsawwassen (near Vancouver) twice a day. The ferry from Long Harbour stops on Galiano,

Mayne and the Pender islands once or twice most days. For more information obtain a BC Ferries schedule or contact BC Ferries. Harbour Air, Seair Seaplanes and Saltspring Air also connect Salt Spring to Vancouver and Victoria by floatplane (see page 320).

## SERVICES AND ACCOMMODATION

Salt Spring's numerous bed and breakfasts range from comfy-casual to luxurious. The island also has a hotel, a number of resorts and inns, two motels, a hostel, two marinas in Ganges and another in Fulford Harbour, private campgrounds and RV and walk-in camping at Ruckle Provincial Park. Salt Spring now has a bus service (buses meet most ferries).

Most of Salt Spring's services are in Ganges. The much smaller village at Fulford Harbour, 17 kilometres away, has a few basic services. For additional information on Salt Spring, contact the Chamber of Commerce Visitor Information Centre (250-537-5252; www.saltspringtourism.com), or the island's accommodation website, www.saltspring-accommodation.com. The information centre also distributes an annual booklet that lists accommodation, activities, services and shopping. Free maps of the island are available at the information centre, from stores and from realtors. The Lions Club annually updates its excellent map of the island, which sells in local bookstores for a nominal price.

## ESPECIALLY FOR WALKERS

In addition to the shore and road walks outlined near the end of this chapter, consider trying one or more of the following relatively easy walks:

- the shoreline and forest trails in Ruckle Park, especially those in the picnic and camping areas (see hike 1)
- Musgrave Greenbelt (see hike 6)
- the summit of Mount Maxwell from the parking area (see hike 8)
- Peter Arnell Park (see hike 9)
- Duck Creek (see hike 14)
- Dunbabin Trail (see hike 16)
- Creekside Rainforest (see page 250)

# HIKES on SALT SPRING

The Salt Spring Trail and Nature Club maintains many trails on the island and schedules outings for ramblers, walkers and hikers every Tuesday from September to June. Salt Spring's weekly newspaper, the *Driftwood*, publishes each month's schedule in its last issue of the month. The island's parks and recreation commission or PARC (250-537-4448) is also a good source of local hiking information.

## 1. RUCKLE PROVINCIAL PARK ★★★★★

| | |
|---|---|
| Trail length | Over 15 kilometres, including 7 kilometres of shoreline |
| Time required | A full day if you plan to hike all the trails |
| Description | A walk along the shore passing many coves and bays and through splendid mixed forest |
| Level | Easy to moderate |
| Access | The park is 8.5 kilometres from the Fulford ferry terminal (turn right on Beaver Point Road) or 20 kilometres from Ganges (look for signs just north of Fulford on the Fulford–Ganges Road). You can begin walking the trails from any of the following accesses: |
| | A. a signed trailhead on the left (north) side of the road shortly after you enter the park |
| | B. the farm buildings adjacent to the first parking area you reach after entering the park (described below) |
| | C. the picnic or camping areas (each of which have parking areas) |
| | D. behind Beaver Point Hall on Beaver Point Road (about 2 kilometres before you reach the Ruckle Park gate) |
| | E. Ruckle Park now includes 40 hectares at adjacent Cusheon Cove, except for the two privately owned houses right on the cove. It |

| | |
|---|---|
| | is possible to enter the park from the now-public driveway almost at the end of the southeast side of Meyer Road (off Bulman Road). If you enter the park in this way, take the second driveway on the right and look for a cairn marking a trail across a creek to your right. From the coastal trail in the park it's also possible to follow the trail from Yeo Point to Cusheon Cove and beyond to the access on Meyer Road. Neither the access nor these trails are officially sanctioned by BC Parks or signed at time of writing. |
| Facilities | Camping sites, outhouses, picnic tables, benches, water |
| Cautions | The Ruckle farm is still active. Keep off the fields and farm roads and respect the residents' privacy. Dogs are best left at home; if you bring one, it must be leashed. |

*Note: In the following description, the numbers correspond to those on the map on page 212.*

Ruckle Park has some of the best hiking in the Gulf Islands and is easy to explore. BC Parks has installed "You Are Here" signboards at most of the trail accesses and intersections, although many of these had been vandalized at time of writing. While you can hike the park's trails in several directions, I think the route described here is the best.

From behind the historic farm buildings (access B; 11 on the map), follow the maple-tree-lined trail along the farm fence down to Grandma's Bay and continue southeast along one of the trails through the stands of arbutus and Garry oak north to Beaver Point. The higher trail is more level but the trail closer to the shore has better views and offers the chance to see waterfowl, seals, otters and other wildlife.

You will reach the walk-in camping area in about 20–30 minutes. From here, I tend to take the rougher trails near the shore as much as possible to avoid the largest camping area and enjoy the views of the water. The camping area ends near Beaver Point—so named because the Hudson's Bay Company paddle steamer *Beaver* went aground here. Steamships stopped at a wharf in the adjoining bay from 1914 to 1951, and there used to be a general store

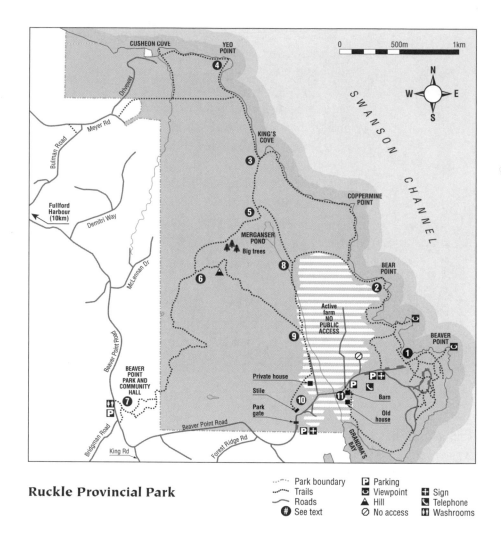

**Ruckle Provincial Park**

| | | |
|---|---|---|
| ····· Park boundary | P Parking | |
| ····· Trails | ◎ Viewpoint | ➕ Sign |
| ── Roads | ▲ Hill | ☏ Telephone |
| # See text | ⊘ No access | ⊞ Washrooms |

and post office nearby. Nothing remains of this building or the wharf, but the area is one of Salt Spring's finest picnic spots.

From Beaver Point, trails lead to the park's picnic area. Walk through this area, past the signboard greeting visitors who enter the park from the nearby parking area (1) and follow the trail that continues along the shoreline. This 4.4-kilometre trail crosses many rocky headlands and passes tiny coves and bays before reaching Yeo Point. Although an informal trail continues from Yeo Point to Cusheon Cove, it is hazardous in places because of erosion and is not an official park trail.

On the way to Yeo Point you can shorten your hike, or vary your route, by taking one of the alternate trails into the forest near Bear Point (2) or King's

Cove (3). The alternate trail from Bear Point (2), about 1.5 kilometres north of Beaver Point, soon reaches a junction (8). If you turn left (south), the trail will take you to the park's entrance road—near "Park Headquarters" at (10). If you go right (north), you will pass Merganser Pond and join a trail (at 5) that links Beaver Point Hall (to the left) and King's Cove (to the right).

King's Cove (3) is named for 1880s settler Leon King. Although it was used as a log dump in the 1920s and again in 1946, some of Salt Spring's largest trees still stand nearby. If you take the 3.8-kilometre trail inland from here toward Beaver Point Hall, about halfway between junctions 5 and 6, you will find a grove of the largest Douglas-firs on Salt Spring, including the one I believe to be the largest—about 8 metres in circumference. This tree can be found about 100 metres to the southeast of the trail.

You can continue along the trail to where it emerges behind Beaver Point Hall (7), turn left and walk along Beaver Point Road to the park entrance, or you can follow one of the trails in the park to the left and make your way to the house that's known as "Park Headquarters" (10) or to Bear Point (2).

## 2. REGINALD HILL ★★★

| | |
|---|---|
| Trail length | 1.5 kilometres each way |
| Time required | 45–60 minutes up, 35–45 minutes down |
| Description | A very steep, winding ascent through second-growth forest to a lookout with views over the Fulford–Burgoyne Valley and the San Juan Islands |
| Level | Strenuous |
| Elevation | 248 metres (elevation gain about 200 metres) |
| Access | Park at the end of Morningside Drive (1 kilometre from the Fulford ferry terminal). Do not drive into the Reginald Hill strata development, as this is a private road and your car could be towed away. Walk through the gate of the strata development. Take the first driveway to the left (100 metres beyond the gate) and follow the red metal markers (bearing left) to the trailhead at the edge of an old quarry. |
| Cautions | Much of the surrounding land is private. Please keep to the trail. |

Note: This hike can be combined with a walk around Fulford.

*Reginald Hill provides a view of the head of Fulford Harbour. From here you can see how the Fulford–Burgoyne Valley cuts a swath through the island to Burgoyne Bay. The snub-nosed peak in the right background is Mount Maxwell, and on the left is Mount Bruce, the island's highest peak.*

This trail is in a small community park. Much of the land to the west and south of the park belongs to the strata development, while the land to the east is part of Wave Hill Farm. There's not much of a view until you reach the top. As you near the top, the trail splits; however, the two trails meet at the top.

Reginald Hill is not nearly as high as Salt Spring's mountains, so the outlook is more intimate and accessible—perhaps a sparrow's rather than an eagle's view. From here you have the island's finest view of Fulford Harbour, the nearby Fulford–Burgoyne Valley and Vancouver Island in the distance. You can also admire Baynes Peak on Mount Maxwell, Bruce Peak on Mount Bruce and the San Juan Islands in the east. Return the way you came.

## 3. HOPE HILL TRAILS ★★★★

| | |
|---|---|
| Trail length | Up to 7 kilometres |
| Time required | Half to full day |
| Description | A hike through fir and cedar forest, with excellent views of Fulford Harbour, much of southern Salt Spring, and on a clear day, other southern Gulf Islands, the San Juan Islands, Vancouver, the Coast Mountains and Washington's splendid Mount Baker |
| Level | Strenuous |
| Elevation | 625 metres (elevation gain about 300 metres) |
| Access | On the west side of Musgrave Road, about 3.5 kilometres from Isabella Point Road and 500 metres beyond a hairpin bend (about 6 kilometres in total from the Fulford ferry terminal and about 18 kilometres from Ganges) |
| Cautions | A. The trails described here and shown on the map have become increasingly difficult to follow, partly because they are often overgrown, are subject to many deadfalls that block them and may easily be confused by the large number of off-road motorbike trails that increase each year. Follow only the trails marked with ribbons or red metal markers and don't proceed unless you are sure you're on the trail you want to follow. I've placed numbers on trees to correspond to the numbers on the map on page 217 so that you can tell where you are on the map from where you are on the ground. I hope the numbers are still there when you are. |
| | B. These trails cross quite steep, rocky terrain that can be very slippery when wet. |
| | C. There is no public trail to the top of Hope Hill, which is on private property and has no view. Respect the landowner's rights. |

*Note: In the following description, the numbers correspond to those on the map on page 217.*

*The top of Hope Hill is a good place to picnic and take in the view of nearby islands.* Lynn Thompson

The trails on this 173-hectare piece of Crown land are often hard to find, and you should hike here with great caution. People regularly report getting lost here, and one poor fellow actually spent a night sitting on a log when he couldn't find the trail out (a good reason to start your hike early in the day).

The trails begin on an old logging road (1). You will soon see a junction of two roads. Keep to the right. In another 5 minutes or so you will reach a junction (2) marked by a red metal arrow and ribbons. You can follow either the trail that starts on your left or continue along the logging road straight ahead. This description follows the trail to the left and returns down the logging road.

This trail quickly becomes another old logging road. However, after about 5 minutes you must turn right onto a very narrow, steep trail. (The logging road continues onto private land and was blocked by large branches at time of writing.) About 25 minutes from the trailhead is a junction (3) with a trail marker on a fallen log. The trail continues slightly to the left, but note the trail going off to the right as it connects with the logging road you left at junction 2, and you may be using it later on. After another 10 minutes of steep climbing you will reach the first viewpoint (4). Enjoy the view as it's terrific.

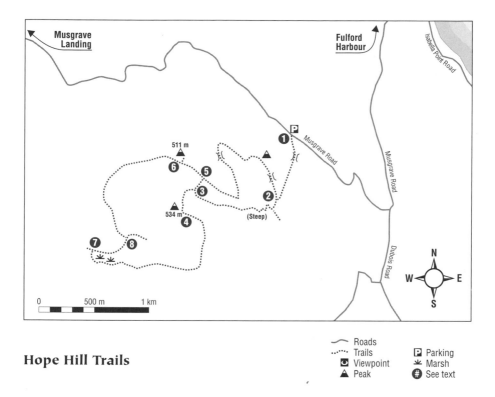

**Hope Hill Trails**

Roads
Trails ⬚ Parking
◙ Viewpoint ⚲ Marsh
▲ Peak ⬤ See text

When you're ready to carry on, I suggest you return to the junction (3) and take the very short (5-minute) trail to the logging road (5), turn left and walk another 5–10 minutes until you reach a short trail on the right (6) that will take you to another viewpoint. This trail climbs steeply over a rock face that can be seen from the logging road, before emerging on a spectacular view. When you have fully enjoyed it, return the way you came, turning left along the logging road and returning to the trailhead (about 45 minutes).

As you can see from the map, there are other trails to walk here, but they can be difficult to find. At the first viewpoint (4), you can walk south along the cliff edge until you reach a trail that descends through mixed forest to one of Salt Spring's largest stands of white pine. This trail ends at another logging road (7), where you will turn right (the left side was impassable at time of writing because of the many deadfalls). You then continue along this logging road past a reedy, wet area to a junction with another trail (8) that continues uphill and left off the logging road. Note that the logging road continues straight on at 8 and leads back toward the viewpoint at 4. However, this trail was totally overgrown and thus very hard to follow at time of writing, so it would not be a good idea to take it.

The trail from 8 crosses a couple of rocky knolls with the faint trail marked with ribbons. (From one of these knolls you can see the tall transmission tower on the summit of Hope Hill on the adjacent privately owned land.) The trail eventually reaches the logging road leading to the viewpoint on the left at 6. This will have taken you about 20 minutes. En route you may have seen a trail on the left with the sign "Mary's Trail." It's overgrown, uninteresting and difficult to follow, so don't take it. From 6, you return down the logging road back to the trailhead.

Note that if for some reason you decide to do all these trails but in reverse— climbing the logging road to the viewpoint at 6 and then continuing down to 8, then to 7 and eventually to the viewpoint at 4—you must be careful at 7 not to continue straight along a very clear and well-marked trail that you will find almost immediately after turning left at 7. The trail you want climbs to the left at this point and is not as clearly evident as the one in front of you.

## 4. MILL FARM REGIONAL PARK RESERVE ★★★★

| | |
|---|---|
| Trail length | About 4 kilometres if you follow all the old logging roads |
| Time required | Plan to spend at least 2 hours in the park reserve; 5–6 hours (or more) if you plan to climb Mount Bruce (see hike 5). |
| Description | Old roads on a 1919 homestead lead to ponds, viewpoints and old-growth forest. |
| Level | Moderate |
| Elevation | About 550 metres (elevation gain about 175 metres) |
| Access | On the right (north) side of Musgrave Road, about 11 kilometres from its junction with Isabella Point Road. Park near the locked gate to the park reserve (on the right or north side), or 100 metres farther along in a driveway on the opposite side of the road (also part of the park). |
| Cautions | If you don't like driving on rough, rocky roads, avoid Musgrave Road. Not all trails/old logging roads are shown on the map on page 220. |

*Note: This hike can be combined with hike 5.*

# SAVING MILL FARM

The 65-hectare Mill Farm Regional Park Reserve is the site of the 1919 homestead of Arnold Smith, one of three brothers who came to Salt Spring from Lancashire, England. The entrance to Smith's homesite and the remains of his huge, old millwheel is 130 metres beyond the park gate.

In 1981 eight people bought the property, planning to build separate homes on the communally owned land. Several cabins were built, although only one couple lived on the property full time. By the early 1990s some of the owners had changed and there was pressure to sell the land. As soon as it hit the market it attracted the attention of a logging company interested in the property's 26 hectares of old-growth fir. The fledgling Salt Spring Island Conservancy mobilized support to persuade the provincial and regional governments to buy the property and preserve it as a park. Over $150,000 was raised toward the purchase price of $800,000, and the farm became a Capital Regional District (CRD) park reserve in 1996. The previous owners accepted a slightly lower offer than the logging company was making to save the land from being logged. Although the CRD removed all but one of the buildings, you can still see the various homesites, especially in the spring when the flowers and shrubs in the old gardens are in bloom.

To me, the Mill Farm is a very special place and I encourage you to wander along the many old roads criss-crossing the property and to explore the sites where the previous owners had built dwellings. These were usually near some source of water and had viewpoints. In many places shrubs and plants that these modern-day homesteaders planted still flower. In one spot you'll even find a couple of palm trees.

Here's the route I usually take: Start at the parking space 100 metres beyond the park gate (on the opposite side of the road) and walk down this driveway to one of the homesites. This short walk takes you by a large pond and to a knoll that sports daffodils in the spring. Then return the way you came and walk back along the road to the main gate.

Once through this gate, you'll find yourself at the junction of two roads. The one on the left stays on lower ground and eventually leads to a pond and one of the homesites. I recommend taking the road to the right, which climbs about 140 metres to the top of the reserve (where you'll find a second gate that divides the Mill Farm from the adjacent Crown land) and eventually joins the trail system leading to Bruce Peak (see hike 5). Just before the gate separating the Mill Farm and the adjacent Crown land, you'll pass a spring-fed pond on your right. This was a source of water for some of the previous owners of the property.

If you don't want to climb Mount Bruce, you can return the way you came, exploring some of the other trails/driveways that you passed along the way up. Some of these trails end at old, west-facing homesites with views of Separation Point and Cowichan Bay on Vancouver Island. About halfway along, one of these driveways goes off in the opposite direction to a homesite where a stoneworker built a number of rock walls. When you get back to the main gate at the entrance to the park, you might like to explore the other road that you ignored when you started; it leads to yet another pond and another road that heads back toward, but not to, the farm site and the remains of the mill.

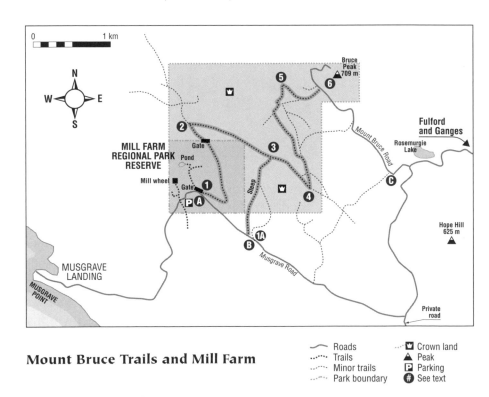

**Mount Bruce Trails and Mill Farm**

| | |
|---|---|
| Roads | Crown land |
| Trails | Peak |
| Minor trails | Parking |
| Park boundary | See text |

To reach the farm site directly, return to the main gate on Musgrave Road, turn right and walk for about 130 metres to another driveway on your right (you'll pass your vehicle if you parked at the second spot I suggested on page 218). Follow this driveway to the farm site, where you'll find the remains of old farm equipment, as well as trees planted by the Smiths that still bear fruit today. If you look carefully, you will also find the rapidly disappearing remains of Arnold Smith's millwheel.

## 5. MOUNT BRUCE TRAILS ★★★★

| | |
|---|---|
| Trail length | About 6 kilometres |
| Time required | 3–4 hours |
| Description | A trail through forest with views to the south, east and west. In late spring look for masses of foxglove in open areas. |
| Level | Moderate to strenuous, some steep climbs |
| Elevation | 709 metres (elevation gain from trailhead to summit 440 metres) |
| Access | A. From the Mill Farm (see hike 4) |
| | B. On the north side of Musgrave Road, 10 kilometres from its junction with Isabella Point Road (about 13 kilometres from the Fulford ferry and about 25 kilometres from Ganges). Look for a number 1A (see map on page 220) on a roadside tree and for red arrows and a red diamond marking the trailhead. |
| | C. From Mount Bruce Road, which veers right off Musgrave Road (just after tiny Rosemurgie Lake) on your right 6.2 kilometres from where Musgrave Road starts at Isabella Point Road. Drive about 300 metres along Mount Bruce Road, park in the driveway on the left and walk from here. You can either follow the road for about 2 kilometres to Bruce Peak (the top of Mount Bruce) or walk for about 10 minutes along the driveway where you parked, turn right at the first intersection and walk another 8 minutes until you reach (4) on the map on page |

|  | 220. This access is through land owned by the Capital Regional District, which is adjacent to the 194 hectares of Crown land on Mount Bruce. |
|---|---|
| Cautions | If you dislike rough rocky roads, avoid the 30-minute drive on Musgrave Road to the trailhead. Stay on the marked trail while hiking. |
|  | This trail follows logging roads for almost its entire length. There are also many other logging roads in the Mount Bruce Crown land. For this reason, people often get lost on Mount Bruce. At time of writing the trail was well marked with ribbons and with the numbers on the map on page 220 also posted on trees where they are located on the trail. But be extra careful not to miss any of the turns shown on the map and described below. Only a few of the logging roads are shown on the map. |

*Note: In the following description the numbers refer to points on the map on page 220 and assume that you will be starting from the Mill Farm (see hike 4). As you hike, look for the corresponding numbers along the actual trail, which, hopefully, no one will have removed. This hike can be combined with hike 4. If you start from access B (1A) on Musgrave Road, you will have a shorter hike, but will miss the Mill Farm.*

From the trailhead at the Mill Farm main gate (1), the trail climbs steeply (215 metres) for 2 kilometres (about 50 minutes) to a junction (2). It will take you about half an hour to reach the gate between the Mill Farm and the Crown land. From here to junction 2, you'll pass a holly tree on your right and soon after that a lookout that gives you a good view of Cowichan Bay. To the left of this viewpoint is a large Pacific dogwood, bedecked with delicate blossoms in the spring. Soon after this, look for the logging road on the right (2).

After about 20 minutes on this road, which climbs only about 30 metres, you'll reach junction 3. You'll see a road on your right that connects with access B on Musgrave Road (1A). Continue straight ahead for another 10 minutes until you reach junction 4. Take the trail on the left, which turns sharply back on itself onto yet another logging road that climbs steeply.

It will take you about 25 to 30 minutes to reach junction 5 and you will climb 120 metres in doing so. You will also have some tremendous views looking south to Shawnigan Lake and west into Cowichan Bay on Vancouver

Island. There are a number of logging roads that intersect this part of the trail, which makes life confusing. You should always take the most-travelled route, which continually climbs generally to the left toward the views. Once you reach the views, the route is less confusing.

At junction 5, you'll see a turnoff to a camping spot with a picnic table used by hunters and people partying, judging from the many beer and pop tins on the ground. Just past this turnoff, you'll see the turn to the right you need to follow to reach the summit. Here, for the first time, you are on trail rather than logging road. It will take about 20 minutes and you will climb 60 metres by the time you reach 6, where you will find a number of communications towers.

You're still not at Bruce Peak. Follow the road to the left until it merges with Mount Bruce Road and turn left to reach the top. At the end of the road (about 500 metres farther) you will find a wooden ladder that climbs to a platform used by hang-gliders. The views to the east here are exceptional—of the Coast Mountains, Mount Baker, the Gulf and San Juan Islands—and then there's Fulford Harbour down below. Take your time to enjoy the wonderful view before retracing your steps. While it may have taken you as long as two and a half hours to get up here, it will probably take you much less time going down.

## 6. Musgrave Greenbelt ★★

| | |
|---|---|
| Trail length | 2 kilometres |
| Time required | 1 hour or more |
| Description | A forest walk to a seasonal waterfall, as well as shore access |
| Level | Easy |
| Access | The entrance to the Greenbelt is a driveway on the left (south) side of Musgrave Road, almost at its end, about 13 kilometres from its junction with Isabella Point Road (about 200 metres before Musgrave Landing). The access is marked with one of the island's 120-centimetre-high cedar trail markers. Park on the grassy fields that make up much of this Crown land. |
| Cautions | Do not drive along Musgrave Road if you don't like rough, rocky roads. |

*Note: The waterfall is on private property. The current owner does not mind hikers visiting the waterfall but the property should be respected; stay on the logging road. Other old roads in this area also cross private property, and you should not follow them without permission from the property owners.*

Walking in this 34-hectare piece of Crown land feels more like exploring than hiking. If you walk straight ahead from where you turned off Musgrave Road, you will be following a very rough, public road leading down to a beach. (Do not attempt to drive down this road!) At very low tides it's possible to walk left (south) along the shore as far as Cape Keppel, where you can access another trail connecting with Mountain Road. However, be sure that you have lots of time between tides if you decide to attempt it.

If you follow the logging road to the left (east) of where you turned into the Greenbelt, you will soon reach a stream crossing the road (dry in summer, a torrent in winter). Cross the creek and look for a trail almost immediately to your left, which will take you to the seasonal waterfall. This lush spot is very beautiful, although the thick growth of trees keeps out the sun. Return the way you came.

While you're in the area, drive down to Musgrave Landing, park along the side of the road and explore the tiny parkette (marked with a cedar post trail sign) that takes in a little knoll overlooking the government dock. Few islanders ever get to this very remote part of Salt Spring. You'll be glad you did.

## 7. BURGOYNE BAY PROVINCIAL PARK ★★★★

| | |
|---|---|
| Trail length | Up to 20 kilometres, depending on route |
| Time required | Up to a day or more, depending on route |
| Description | A number of trails follow the shoreline on both sides of Burgoyne Bay, while others climb Mount Sullivan to the south and Mount Maxwell to the north. |
| Level | Moderate to strenuous |
| Access | The large parking area at the end of Burgoyne Bay Road |
| Cautions | None of the trails in this relatively new provincial park have been officially flagged at time of writing, as there was still no park management plan in place. |

In 1999 the Texada Land Corporation, a development company, acquired 2,024 hectares (about one-tenth of all the land on Salt Spring) and began to log it intensively. This led to wide-scale protests and a massive local drive to protect the land. In 2001 the province, The Land Conservancy of British Columbia (TLC) and the Capital Regional District (CRD) bought 664 hectares of land from the logging company in the Fulford–Burgoyne Valley, Mount Maxwell, Mount Bruce and Mount Tuam areas. Of the total purchase, 334 hectares around Burgoyne Bay were included in Burgoyne Bay Provincial Park in 2004.

While islanders have used the hiking trails in this area for many years to access the shoreline of Burgoyne Bay and to climb the nearby mountains, at time of writing the park was still in its planning stages and an official trail system had yet to be developed. Use the following suggestions to start exploring or ask locals for up-to-date trail information.

From the parking lot follow old logging roads on the north side of the bay for 30–40 minutes before reaching a piece of private property. At this point, either return the way you came or try another logging road in the park. If you try to return along animal trails that follow the shore, be aware that the terrain is treacherous.

Other logging roads from the parking lot lead through the extensive area of Garry oak up to Mount Maxwell Provincial Park. However, as this involves crossing an ecological reserve, BC Parks would prefer that you access Mount Maxwell from above (see hikc 8). Highlights of this higher ground are the many erratics (boulders left behind thousands of years ago by glacial action) and the largest arbutus tree on Salt Spring, with several of its branches held up by two of the huge boulders. Despite all the trees in this area between Burgoyne Bay and Mount Maxwell, the terrain is fairly open, affording great views of Sansum Narrows and Maple Bay on Vancouver Island. However, there is no sanctioned trail through this area, which is owned by the Nature Trust of British Columbia.

South from the parking lot, trails lead up toward Mount Sullivan. One logging road winds its way up the mountain, eventually entering private lands. None of these trails are signed, so be very careful not to get lost if you hike in this area. Lower down along the southern shoreline of the bay, you can walk for up to an hour, alternately along the beach and just above the shoreline, until you reach another piece of private property toward Bold Bluff Point.

## 8. MOUNT MAXWELL PROVINCIAL PARK ★★★★★

| | |
|---|---|
| Trail length | 6–14 kilometres, depending on route chosen |
| Time required | Up to a full day, depending on route chosen |
| Description | A steady climb through second-growth fir forest to the summit of Mount Maxwell (known as Baynes Peak), which offers magnificent views |
| Level | Moderate; some steep sections |
| Elevation | 593 metres (elevation gain 175 metres) |
| Access | A. From the end of Seymour Heights. To get here from the Fulford–Ganges Road, go northwest on Dukes Road (about 6 kilometres from Ganges or 7.5 kilometres from the Fulford ferry terminal) until you reach Seymour Heights (about 1.8 kilometres). The trailhead is on your right at the end of Seymour Heights (another 1.7 kilometres) and is marked with a cedar post trail sign. There's no parking at the trailhead but you can park at the corner of Armand Way and Seymour Heights (800 metres from the trailhead). B. From the end of Armand Way |
| Facilities | Benches, picnic tables, outhouse at the top |
| Cautions | Beware of the steep drop-offs at the viewpoints. |

Many people consider the views from Baynes Peak as Salt Spring's best. Part of a well-signed, 231-hectare provincial park, it is a popular destination for tourists who can drive up the mountain (8.7 kilometres from the intersection of Cranberry and Fulford–Ganges Roads), park in the parking lot and enjoy the expansive views from the viewpoint at the top. Others walk from the top along the fence-line trail that leads down to what locals call the Rim Trail, a beautiful path that crosses rocky outcrops before descending farther down Mount Maxwell Road near the ecological reserve. But most hikers take one of the accesses listed above and climb to the summit.

The trail from Seymour Heights (access A) mainly passes through a second-growth Douglas-fir forest. The trail from Armand Way (access B) passes through wetter terrain that nourishes giant cedar and sword ferns. I prefer

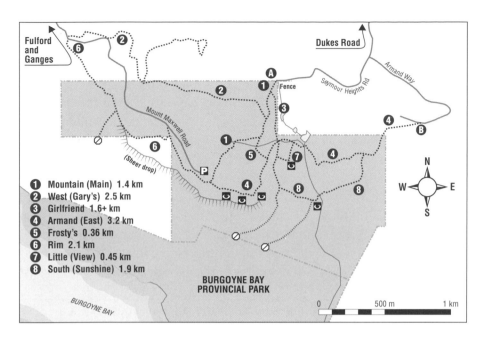

## Mount Maxwell Provincial Park

**1** Mountain (Main) 1.4 km
**2** West (Gary's) 2.5 km
**3** Girlfriend 1.6+ km
**4** Armand (East) 3.2 km
**5** Frosty's 0.36 km
**6** Rim 2.1 km
**7** Little (View) 0.45 km
**8** South (Sunshine) 1.9 km

Roads
Trail s
Park boundary

⊘ No access
◐ Viewpoint
🅿 Parking

*You can see the full length of the beautiful Fulford–Burgoyne Valley from Baynes Peak at the top of Mount Maxwell.*

the Armand Way access, but both are delightful. Either trail will take you an hour to reach the summit, where they merge.

Recently a friend and I walked most of the trails in the park. It took us about 6 hours, including stops for lunch, to take photos and to figure out where we were. Here's how our tour went: We started from the access at Seymour Heights. The trail climbed steeply. We reached the turnoff for trail 3 in about 10 minutes. The trail climbed even more steeply from there until we reached the turnoff to trail 2 in another 10 minutes.

We then continued along trail 2. It took about an hour to reach the junction with Mount Maxwell Road. We turned left (southeast) along the road for about 100 metres until we reached the turnoff for the Rim Trail (trail 6) on the right (west). This up-and-down rocky trail is quite demanding in places, but offers splendid views and goes through wonderful forest. There are trails that diverge from it, but the Rim Trail is fairly obvious and mainly to the left when you have choices.

It took us another 40 minutes to reach the summit (about 2 kilometres). From the top of Mount Maxwell (Baynes Peak) you look over the Fulford–Burgoyne Valley all the way to Fulford Harbour, Burgoyne Bay and the boat activity on Sansum Narrows and in Maple Bay on Vancouver Island.

We were ready for lunch, but we first looked for the trail connections behind the parking lot. Trails 1 and 4 connect there. We started along trail 4, but soon found a trail to the southwest that climbed to a large, moss-covered bluff from which we had a 180-degree view. To the north, in the far distance, was Vancouver; to the east, Mount Baker; and to the south, the Olympic Mountains in Washington State. On a clear day you can see Mount Baker and as far as Mount Rainier. This is where we had our lunch.

After lunch we descended to intercept trail 4 and followed it. It took us 10 minutes to reach trail 5 (Frosty's, named after a hiker's feisty poodle that always accompanied him on his walks), a short trail that connects trails 1 and 4; we didn't take this. In another 8 minutes we reached trail 3 (Girlfriend, named for the girlfriend of a trailblazer who established the trail). We continued on trail 4 and in 25 minutes we reached the junction with trail 8. We particularly enjoyed trail 4 with its wonderful huge cedars, enchanting forest and pretty ponds on its north side. We didn't take trail 7, which leads to a viewpoint and connects trails 3 and 4.

We found trail 8, a more recently developed trail, hard to follow in spots. It also descends over 100 metres, which you then have to regain. I would only recommend this trail for the strong, experienced hiker. Much of the trail is marked by orange spray paint on trees and rocks. This trail has one exquisite viewpoint overlooking the Fulford–Burgoyne Valley and some beautiful cedars.

When we reached trail 3, we took it north (the alternative being to descend to the edge of the cliff and down to the sea). This trail climbs extremely steeply. It took us only 15 minutes to reach the junction with trail 4 and another 10 minutes to reach the junction with trail 1. We then retraced our steps to the trailhead on Seymour Heights and drove back to town for coffee.

I recommend the trails from the two accesses to the summit (trails 1 and 4) and trails 2 (Gary's) and 6 (Rim), but I would skip the rest unless you have a whole day to spend here as we did. If you hike trails 3 and 8 be sure to leave lots of daylight in case you miss the trail.

## 9. PETER ARNELL PARK ★

| | |
|---|---|
| Trail length | About 3 kilometres |
| Time required | 45 minutes |
| Description | A short hike over moss-covered rocky terrain through young forest |
| Level | Easy, with some moderate sections |
| Access | Take Stewart Road south from Cusheon Lake Road for about 1.5 kilometres. The signed trailhead is on your left (east) at a wide bend in the road (see map on page 230). The trail comes out again on Stewart Road, about 200 metres south, just past the sign for Peter Arnell Park on the west side of the road. |
| Cautions | Some of these trails cross into the neighbouring Islands Trust Fund property called Deep Ridge Nature Reserve. One of these descends steeply and dangerously to the sea. Don't be tempted to take this treacherous trail as fallen trees eventually completely block the path. |

This is a pleasant, if unspectacular, hike in a 13-hectare park that commemorates a surveyor who died accidentally and whose family had close connections with Salt Spring. The park extends on both sides of Stewart Road, but the main trail is on the east side of the road. The trail crosses moss-covered, rocky terrain and provides partial views of Galiano Island and Active Pass. Most but not all of the various trails are shown on the accompanying map. To complete an easy loop, take the trail to the right whenever you have a choice.

The signposted section of Peter Arnell Park on the west side of Stewart Road has no trail network but provides the access for hike 10.

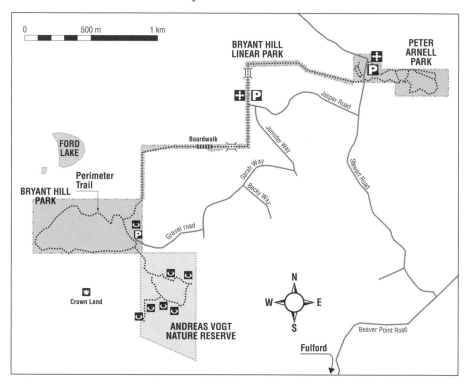

## Peter Arnell Park to Bryant Hill Park

Roads
Trails
Park boundary

Viewpoint
Parking
Sign

| 10. PETER ARNELL PARK TO BRYANT HILL PARK ★★ | |
|---|---|
| Trail length | About 6 kilometres to get to Bryant Hill Park and another 5 kilometres of trail circling this park |
| Time required | Up to 2 hours each way, plus another hour if combined with the trail in Bryant Hill Park or with hike 11 |

| Description | Steep climb with some views to a 32-hectare park |
| --- | --- |
| Level | Strenuous climb. The trails in Bryant Hill Park are of moderate difficulty. |
| Elevation | 80 metres, although the trail descends and then reascends much of this, so that the total climb is two or three times this figure |
| Access | A. From Peter Arnell Park on the west side of Stewart Road (1.6 kilometres from the junction of Cusheon Lake and Stewart roads), the trailhead leading to Bryant Hill Park is on the left (south) side of the park. |
| | B. From the meeting point of Jasper Road and Jennifer Way marked, at time of writing, by rusting diesel tanks. From this access you are partway up the trail. |
| | C. If you prefer to avoid the steep climb to Bryant Hill Park, you can drive directly there. Take Jasper Road (off Stewart Road just past Peter Arnell Park) and continue along Jennifer Way to Sarah Way. Proceed almost to the end of Sarah Way, turn right on a signed gravel driveway and drive 1 kilometre to its end, where you'll find a small parking area. On the west side, you'll see a trail leading to the gate for Bryant Hill Park on the right and the access to Andreas Vogt Nature Reserve (see hike 11) on the left. |
| Cautions | The trail up to Bryant Hill Park has been marked with white markers, but is still somewhat difficult to find in places. Several places on the trail tend to be overgrown—with broom or salal or stinging nettle. The Salt Spring Parks and Recreation Commission is currently improving both the trails and the signage. In the summer slippery arbutus leaves cover much of the trail. Walk carefully. |

*Note: This hike can be combined with hike 11. As the first part of this hike is steep and not as interesting, I recommend that you take access C and spend more time exploring the trails on the higher ground in the park, the neighbouring Crown land and nearby Andreas Vogt Nature Reserve.*

From access A, the first half of the trail is fairly steep, crossing a number of driveways. Look for white metal triangles, diamonds and directional markers, and always take the trails facing you, rather than the logging road/driveway offshoots that you'll cross from time to time. If you do not see a metal marker indicating the trail, be sure to find one before continuing. It's easy to get lost on this linear trail and stray onto private property.

After about half an hour of walking, just past a green metal bridge you'll reach a signboard with an inaccurate (at time of writing) map of the trail and the park. This spot is very close to access B (where Jasper Avenue meets Jennifer Way). Within another 5 minutes you'll pass a picnic table before reaching a viewpoint over Ganges Harbour to Galiano Island in the distance. Shortly beyond the viewpoint you'll cross a second green metal bridge.

Soon after the second bridge you'll reach a long boardwalk. Follow it to its end and then continue on the trail west; the trail starts to descend fairly steeply. It joins an overgrown logging road, but after a few metres it leaves the road to continue on the left (south). It meets another overgrown logging road but doesn't cross it. Make sure that you don't either. The trail is now heading west and still descending. By the time you have walked about 10 minutes from the boardwalk, you will notice that the trail crosses short wooden bridges over seasonal creeks.

## ROQUEFORT ANYONE?

Bryant Hill is named after Colonel Jasper and Dr. Meta Bryant, a remarkable couple who retired to Salt Spring. For several decades from the 1920s on they kept a herd of goats, making cheese each day and aging it in a cave on their property. With advice from Professor Golding of UBC, they developed a prize-winning Roquefort-type cheese that they shipped to market at Spencer's—then Victoria's largest store.

Although they eventually had a phone installed, the Bryants led a spare lifestyle, relying on a generator for power and using bicycles to get around the island after giving up their car to save gas during the war. Although supposedly retired, Meta still worked in the hospital in the late 1940s. In the 1970s their deserted goat farm became a hippie commune.

After a few more minutes of walking you'll cross another overgrown logging road. Don't take it. Look for the directional sign on the ground. The trail switchbacks steeply downward in a southwesterly direction. Follow the trail's switchbacks and don't be tempted by animal paths. When you reach the valley bottom you will then start back up the other side, climbing steeply to the park. When you reach the park, turn left along an old logging road and either follow signs to the Andreas Vogt Nature Reserve or take the circular path around Bryant Hill Park, which will also eventually lead to the trailhead for the nature reserve.

As you can see on the map on page 230, the perimeter trail in Bryant Hill Park (5 kilometres) circles the park and will take you about an hour to walk. At its start it descends and then reascends before passing a pretty pond around its halfway point. The last part of the trail follows the border between Bryant Hill Park and the adjacent Crown land, eventually passing the trailhead for the Andreas Vogt Nature Reserve and the adjacent Crown land (see hike 11).

## 11. ANDREAS VOGT NATURE RESERVE ★★★

| | |
|---|---|
| Trail length | 2 kilometres; more if combined with hike 12 or the adjacent Crown land trails |
| Time required | 1 hour; more if combined with hike 10 or the adjacent Crown land trails |
| Description | A walk over rocky knolls in Garry oak and arbutus habitat with views of most of Salt Spring's peaks and the San Juan Islands |
| Level | Moderate |
| Access | See the map on page 230. Take Jasper Road (off Stewart Road) and continue along Jennifer Way to Sarah Way. Near the end of Sarah Way, turn right on a gravel road and drive 1 kilometre to the small parking area at its end. Next to the parking area is a gate for Bryant Hill Park (see hike 10). Take the signed trail to the left (south) of the gate and, after a few minutes, turn left again into the reserve, just past a streambed. |

In 2002 Cordula Vogt and her mother, Oda Nowrath, gave this 29-hectare piece of land to the Salt Spring Island Conservancy to preserve, with the hope that future generations would enjoy it as much as they had. It is named for Cordula's late husband.

The loop trail into the property passes a huge cedar and many fine firs on the adjacent piece of Crown land that, unlike Bryant Hill Park and the nature reserve, was not logged in the 1980s. The trail soon climbs to the first of many rocky knolls that offer views of islands and mountains in the distance, although these views are filling in as the trees grow.

Stay on the marked trail to preserve the vegetation on this beautiful piece of land. You can complete a loop trail, returning to where you started, or carry on to trails in the Crown land that eventually lead to a trail junction with Bryant Hill Park, where you turn right to return to the parking area. At time of writing the Crown land trails were poorly marked and somewhat confusing, although there were plans to improve them. Avoid them unless you have a good sense of direction and lots of time to find your way out of the thick forest.

*Remnants of Salt Spring's early architecture still exist. Fortunately, they aren't all this dilapidated.* K. Hagerty

## 12. MOUNT ERSKINE PROVINCIAL PARK AND MANZANITA RIDGE ★★★★

| | |
|---|---|
| Trail length | About 11 kilometres |
| Time required | One-half to a full day |
| Description | A steep climb through arbutus groves, Douglas-fir, pine and manzanita to a splendid viewpoint |
| Level | Strenuous; some very steep, slippery sections |
| Elevation | 448 metres; elevation gain 370 metres |
| Access | A. The east side of Collins Road (see page 236), 700 metres from the point at which Rainbow Road becomes Collins Road. Look for the trailhead sign on the left (east) side of the road.<br><br>B. North side of Toynbee Road (500 metres from its intersection with Cranberry and Mount Maxwell roads). Look for the trailhead on the right just past the gate for 181 Toynbee Road.<br><br>C. The end of Trustees Trail (off Spring Gold Way off Juniper Place) |
| Cautions | There are slippery sections, ridges and sharp drop-offs from some of the trails. Stay on the trails and hike with care. |

*Note: In the following description, the numbers correspond to those on the map on page 236.*

From access A, the first part of the trail is not in the provincial park, which is mainly landlocked, but is in Lower Mount Erskine Nature Reserve, 22 hectares owned by the Islands Trust Fund. It will take you about 45 minutes to reach the junction at (1), where a trail from access C joins. You will have found the trail very easy to follow to this point, although an old trail leading to private land goes off to the left about halfway up. Continue climbing to junction 2, where you can turn right. This is the beginning of a loop, and you will return to this junction from the other direction on your return. As you continue look for small elfin doors placed in front of large rocks or tree stumps. In recent years several of these charming miniatures have been anonymously installed, often accompanied by curtained windows, baskets of firewood and other accoutrements.

After another 20 minutes you will reach junction 4. Continue straight ahead to the viewpoint at the top of the mountain. It looks west over

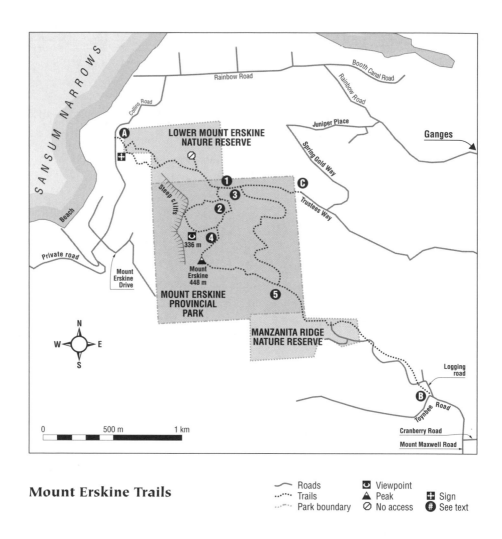

**Mount Erskine Trails**

Roads
Trails
Park boundary

◯ Viewpoint
▲ Peak
⊘ No access

✚ Sign
❸ See text

Sansum Narrows to Quamichan Lake on Vancouver Island, south as far as Shawnigan Lake and north over Booth Bay and St. Mary Lake on Salt Spring, and then to Tent, Penelakut (formerly Kuper) and Galiano islands beyond.

If you decide not to continue to Manzanita Ridge, return to the main trail and turn right when you get to junction 4 to complete the loop described earlier. When you reach 2, keep descending the way you came, making sure to keep to the left at junction 1 and again at the trail leading to private property farther down. You may see some other minor trails, which you can take if you like, as most of them end up merging with the main trail at some point.

# TRAILS AND PARTNERSHIPS

The story of Mount Erskine Provincial Park and the trail system with the neighbouring lands is one of partnerships and determination. It began when Jack Fisher donated 22 hectares of his property on Collins Road to allow public access to the trails on Mount Erskine. The Islands Trust Fund eventually became the owners of this piece of land, calling it the Lower Mount Erskine Nature Reserve. The public trail allowed walkers to access a viewpoint just below the summit of Mount Erskine, which was still private property.

In 2003 the Salt Spring Island Conservancy (SSIC) mounted a campaign to raise $85,000 to buy 20 hectares of land and a right-of-way to it from Toynbee Road from long-time resident Martin Williams. Islanders responded favourably, and the money was quickly raised. With views over Trincomali Channel to Galiano Island and over the Shepherd Hills to Sansum Narrows, Manzanita Ridge Nature Reserve includes beautiful rocky terrain and a stand of 200-year-old Douglas-firs.

In 2006 the SSIC was offered the opportunity to buy the 40 hectares of land at the top of Mount Erskine. The price of $650,000 plus expenses seemed insurmountable, but, once more, islanders responded with enthusiasm, and in a few months more than enough money was raised to make the purchase happen. The final purchase included three partners—the SSIC with a 60 percent share, the Nature Conservancy of Canada with 20 percent and the provincial government (BC Parks) with 20 percent. Through an agreement with the province, BC Parks leased the land for 99 years and agreed to combine it with the adjacent Crown lands (an additional 67 hectares) to create Salt Spring's fourth provincial park.

As a result of this partnership of government and private owners islanders can now walk through 149 hectares of some of the most beautiful land on Salt Spring—all the way from Collins Road to the northwest to Toynbee Road to the southeast.

If you decide to continue to Manzanita Ridge (20 hectares owned by the Salt Spring Island Conservancy), keep on the trail from the viewpoint, ignoring junction 5, which leads down to access C. Signs will inform you when you reach the Conservancy property—under hydro wires in a clearing that provides views east to Montague Harbour on Galiano Island and west to the Shepherd Hills on Salt Spring. As you continue toward Toynbee Road, the trail intersects a logging road from time to time. Very little of the trail is actually on the road, which is on the adjoining property and is a private hydro access road. So stay on the clearly marked trail until you reach Toynbee Road (access B). From here you can return the way you came, or if you have more ambitious plans, carry on.

Climbing Mount Erskine from either access A or access B is steep. A more pleasant alternative is to start from access C and turn left at junction 3. Watch carefully for this junction as it's easy to pass by the hairpin turn to the left; if you do miss it and walk the very short distance to junction 1, you can just turn around and easily find junction 3 on the way back (less than 5 minutes). This trail goes through some beautiful forest, moss-covered rocky knolls and perhaps the largest old-growth Douglas-fir in the park. When you reach junction 5, turn right to reach the summit and left to continue to Manzanita Ridge and eventually Toynbee Road.

## 13. Channel Ridge Trails ★★★

| | |
|---|---|
| Trail length | 16 kilometres |
| Time required | 4–5 hours |
| Description | A ridge walk through Douglas-fir and arbutus forest with occasional ocean views |
| Level | Easy to moderate with some steep sections |
| Elevation | 265 metres |
| Access | A. North end: Across from 1110 Sunset Drive (just south of West Eagle Road). There's limited parking along the edge of Sunset Drive. |
| | B. South end: On the left (west) side of Broadwell Road, just north of Tern Road. The trail begins along a row of hydro poles. |
| | C. The accompanying map shows a number of additional entry points to the trail system. |

| Cautions | These trails surround a large strata development (at time of writing as-yet unbuilt) and are administered by the Salt Spring Parks and Recreation Commission (PARC) through an agreement with Channel Ridge Properties. The "village" may be under construction when you hike the trails, so stay on the trails shown on this map. |
| --- | --- |
| | Much of the area on the east side of the map is watershed and is owned by the Salt Spring Water Preservation Society, which allows only hikers (no bikes or horses) on its trails. |

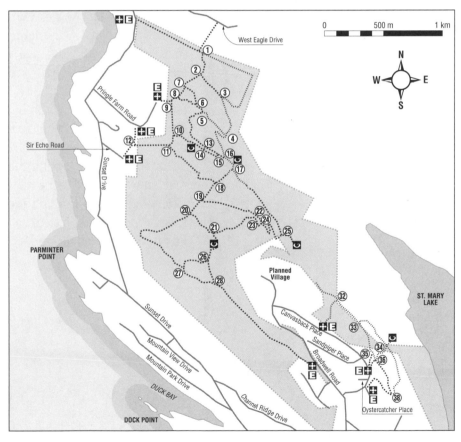

**Channel Ridge Trails**

| | | |
| --- | --- | --- |
| ⌒ Roads | | E Entrance |
| ....... PARC trails | | ✚ Sign |
| ......... Water Preservation Society trails | | ◖ Viewpoint |
| | | ⓕ Trail marker |

Channel Ridge is formed of sandstone and conglomerate rock. The trails pass by spectacular moss- and fern-covered rock faces, views of Crofton, the Shoal Islands, Chemainus and even Ladysmith from the arbutus and Garry oak meadows on the west, and St. Mary Lake, the Strait of Georgia, the Coast Mountains and, on a clear day, Mount Baker to the east.

PARC has developed a system of trails that avoids the village area, where construction is scheduled to take place. The comprehensive numbering system and signage will make it difficult for you to get lost if you have this map and can relate it to the numbers on the ground. I suggest you start at one end

and walk as far as you can to the other, returning as much as possible using a different route. The trails are prettiest in the winter when the rains enhance the greens in the landscape and activate the many seasonal creeks. It's drier and dustier here in the summer, although the forest has a cooling effect when the island has one of its rare heat waves.

In the future, additional routes may be added to the trails system, and paths through the village (once it is completed) will link to the trails all around it.

*Many of Salt Spring's trails, beach accesses and local parks are identified with cedar signs like this.* Philip Grange

## 14. DUCK CREEK ★★★

| Trail length | 1.5 kilometres each way |
| --- | --- |
| Time required | 45 minutes |
| Description | A pleasant stroll along a creek |
| Level | Easy |
| Access | A. On the east side of Sunset Drive less than 500 metres from Vesuvius Bay Road (directly across from the mailboxes just south of 208 Sunset Drive) |
| | B. On the west side of Broadwell Road just north of Vesuvius Bay Road |

The trail stretches from Sunset Drive east to Broadwell Road and includes a series of stairs, bridges, viewpoints and rest spots. As it follows the creek, it passes through old-growth fir and cedar forest. Salmon enhancement workers adjusted the flow of water in the creek to create rearing pools and spawning beds for salmon and steelhead trout. The creek is a rushing stream in the rainy months but dwindles to a trickle in the summer. Dog walkers like to use the trails through the fields above the creek. You could start out along the creek and return by the fields or vice versa.

## 15. JACK FOSTER TRAIL (SOUTHEY POINT) ★★★

| Trail length | 4 kilometres round trip (at low tide) |
| --- | --- |
| Time required | 70–80 minutes total |
| Description | A circle route that begins in a lovely wooded area, continues on the beach along Trincomali Channel and returns along a road |
| Level | Moderate |
| Access | A. On the east side of Southey Point Road at its junction with Sunset Drive and North End Road. The trailhead is marked with a red metal marker. There's limited parking just across the road but be sure not to block any driveways. |
| | B. From the right (east) side of the driveway to the farm at 2521 North End Road |

| Cautions | If you do all of this hike, including the bit along the beach, it must be done at very low tide (definitely not more than half a metre). Be careful on the steep descent to the beach on the first part of the hike. Be sure to stay on the trail and off the neighbouring private property. The last section of the beach is covered with large boulders that you will have to scramble across. Be careful, as the rocks can be slippery. If you have a dog, keep it leashed on the last part of the trail, as you will be passing a sheep farm. |
|---|---|

From access A the first section of this hike is through a fine forest of arbutus, cedar and fir. This area can be quite wet at times. It will take you about 20–25 minutes to reach the beach.

When you reach the shore you can follow it in either direction; however, if you turn left (toward Southey Point), you cannot leave the shore without trespassing on private property. So turn right (south) and walk along the beach for about 1 kilometre (20 minutes) until you reach a small breakwater. Along the way you will have views of other islands in Trincomali Channel: the Secretaries to the northeast, Wallace directly to the east and Galiano behind it.

You could choose to turn around at this point, as you have just completed the most beautiful part of the hike. However, just before the breakwater, a boulder stairway leads to a public trail that leads to North End Road (access B). The trail comes out just before the end of the driveway to the farm at 2521 North End Road. To complete the loop, continue along the driveway to the road, turn right (west) and walk about 1 kilometre to the trailhead on Southey Point Road where you started.

## 16. DUNBABIN TRAIL ★★★

| Trail length | 1.6 kilometres return |
|---|---|
| Time required | 20 minutes return |
| Description | Pleasant trail following a small creek through rain forest |
| Level | Easy |

| Access | A. On the south side of Stark Road, 500 metres west of Robinson Road |
|---|---|
| | B. On the west side of Robinson Road, 200 metres south of Stark Road |

While this trail is much shorter than any of the other hikes, I have included it here because of its beauty. The walk features large cedars, firs and ferny hollows. It is accessible to most walkers and is well worth the visit.

## 17. QUARRY DRIVE PARK-BAKER RIDGE TRAIL LOOP ★★

| Trail length | 2 kilometres |
|---|---|
| Time required | 30–40-minute loop trail |
| Description | A pleasant trail through forest and along the shore, followed by a steep, tricky trail over rocky ground |
| Level | Moderate |
| Access | A. From Quarry Drive Park just past 221 Quarry Drive on the south side of the street (Quarry Drive runs east off Chu-an Drive.) |
| | B. On the north side of Baker Road near its end |

From access A, a 400-metre trail leads up and over a mossy ridge to the shore, where you can walk in both directions for some way. The trail will take you about 10 minutes. On the way you will pass a bench at a point where there is a view of the water. Once on the beach you can return the way you came or turn left (east) and walk for about another 10 minutes until you reach a wooden stairway that leads to the public access at the end of Baker Road. From here, walk a short way east along the road until you see the start of the Baker Ridge trail on your left. This 10–15-minute trail is steep and treacherous in places, so be very careful if you take it. On the positive side, it is well flagged and easy to follow. It emerges on the north side of the end of Quarry Drive (about 2 minutes from where you started).

# SHORE WALKS

There are a number of fine walks along Salt Spring's mostly rocky shore. The following selection of public accesses are listed roughly from north to south and have been grouped by area. Some of the accesses indicated on the Salt Spring map have not been described, as they offer limited walking opportunities. However, they are often excellent places to launch a kayak or canoe. Look for the 120-centimetre-high cedar beach access signs.

**Southey Point area:** One of the prettiest spots on Salt Spring is the pock-marked sandstone shore at the foot of Arbutus Road. You can walk south at low tide, enjoying the views toward Penelakut (formerly Kuper) and Thetis islands and examining tide pools and sea stars clinging to the rocks. You can also walk north for a short distance along this shore. Swimming from the sandstone rocks is lovely in the summer.

There is a second shore access at the end of Southey Point Road (a narrow path between two private properties). Although you cannot walk very far (the tiny beach is exposed even at low tide), this is a pretty place to swim, to clamber over the rocks or just to enjoy the view.

You can also walk some distance along the eastern shore of Southey Point (see hike 15).

**Sunset Drive:** Between 1076 and 1100 Sunset Drive (south of West Eagle Road), a path descends west to the shore and provides excellent views of Idol Island just offshore and Tent Island in the distance. You can walk south along the beach for a short distance at low tide.

A second access just south of 856 Sunset Drive (across and to the south of Sir Echo Road) has a short trail to an appealing little bay that dries at low tide.

**Hudson Point:** A road descends to the beach 800 metres north of Fernwood. This access doubles as a boat launch. You can walk along the shore for some way in both directions at low tide. In the distance is Wallace Island and behind it Galiano Island.

**Fernwood:** A government dock is located at the foot of Fernwood Road (where North Beach Road becomes Walker's Hook Road). It's possible to reach the shore just to the right of the dock and then walk south along the beach.

**Maliview Drive:** The beach at the foot of Maliview Drive is the same beach accessed at Hudson Point, Fernwood Road and along Walker's Hook Drive.

This long beach is a good place to examine intertidal life and to watch great blue herons fishing.

**Vesuvius Beach:** A short flight of stairs from Langley Street (off Vesuvius Bay Road) leads to the most popular bathing beach on Salt Spring. This lovely bay is known to have the warmest ocean swimming on the island; however, the walking here is limited.

**Quarry Drive Park:** See hike 17.

**Booth Bay:** Stairs lead to the beach at the end of Baker Road (off Lower Ganges Road). You can walk for some distance in both directions at low tide, although if you walk southeast and turn into Booth Canal, you soon begin to sink into the mud.

*When the tide is in, Booth Canal looks splendid.*

**Collins Road:** The beach at the end of Collins Road (off Rainbow Road), beneath Mount Erskine, is known locally as Cranberry Outlet (a.k.a. Bader's Beach, Erskine Beach and Collins Beach). The best walking here is right (north) along the shore at low tide. You might also like to hike the short trail

*While blue herons are on the endangered species list, they are frequently seen in the Gulf Islands, where there are many rookeries.* Kim Thompson

that parallels the beach at a slightly higher elevation. It begins beside the parking area at the end of Collins Road, near where Maxwell Creek (a.k.a. Cranberry Creek) flows into the sea.

**Long Harbour area:** There are two accesses to the shore of Long Harbour, one by a path at the end of Beachside Drive (off Harbourside Place) and the other at a boat launch at the bottom of Ontario Place (off Quebec Road). Both accesses offer limited walking at low tide.

**Churchill Road:** Stairs lead down to the pretty beach at the end of Churchill Road (off Upper Ganges Road), where you can walk a short distance along the shore at low tide. From here there's a good view of the Chain Islands in Ganges Harbour and the shoreline along Long Harbour Road.

**Harbour's End:** A regal set of stairs leads down to the beach across from the Harbour House Hotel on Upper Ganges Road. At low tide you can walk south along the shore as far as the Ganges Marina. You will find interesting rock formations and tidal life to examine here.

**Price Road:** Take Beddis Road to Price Road (about 1.8 kilometres). Turn left (east) onto Price Road and continue for 900 metres. This excellent access (which looks like a driveway to the south of 289 Price Road) allows you to walk the beach either way for some distance at low tide.

**Beddis Beach:** Toward the end of Beddis Road (about 6 kilometres from the Fulford–Ganges Road), south of the Cusheon Lake Road turnoff and before Beddis turns sharply right (south). Look for the sign and the gate across the driveway to the beach. There's a small parking area on the east side of the road just past the gate. Many consider this to be the island's loveliest beach. You can walk north for some distance at low tide.

**Burgoyne Bay:** There's a parking area in the provincial park at the end of Burgoyne Bay Road. You can combine a beach walk with a walk along the trails higher up above the bank (see hike 7). There are excellent views of Baynes Peak on Mount Maxwell directly above the bay and across to Maple Bay on Vancouver Island.

**Ruckle Park:** This outstanding park, at the end of Beaver Point Road, has a rocky shoreline with beautiful little coves and bays that you can explore at length. (See hike 1.)

**Kingfisher Cove:** This access at the end of Fraser Road (off Bridgman Road) leads down to an expansive beach. This is a good spot for a picnic at low tide or to launch a kayak at a higher tide (the beach gets soft and muddy when the tide is out).

**Eagles Way (off Stevens Road):** Walk 800 metres east along Stevens Road from its intersection with Forest Ridge Road. A path on the south side of Stevens Road leads to the shore at Eleanor Point where you can walk along the beach in both directions for a short distance. From here you can see Russell Island and the Swartz Bay ferry terminal in the distance.

**Musgrave Landing:** See hike 6.

**Drummond Park:** Take the Fulford–Ganges Road to Isabella Point Road. The parking area is on the left of Isabella Point Road, just past the intersection, and steps lead down to the shore. At low tide this small local park opens on a wide beach where you can walk in either direction for some way. This flat beach is likely to be quite muddy just after the tide has gone out. There's a petroglyph of a seal on a large, smooth boulder under some cedar trees next to the north end of the parking lot.

**Hamilton Beach:** Park on the left side of Isabella Point Road in an open area about 1.8 kilometres from the Fulford–Ganges Road and walk down to the beach. (The road is adjacent to the beach and there's some limited parking along the side of the road.) This is the same kind of walk as Drummond Park (above). There is also a public trail in Fern Creek Park (see page 251) across the road (on the west side of the road). You might like to combine this with your shore walk.

*The author and friend check on the dinner menu from Hope Hill.* Lynn Thompson

## ROAD WALKS AND SHORT TRAILS

There are many beautiful roads to walk on Salt Spring, although few of them are as peaceful as they once were. The following selection is based on tranquility and beauty. These walks are described in roughly a north-south order. (I have also included a few short and easy off-road walks.)

**Southey Point area:** Arbutus Road, Southey Point Road and Dogwood Lane are all pleasant. They are well treed and quiet, but provide few glimpses of the water.

**Sun Eagle Road to North View Road:** This steep, 10-minute connector trail descends from just left (south) of 268 Sun Eagle Road to the end of Northview Road. The trail offers views west to Penelakut (formerly Kuper) and Tent islands from its top end.

**North Beach Road to Walker's Hook Road:** This is the longest stretch of low-bank seaside road walking you'll find on Salt Spring. For much of the way the houses are on the west side, while the east (water) side is clear. The views are of Wallace and Galiano islands. You might like to combine this with a beach walk. There are many places to access the shore along here.

**St. Mary Lake area:** There are good water views from Tripp Road on the quiet, west side of the lake, where you'll also find a few relatively private swimming spots. The walk along North End Road, on the east side of the lake, is also pretty but the traffic is heavy. The area along and off Lang's Road, at the north end of the lake, is quiet but there is no public access to the water here.

**Vesuvius:** This residential area off Vesuvius Bay Road, southeast of the ferry dock, is a lovely, quiet area for walking. Start with Chu-An Road, which runs south off Vesuvius Bay Road, and then meander through the labyrinth of neighbourhood roads. There's another small pocket of interesting, quiet roads off Langley and Bayview roads, which also run south off Vesuvius Bay Road just before the ferry dock. You might want to combine this walk with a swim at Vesuvius Beach.

**Harrison Road to Baker Road:** This linear trail connects the end of Harrison Road to the end of Baker Road. It is well signed and fenced and will take you about 20 minutes to walk. This trail can be combined with hike 17.

**Long Harbour area:** Some of Salt Spring's most interesting homes and loveliest shoreline are along Old Scott Road and Scott Point Drive. Start walking on either of these from Long Harbour Road. Both roads are narrow, well treed and quite beautiful.

A 10-minute off-road walk beside the ferry terminal (on the north side of Long Harbour Road) climbs to a beautiful view over Welbury Bay and then descends to rejoin Long Harbour Road opposite Welbury Road. Try this one while you wait for the ferry.

**Madrona Bay Trail:** A steep loop trail off Long Harbour Road almost directly across from Eagle Ridge Drive leads into a very small community park and approaches but does not quite reach the shoreline (there is no trail directly to the water here).

**Ganges area:** To ensure that the village of Ganges remains a pedestrian-friendly area, the Salt Spring Parks and Recreation Commission (PARC) is developing pathways to connect the various parts of the village. Inquire at the Tourist Information Centre or the PARC office for a map of the entire pathways system and use some of these paths to explore the village. Some paths connect with the trails in Mouat Park (see page 250).

**Mouat Park:** At the end of Seaview Avenue (off the Fulford–Ganges Road) in Ganges. The trails follow McPhillips Creek and go through second-growth forest. The island's only public disc golf course is in this park.

**Grace Point Park:** Walk along the water beside the Grace Point condominium strata at the end of Purvis Road in downtown Ganges. Continue past the condominiums on the left and through the condominium gate out to Grace Point at the end of the peninsula. Be careful, as the trail climbing the rocky headland is a bit treacherous. You'll have lovely views of Ganges Harbour and the surrounding shore from the point. Nearby Grace Point Island is privately owned.

**Beddis Road:** Beddis is a joy to walk. It meanders like a country road should, and affords good views of the water every so often and lovely vistas of the surrounding land. If you have the stamina, walk the 8.5 kilometres (each way) from the Fulford–Ganges Road as far as Beddis Beach.

**Creekside Rainforest:** On the south side of Creekside Road, 300 metres from its intersection with Beddis Road, 500 metres from Beddis Beach and 8.4 kilometres from downtown Ganges. Almost one million dollars was raised on Salt Spring to buy this 8-hectare property owned by The Land Conservancy of British Columbia (TLC). The 10-minute trail above the creek is very atmospheric, as it passes moss-covered maples and fir trees and a very green ravine descending to salmon-enhanced Cusheon Creek below. A sign indicates the boundary between this property and its neighbour, despite the fact that the trail continues through the private land. Respect the sign and return the way you came.

**Sky Valley–Cusheon Lake circuit:** This walk goes through arbutus forest and along Cusheon Lake, where you can swim. Park on Sky Valley Road, just off the Fulford–Ganges Road (about 3.5 kilometres south of Ganges). Walk to the end of Sky Valley Road and take the trail heading off on the left (southeast). When you have choices, keep to the right or go straight (the offshoots to the left lead to private property). This is a very short trail, and in about 5 minutes you will emerge on the continuation of Sky Valley Road. Follow it 200 metres to Lord Mikes Road and turn right. Walk along Lord Mikes for 500 metres, then turn right again on Cusheon Lake Road. There are good views of the lake and of Bruce Peak. When you return to the Fulford–Ganges Road, turn right (north) toward Ganges and walk the short distance back to Sky Valley Road, where you started. The whole walk will take you about an hour.

**Beaver Point Road area:** Beaver Point Road is a great country-road walk along a verdant valley lined with farms encircled by cedar rail fences. Two of Salt Spring's prettiest lakes—Stowell and Weston—are on this road. Be sure to look at charming Beaver Point Hall (at the corner of Bridgman Road) and the little red Beaver Point School behind it.

**Forest Ridge Park:** This beautiful area is often overlooked because it's so close to Ruckle Provincial Park. From Beaver Point Road walk down Forest Ridge Road to its end at Stevens Road. Just before the Stevens Road junction you'll see a signed trail entering the forest. Follow it for a short distance through some mature trees until you see a giant Douglas-fir on your left. Known to locals as the Grandmother Tree, this is the second-largest Douglas-fir I've seen on Salt Spring (the largest is in Ruckle Park) and seems to be a popular spot for some islanders to leave tributes either to the tree or to important people in their lives. From here you can walk 800 metres east along Stevens Road to Eagles Way, an old road (now a path) which descends south to the shore (see page 247).

**Fulford Harbour:** Walk along Morningside Road from the ferry, exploring the side roads as you go. There are good views of Fulford Harbour along the way. This is a good walk to combine with hike 2.

**Fern Creek Park:** This trail starts across from Hamilton Beach, about 1.8 kilometres along Isabella Point Road from its intersection with the Fulford–Ganges Road. Look for the trailhead about 25 metres south of the road leading into a development. This pretty but steep trail follows a creek bed through a fern-filled ravine, which is part of 2-hectare Fern Creek Park. Look for western hemlock, immense red cedars and some large holly trees. The trail meanders through woods and crosses a seasonal creek, making it a pleasant place to spend an hour, although the 1.2-kilometre trail will only take you half an hour to walk. The trail can be slippery and muddy after rain, as the ground is fairly moist and doesn't drain well.

**Isabella Point Road–Roland Road:** Walk south along Isabella Point Road from Drummond Park. Turn left at Roland Road to continue along the shore. The road is quiet and pretty, and there are good views of Fulford Harbour. It's about 4 kilometres from Drummond Park to the end of Roland Road. You might like to combine this road walk with a shore walk at low tide. (See the Drummond Park shore walk, page 247.)

**Mountain Road:** Mountain Road runs southwest off Isabella Point Road, slightly over 3 kilometres from the Fulford–Ganges Road. You can walk this beautiful, seldom-travelled, forested road for at least 4 kilometres before you reach a private development. From here a public road allowance continues toward Musgrave Landing. Look for one of Salt Spring's two waterfalls on the north side of the road about 3 kilometres from Isabella Point Road. You'll also find a number of well-used trails to explore in the Mount Tuam Ecological Reserve, which straddles Mountain Road. Just before the end of Mountain Road, you'll see hydro poles heading up the mountain. A trail beside them leads through the forest and up Mount Tuam. After about 20 minutes you'll find yourself in the open on the flank of Mount Tuam. From here you must find your own way up the mountain, as there is no distinct trail. Although the area around the top of the mountain is private property, there are good views on the steep hike up the flank of the mountain before you reach the private property. The land you are walking on is ecological reserve administered by BC Parks.

**Refrigerator Trail:** This trail at the end of Isabella Point Road is so named because of a discarded appliance at its north end. The trail connects Isabella Point and Mountain roads and is part of the Mount Tuam Ecological Reserve, which has very well-developed trails throughout and is regularly used by locals. This trail is not signed, is somewhat overgrown and can be hard to follow in places. When you have a choice, stick to the left and bear west until you reach Mountain Road. The trail is about 1 kilometre long and will take you 10–15 minutes if you don't get lost.

## AND IF YOU PADDLE . . .

With many good launch spots, little in the way of current to worry about and mostly protected water, Salt Spring has some of the best paddling in the Gulf Islands. In addition to the cautions detailed below, be very careful to avoid Salt Spring's three ferries and other boat traffic. Here are a few ideas from the easiest of Salt Spring's launch sites:

**Arbutus Road:** Put in at the end of Arbutus Road and paddle south along the well-developed shore of Stuart Channel to Vesuvius; east to Wallace Island Marine Provincial Park (see page 314); even farther east to Dionisio Point Provincial Park (see page 104) or Montague Harbour Marine Provincial Park on Galiano Island (see page 99); or west around the beautiful sandstone formations of the Tent and Penelakut (formerly Kuper) Island shoreline, possibly stopping for lunch at one or other of the two marinas in Telegraph Harbour on Thetis Island (see page 296).

**Hudson Point:** This popular boat launch on North Beach Road gives you access to Salt Spring's fairly developed northeast shore and an easy trip to Wallace Island Marine Provincial Park (see page 314) or farther south to Montague Harbour Marine Provincial Park on Galiano Island (see page 99). Caution: The wind can come up suddenly in Houstoun Passage, especially on summer afternoons.

**Cranberry Outlet:** Put in at the end of Collins Road and paddle south along the mostly undeveloped shoreline to Burgoyne Bay; paddle north along the island's more heavily developed northwest shore to Southey Point; or paddle west over to Maple Bay on Vancouver Island for lunch at a restaurant or the pub.

**Quebec Drive:** Launch at the end of Quebec Drive, in the middle of Long Harbour, and paddle along the Athol Peninsula shoreline to Nose Point. From here you could paddle east over to James Bay on Prevost Island (part of the Gulf Islands National Park Reserve). Local paddlers enjoy the paddle all around Prevost Island, which offers some of the most scenic and varied shoreline in the Gulf Islands. Alternatively, if you prefer something less remote, you can paddle west around heavily developed Scott Point into Welbury Bay and on to busy Ganges Harbour. Caution: If you paddle to Prevost Island, be careful of turbulence around Nose Point when the current is running; strong tidal flows where Captain Passage meets Trincomali Channel, especially on a flood tide (time your paddle for slack current); and rough water around Selby Point on Prevost.

**Churchill Road:** From the shore access at the end of Churchill Road you have easy access to the Chain Islands (Goat, Deadman and the Sisters). While all of these islands are privately owned, you are allowed to stop on the beaches below the high tide line. Plan to stop for tea or lunch at the stunning shell beach on privately owned but uninhabited Third Sister Island. (Locals have built a charming outhouse here with the owner's permission.) The shore access on Price Road (see page 246) is another good launch site for visits to these islands. Cautions: The beach at the end of Churchill Road is almost non-existent at very high tides. Walter Bay, on the south side of Ganges Harbour, is a protected bird sanctuary.

**Beddis Beach:** You can paddle to Prevost Island and the islands on its western shore from this launch site. Of particular interest is tiny, privately owned Owl Island (beside Secret Island) in the spring when it is covered with wildflowers. Beddis Beach is also a good place to put in for a paddle along Salt Spring's southeast shore toward the Channel Islands and the beautiful Ruckle Park shoreline.

**Burgoyne Bay:** Launch from the government dock or the nearby beach at the end of Burgoyne Bay Road and paddle south to Musgrave Landing, north to Cranberry Outlet or west to Genoa Bay or Cowichan Bay on Vancouver Island. The Salt Spring shoreline from Burgoyne Bay is largely undeveloped. Musgrave Landing is a fascinating little backwater that contains a lot of Salt Spring history. There's a small, upscale strata development here. Caution: The water around Bold Bluff Point in Sansum Narrows can be rough, especially when a southerly wind meets an ebbing tide. To avoid paddling against a potentially strong current, paddle north with the flooding tide or south when the tide is on the ebb.

**Menhinick Road:** Launch from an access across from 130 Menhinick. This access is down a right-of-way beside a house. Walk down the path to the water and carefully take your boat down the rickety stairs to the small beach below. You can cross to Russell and Portland islands (both part of Gulf Islands National Park Reserve) from here. Either of these islands makes a good lunch stop and both have trails to walk. (For more information on Portland Island, see page 310.) You can then tour the shoreline of either or both of these islands. From the Menhinick launch site you can also paddle along the shoreline of the Tsawout Indian reserve and the beautiful shoreline along the east side of Fulford Harbour. There is a second launch site from the end of Seabright Road, which runs south off Menhinick. The only disadvantage of this water access is that the beach disappears at very high tides. You can also continue along the shoreline to explore the Ruckle Park shore from here, or if you prefer to spend more time around Ruckle Park, you can launch from the picnic area of the park.

**Drummond Park or Hamilton Beach:** Either of these launch sites on Isabella Point Road gives you access to the diverse shoreline of Fulford Harbour. From Hamilton Beach you can easily round Isabella Point to tour the exquisite Isabella Islets and continue along the relatively undeveloped southern shoreline of the island to Cape Keppel.

*Most of Prevost Island still belongs to the descendants of Digby Hussey de Burgh, the Irish farmer who bought it in 1924. Kayakers can camp and hike on the Gulf Islands National Park Reserve's land around James Bay and Selby Cove and explore the land around Portlock Point and Richardson Bay, where the light beacon established in 1895 still shines its warning.* Parks Canada

*Prevost Island offers some of the most scenic and varied shoreline in the Gulf Islands.*

# Saturna

*L*ocated at the end of a chain of islands that includes Mayne and Galiano, Saturna is the most southern Gulf Island and considered by many the most lovely. Much of Saturna's 31 square kilometres is part of the Gulf Islands National Park Reserve (GINPR), including Winter Cove, Narvaez Bay and East Point; land around the summits of Mount Warburton Pike, Mount Elford and Mount David; the former Saturna Island Ecological Reserve; and parts of Brown Ridge and Taylor Point. Saturna's lovely beaches and ridge walks make it one of the best hiking destinations in the Gulf Islands, and because of its small population of 359 (Capital Regional District 2006 estimate), its charming roads are serenely quiet. East Point Road on the north shore has sea views and many beach accesses for almost all of its length. Other roads lead to delightful coves and bays, and one leads to a splendid cliff walk overlooking other Gulf Islands, the San Juan Islands and the peaks of Washington State. Two ridges run the length of Saturna. The deep valley between them extends from Narvaez Bay in the east to Lyall Harbour in the west, with Narvaez Bay Road running through it. Most of the island's limited services are located near the ferry terminal, from where there are daily sailings to Swartz Bay (near Victoria).

## HISTORY

Saturna Island was named after the *Santa Saturnina*, a Spanish ship that explored the area in 1791. This island grew more slowly than its neighbours—Mayne, the Penders, Salt Spring and Galiano—largely because it had little good farmland and because it was the farthest away from the main shipping routes. The first settlers had orchards and cows (for milk and butter) but kept mostly sheep, as is still the case with the few farmers on Saturna today. Some sandstone quarries were established on the island at the end of the 19th century. Sandstone quarried at Taylor Point was exported to Victoria and as far away as Winnipeg.

The riptides and strong currents in Boundary Pass, east of Saturna's East Point, have always made it a dangerous waterway. The East Point lighthouse was built in 1888, two years after a ship went aground on Boiling Reef.

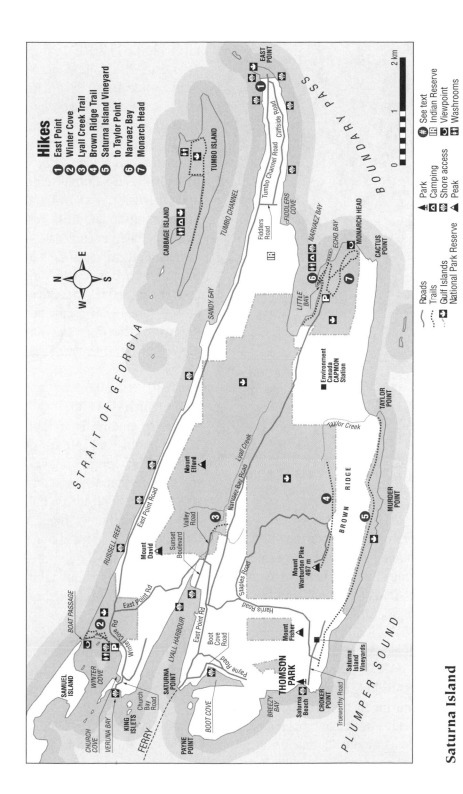

## Hikes

1. East Point
2. Winter Cove
3. Lyall Creek Trail
4. Brown Ridge Trail
5. Saturna Island Vineyard to Taylor Point
6. Narvaez Bay
7. Monarch Head

2 km

- See text
- Indian Reserve
- Viewpoint
- Washrooms

- Park
- Camping
- Shore access
- Peak

- Roads
- Trails
- Gulf Islands National Park Reserve

**Saturna Island**

*This charming little church was once used by visitors to Saturna but is now on private land and best viewed from the water.*

## GETTING THERE

There are ferries to Saturna from Swartz Bay (near Victoria), Tsawwassen (near Vancouver), Galiano, Mayne and North Pender Island. Reservations are recommended for travel between Saturna Island and Tsawwassen. For more information obtain a BC Ferries schedule or contact BC Ferries. Saltspring Air flies to Saturna from downtown Vancouver and the Vancouver airport, and Seair Seaplanes flies to Saturna from the Vancouver airport (see page 320).

## SERVICES AND ACCOMMODATION

The ferry landing is at Lyall Harbour, adjacent to most of Saturna's few services, including a store that sells gas and diesel fuel, a bookstore, a pub and the community hall. A general store on nearby Narvaez Bay Road sells delicacies from the island's excellent bakery; you'll also find a café, post office, mechanic and liquor store there. At time of writing there were no pharmacies or banks on Saturna, but there were ATMs at the pub and the lower store. The island has a medical clinic and a doctor visits once a week.

Many of the island's bed and breakfasts are within a few kilometres of the ferry dock. At time of writing there were no private campgrounds and only seven walk-in campsites in GINPR at Narvaez Bay. Be sure to make arrangements for lodging in advance, as accommodation is extremely limited, especially during the summer.

An annually updated information pamphlet is available on the ferries and in island stores. For more information on Saturna visit www.saturnatourism.com.

About one-half of Saturna's land base is within the national park; for more information on the park call 1-866-944-1744 or visit www.parkscanada. gc.ca/gulf.

## ESPECIALLY FOR WALKERS
In addition to the Shore and Road Walks listed at the end of this chapter, there are many easy walks on Saturna. Try the following:

- the area around East Point lighthouse (see hike 1)
- the short loops in Winter Cove (see hike 2)
- the walk down to Narvaez Bay (see hike 6) or up to the Monarch Head viewpoint (see hike 7). The access trail to Narvaez Bay is quite steep (a long, 45 percent grade). The trail to the Monarch Head viewpoint also has some steep areas.
- Although there is no official park trail along Brown Ridge, the Mount Warburton Pike viewpoint offers a magnificent panorama and parking area. Informal "goat paths" provide a ridge walk along gentle terrain; these paths are right on the edge of a cliff so be cautious (see hike 4).

Three cultural spots are worth visiting:

- A short walk from the ferry, along East Point Road, is the current St. Christopher's Anglican Church, which I found appealing.
- The exterior of the original St. Christopher's Church (see page 258) can be seen from Church Bay Road. From its intersection with East Point Road, walk along Winter Cove Road 1 kilometre to Church Bay Road and then down this road to where you can see Church Bay. The charming little church (capacity 20) started out as a Japanese boat-house. It is now on private property and no longer in use.
- If you like exploring old cemeteries, visit the Saturna Cemetery, 1.3 kilometres along Narvaez Bay Road east of the store.

## HIKES on SATURNA

Most of the hikes described here are part of the GINPR. Parks Canada recommends that you hike only on the officially designated trails, as indicated on park maps, at trailheads and on park information boards. These trails will have been assessed for public safety concerns and routed to ensure that sensitive ecosystems are not impacted.

## 1. EAST POINT (GINPR) ★★★

| | |
|---|---|
| Trail length | 1.5 kilometres |
| Time required | 35 minutes or more |
| Description | A walk at the East Point lighthouse property offers great views of the churning waters of Boundary Pass and Washington's majestic Mount Baker, as well as the chance to see killer whales. There is an accessible beach on the northwest bay overlooking Tumbo Island. |
| Level | Easy |
| Access | The end of Tumbo Channel Road |
| Facilities | Small museum in the foghorn building, outhouse, benches, bicycle rack, information board, picnic tables, telephone on road at entrance |

The views from East Point over the busy, churning waters of Boundary Pass are magnificent. This is perhaps the best place in the Gulf Islands to see killer whales—pods of whales pass by regularly from May to November.

The trail to the left of the parking area and paths on-site provide access to the beach below. Walk as far as you can along the stunning shoreline, with its intricate sandstone formations. At low tide you can walk right around the point on the boulders, examining tide pools and admiring the large rocks. Then walk around the meadow passing the lighthouse and other buildings.

## 2. WINTER COVE (GINPR) ★★★

| | |
|---|---|
| Trail length | 2-kilometre loop from the parking area |
| Time required | 40 minutes |
| Description | A walk through forest, wetland and along the shore of Winter Cove to the open water of the Strait of Georgia |
| Level | Easy |
| Access | To the west of the intersection of East Point Road and Winter Cove Road. The trail enters the woods on the right (east) side of the parking area, just up from the water. |

| Facilities | Picnic tables, outhouses, boat launch, sports fields across the road. The park has no camp-sites. |
|---|---|

Winter Cove occupies 75 hectares of land and an additional 16 hectares of intertidal foreshore. The park contains a fine salt marsh and the typical dry, coastal Douglas-fir vegetation. The shoreline is made up of sandstone, shale and middens left over from aboriginal use in the past. Middens are considered significant cultural features and should be respected; please stay on the designated trails.

This short hike is well worth doing for the fine views of Winter Cove and the Strait of Georgia, as well as the restful ambience of the park. After about 10 minutes you reach a point at the edge of Boat Passage, the narrow stretch of water that rushes between Saturna and neighbouring Samuel Island. Park benches on the edge of these rocks and elsewhere make pleasant places to stop and contemplate the power of the water. From there the trail winds back through the forest to the day-use area. Walks along the Winter Cove shoreline are also pleasant, but, for protection purposes, the national park discourages links between the shoreline and the trail above. Winter Cove appears remarkably different at high and low tide.

*These fantastic sandstone formations greet you as you walk around East Point Light Station on the foreshore.*

## 3. Lyall Creek Trail (GINPR) ★★

| | |
|---|---|
| Trail length | 1.5 kilometres one way |
| Time required | 20 minutes one way |
| Description | A descent to a ferny forest and along a creek. This trail was developed by the local parks and recreation department and is now part of GINPR. |
| Level | Easy |
| Access | A. On the north side of Narvaez Bay Road, 1.4 kilometres east of the store |
| | B. At the end of Valley Road (east off East Point Road). It is recommended that you use access A, as it is easier to find and the trail is clearer from that side. |

From the Narvaez Bay Road access, the trail drops steeply about 50 metres to the ferny canyon floor below. On the way, about 5 minutes from the trailhead, you will find a bench where you can sit and watch an exquisite seasonal waterfall as it flows gently over a mossy rock face. The trail joins the two accesses and passes through a great number of large cedar, mature alder and fir.

## 4. Brown Ridge from Mount Warburton Pike ★★★★★

| | |
|---|---|
| Trail length | Up to 4 kilometres round trip if you stay on the ridge |
| Time required | Allow 2 hours for the ridge walk. Don't rush; this is one of the finest hikes in the Gulf Islands. |
| Description | Glorious cliff walk looking southwest over Plumper Sound and the Pender Islands and south to the San Juan Islands and the mainland peaks in the US beyond. |
| Level | Easy if you stay at the top |
| Elevation | 497 metres |

| Access | The trail begins at the end of Staples Road (4 kilometres southeast off Harris Road) at the top of Mount Warburton Pike and continues east along Brown Ridge. |
| --- | --- |
| Cautions | A. The TV tower is on land leased from the federal government. It is private property and should not be disturbed in any way. This trail follows the edge of a steep cliff. Proceed carefully. |
| | B. If you descend to Taylor Point from Brown Ridge, a way of combining this hike with hike 5, you will be walking on land owned by the Campbell family. Although Parks Canada has an easement for future trail development down to Taylor Point, which is in the park, this trail has not been built at time of writing. For this reason, you should obtain permission to walk here from the Campbells (250-539-2470). |

Mount Warburton Pike is the highest point on Saturna. The trail that follows the edge of Brown Ridge is to the left (east) of the TV towers at the end of Staples Road. From the towers drop down until you find the trail; otherwise you will be in the woods. You will probably find several trails, as you make your way east along the ridge. Many of these are goat trails, and if you're lucky, you'll see the large feral goats that inhabit the ridge area.

On a clear day—and there is really no point in doing a hike like this if it isn't clear—the views are fantastic. At the beginning of the hike, you look down over the Pender Islands and beyond to Moresby, Portland and Salt Spring islands. As you proceed farther, you can see the San Juan Islands and the Washington coast. Below, grassy meadow drops away, at first gradually and then very steeply, to the farm below. Behind you is a magnificent stand of what are perhaps the largest firs on the island.

Return the way you came. At time of writing there was no developed trail to Taylor Point. Parks Canada has obtained a trail easement through the Campbell farm property, and this roughly follows Taylor Creek. However Parks Canada has not yet assessed the area for natural or cultural sensitivity or public safety and hence does not promote trail use at this time. At some point Parks Canada may develop a proper trail. Until this happens, the going is rough, dangerous and not particularly pleasant.

*As you descend from Mount Warburton Pike, you'll see the tip of Taylor Point curling out into the sea.* Parks Canada

*Mount Warburton Pike is on land once owned by its namesake, the youngest son of an upper-class English family. At one time Pike owned 567 hectares of land on Saturna.* Lynn Thompson

*Hiking and kayaking in the Gulf Islands is always full of surprises.*

## 5. Saturna Island Vineyard (Trueworthy Road) to Taylor Point ★★★

| | |
|---|---|
| Trail length | 4 kilometres each way |
| Time required | 2 hours each way |
| Description | A precipitous walk along the top of a bluff with occasional magnificent views out across Plumper Sound to the Pender Islands |
| Level | Moderate to strenuous |
| Access | The eastern end of Trueworthy Road (off Harris Road), where you will find a gate and a Gulf Islands National Park Reserve (GINPR) sign-board |
| Cautions | At time of writing Parks Canada was discouraging people from hiking this route until public safety concerns have been addressed and routing determined that minimizes impacts on sensitive ecosystems. The animal trails that now exist cross steep terrain. The Campbell farmland is to the north of the parkland; if you take this route, respect the private property and stay within the park. |

It's possible to follow a route along animal trails below the Campbell farm between the Saturna Island Family Estate Winery (the vineyard) and Taylor Point. This 54-hectare strip of parkland falls sharply toward the sea, rising to over 100 metres in places. There is no developed trail, although when I hiked it, I found blue and pink flagging that followed a rough, but mostly distinct trail. You will often find yourself on rocky ledges, and in a couple of places you will have to descend down one side of a shallow gorge and climb up the other.

Taylor Point is an exquisite headland where you will want to have your lunch or stop for tea. Nearby is the ruin of a two-storey sandstone house built by stonemason George Taylor in 1892. The house burned down some years later. You can also visit Taylor Point by kayak or canoe. Land at the expansive beach just east of the point and ascend the point by the access at the west side of the beach. This is the approximate boundary between GINPR and the Campbell farm.

## 6. Narvaez Bay (GINPR) ★★★★

| | |
|---|---|
| Trail length | 2–3 kilometres return (5 kilometres if combined with hike 7 to Monarch Head) |
| Time required | 1–2 hours |
| Description | A walk to stunning shoreline, with the possibility of combining this walk with hike 7 to Monarch Head |
| Level | Mostly easy, with a steep descent to the water and a steep ascent back |
| Access | The end of Narvaez Bay Road (6.4 kilometres from the general store at the corner of Narvaez Bay Road and East Point Road). This is also the access for hike 7 to Monarch Head. |
| Facilities | Outhouses, picnic tables, seven walk-in camp-sites, signboards |

At the end of Narvaez Bay Road you'll find a parking lot and Parks Canada's signboard marking what I consider the most beautiful part of the 252 hectares of the Narvaez Bay section of GINPR. A 1-kilometre walk along a former driveway takes you down to the water. You'll need only 20 minutes or so, but you'll want even more time to enjoy the ambience of this lovely spot.

Parks Canada has installed excellent signage that leads you to the anvil-like protrusion in the shoreline that creates Little Bay to the northwest and Echo Bay to the southeast. There's a separate short trail to Echo Bay from a fork that you will reach before you get to the anvil.

The solid stone walls lining the sides of Echo Bay create an echo effect. Once you have finished admiring the magnificent walls and trying out the echo, you can return to the fork and continue to the larger part of Narvaez Bay on the other side of the anvil. Here you'll find another park sign, an outhouse, seven walk-in campsites with picnic tables, more beautiful shoreline and views of Fiddlers Cove and the houses along Cliffside Road to the northeast and Washington State to the east.

When you're ready to return, start back up the road following signs to the parking lot. If you haven't already walked to Monarch Head (hike 7), you might do that now.

## 7. NARVAEZ BAY TO MONARCH HEAD

| | |
|---|---|
| Trail length | 3 kilometres |
| Time required | Up to an hour |
| Description | A figure-eight trail to a viewpoint through mixed cedar and fir forest, with the possibility of descending to Narvaez Bay (see hike 6) |
| Level | Moderate (a steep, 55-metre climb to the viewpoint) |
| Access | The end of Narvaez Bay Road (6.4 kilometres from the general store at the corner of Narvaez Bay Road and East Point Road). This is also the access for hike 6 to Narvaez Bay. |
| Cautions | Although Parks Canada has built the trail leading to Monarch Head, the head itself is not part of GINPR, and the end of the trail is marked with a fence and a sign. Please respect the private property. |

*The view from Monarch Head.*

The trail follows a wide and spacious old grassy road that climbs for 1.2 kilometres from the parking area. The viewing area at Monarch Head sits on top of a craggy cliff with beautiful sandstone formations on the shore below and picturesque kelp floating on the water offshore. The spectacular viewpoint faces east to Patos and Sucia islands in the American San Juan Islands.

## SHORE AND ROAD WALKS

### Shore Walks

The Saturna Island Parks and Recreation Commission (SIPRC) has been very busy improving the island's beach accesses. Signage is generally good, and accesses are often equipped with benches and picnic tables. Here are some of the best beach accesses. The names are the ones used by SIPRC. The trailhead for each access is marked with a red-and-white reflective sign (a number beginning with the letter "A"). The accesses are listed roughly from east to west.

**Pine Tree:** This small community park is at the end of a path to the shore at the western edge of East Point Park.

**Trillium:** A signed path leads to stone steps to the beach at the western edge of East Point Park.

**Lily:** A path between 721 Tumbo Road and East Point Resort Ocean Cottages leads to steps to the beach.

**Peacock:** A signed trail between 228 and 230 Cliffside Road leads to a bench overlooking a viewpoint.

**Orcas:** A signed path between 154 and 156 Cliffside Road leads to a viewpoint with a bench to sit on while enjoying it.

**Strait Road:** A short path leads to a bench and a viewpoint at the end of Strait Road (off East Point Road about 5 kilometres east of the turnoff to Winter Cove). This access is on the edge of a bank and is fenced for safety.

**Russell Reef (GINPR):** The access to this little park is on the north side of East Point Road, 1.1 kilometres east of Winter Cove Road. You can walk on this beach for some distance at low tide.

**Winter Cove:** This large boat launch is a good place to put in a canoe or kayak.

**Veruna Bay:** This signed access between 103 and 104 Church Bay Road (off Winter Cove Road) is a good place to launch a canoe or kayak or just walk along the very pretty beach.

**Cascade Glade:** A rough, 5-minute trail at the west end of Bonnybank Road leads down to the water where you have a lovely view over Lyall Harbour.

**Sunset Beach:** You can drive right down to this access at the end of Sunset Road at the head of Lyall Harbour. You might watch the sunset as you have your dinner on the picnic table provided, or you might launch your canoe or kayak and watch the sunset from the water. I'm told that the beach can be very muddy, although it was fine when I walked it.

**Ralph:** A signed trail leads down to this access between 106 and 108 Boot Cove, where you'll find a picnic table, a bench and lovely views of charming Boot Cove.

**Thomson Park (Saturna Beach):** The access is from the western end of True-worthy Road (behind the Saturna vineyard) off Harris Road or through the right-of-way at the end of the vineyard's parking lot. Named after the Thomson family, one of Saturna's oldest families, this beach was the original home of the Saturna Canada Day lamb barbecue, an island fundraising tradition now held in Winter Cove. The park has picnic tables and an outhouse. The dock is privately owned.

## Road Walks

The roads on Saturna are almost always quiet and pleasant for walking. For example, you can walk along East Point Road from Russell Reef just east of Winter Cove for about a half-hour following the beautiful shoreline, with easy access to the rocky beach. This makes a good beach walk at low tide.

## AND IF YOU PADDLE . . .

Saturna's deep bays and coves, as well as the many neighbouring islands, make paddling here a delight. However, the currents in Boat Passage and around East Point can be dangerous, and only experienced paddlers should even consider paddling here without a guide. If you do go, study your tide and current tables carefully and paddle these areas only at slack tide.

Both Cabbage Island (4.5 hectares) and Tumbo Island (121 hectares), just north of Saturna, are part of GINPR and are accessible only by water. Although there are no hiking trails on Cabbage Island, there is a lovely sand beach and the views are excellent. There are five campsites with picnic tables and a composting toilet but no drinking water on the island. In addition to beachcombing, you can swim and fish from the island's beautiful beaches. Tumbo Island has no camping, but does have a wonderful trail system. It too has beautiful views and beaches.

*At high tide the water funnels furiously through Boat Passage between Saturna and Samuel Islands. Some small boats use this shortcut to reach the open water of the Strait of Georgia.* Rick Tipple

Here are some good places to launch:

**Winter Cove:** The informal boat launch at Winter Cove (GINPR) is an easy place to launch. From here you can paddle southwest around the cove and along the shore to Veruna Bay and on to Lyall Harbour. If you are an experienced paddler, you can also paddle around neighbouring Samuel Island, but do this in a counterclockwise direction, returning the way you came and avoiding Boat Passage except at slack tide: the stories of dumpings in Boat Passage are legendary. The flood tide also flows swiftly northwest in Georgeson Passage between Samuel and Lizard islands. Be very cautious in these narrow channels.

**Veruna Bay:** The access is at the end of Church Bay Road. Paddle south to the King Islets and around the shoreline of Lyall Harbour.

**Sunset Boulevard:** This boat launch at the end of Sunset Boulevard puts you in the middle of Lyall Harbour, which, though large, is not very interesting.

**Boot Cove:** The access is across from 121 Boot Cove Road, to the right of 120 Boot Cove Road. This is a good place to launch at high tide. However, at low tide you will find yourself in oozy mud. Boot Cove is a pleasant and interesting place to paddle. From here you can paddle north across Lyall Harbour to the King Islets, Veruna Bay, Winter Cove and Samuel Island, or south to Breezy Bay and Saturna's Plumper Sound shoreline.

**Thomson Park (Saturna Beach):** The access is from the western end of Trueworthy Road (behind the Saturna vineyard) off Harris Road or through the right-of-way at the end of the vineyard's parking lot. This gives you easy access to the Plumper Sound shoreline east as far as Narvaez Bay, or north to Breezy Bay and Payne Point.

*Boot Cove is very protected and interesting to explore. It also gives you access to the impressive cliffs that form much of Saturna's southern shore.*

# Texada

$N$ ot only is Texada the largest of the Gulf islands—50 kilometres long and 10 kilometres at its widest point—it is also the tallest. Its highest peak, Mount Shepherd, is an impressive 891 metres. Like the other islands in this book, it has a mild climate and lush forests. However, it is often over-looked as a tourist destination, as it has long been considered an industrial island. Its three massive limestone quarries produce several million tonnes of limestone a year for the chemical, cement and pulp industries. Many of the island's approximately 1,107 (2006 census) residents are employed by the quarries and don't depend on tourism. Texada's links are to the mainland, with ferries connecting it to Powell River rather than to Vancouver Island or to another Gulf Island. Good farmland is scarce, there are few safe

*This lovely view is from the north peak at Twin Peaks looking south.* Tom Scott

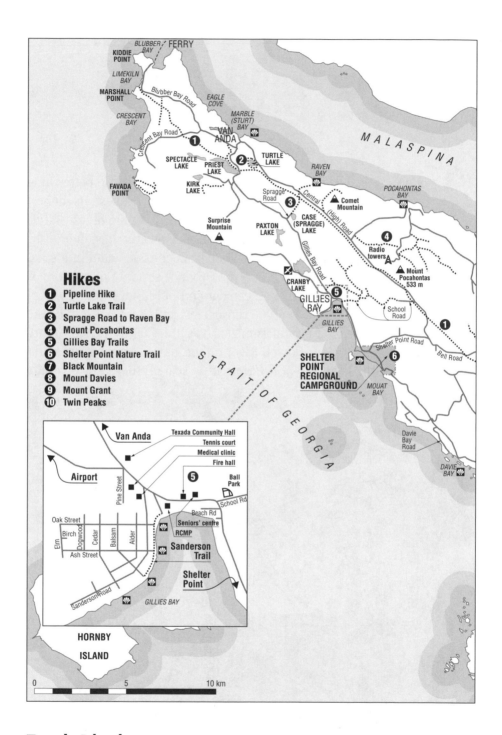

**Hikes**

1. Pipeline Hike
2. Turtle Lake Trail
3. Spragge Road to Raven Bay
4. Mount Pocahontas
5. Gillies Bay Trails
6. Shelter Point Nature Trail
7. Black Mountain
8. Mount Davies
9. Mount Grant
10. Twin Peaks

**Texada Island**

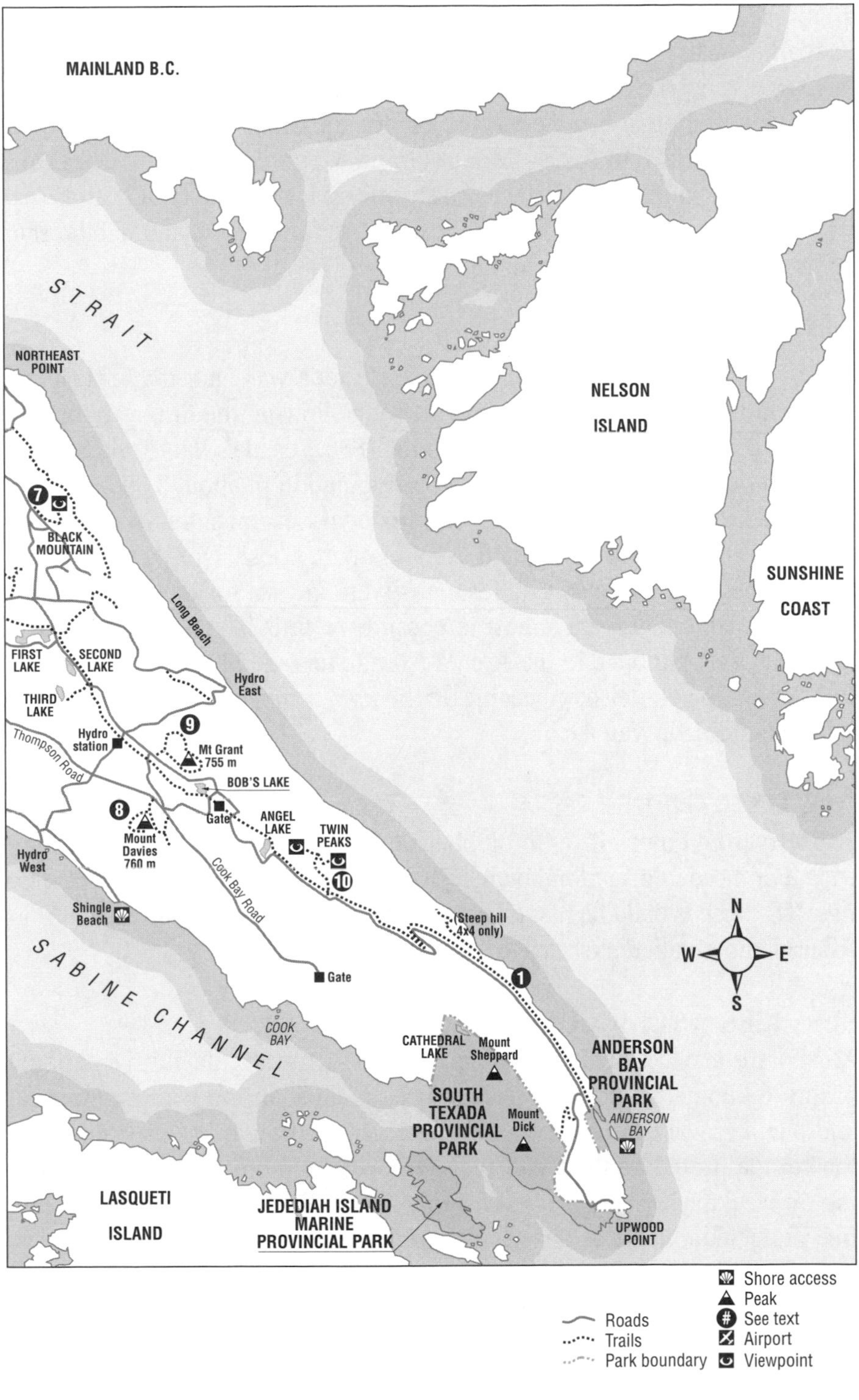
MAINLAND B.C.
STRAIT
NORTHEAST POINT
NELSON ISLAND
SUNSHINE COAST
BLACK MOUNTAIN
Long Beach
FIRST LAKE
SECOND LAKE
THIRD LAKE
Hydro East
Hydro station
Thompson Road
Mt Grant 755 m
BOB'S LAKE
Gate
ANGEL LAKE
TWIN PEAKS
Mount Davies 760 m
Hydro West
Cook Bay Road
Shingle Beach
(Steep hill 4x4 only)
SABINE CHANNEL
Gate
N
W
E
S
COOK BAY
CATHEDRAL LAKE
Mount Sheppard
ANDERSON BAY PROVINCIAL PARK
SOUTH TEXADA PROVINCIAL PARK
Mount Dick
ANDERSON BAY
LASQUETI ISLAND
JEDEDIAH ISLAND MARINE PROVINCIAL PARK
UPWOOD POINT
Shore access
Peak
Roads
See text
Trails
Airport
Park boundary
Viewpoint

anchorages and the island's main towns of Van Anda and Gillies Bay reflect its working-class roots, with little in the way of typical island craft boutiques or tourist-savvy shops. Nevertheless, Texada does have a strong arts community, a coffee shop, a commercial art gallery and an array of craft boutiques and artists' studios. Its hikes—Mount Grant, Mount Davies and Twin Peaks in particular—offer some of the more stunning views in the Gulf Islands and make it well worth a visit. As well, Texada has flora, fauna and habitat that are not found anywhere else in the Gulf Islands.

## HISTORY
Discovered by Spanish explorers in 1791, Texada was named after Felix de Tejada, a rear admiral in the Spanish navy. Following the discovery of iron ore in 1871 and copper and gold in about 1880, Texada's Van Anda became a boom town. By 1910 the island had a population of about 3,000 and Van Anda had three hotels with saloons, a hospital, several stores, a bimonthly newspaper (the *Coast Miner*) and even an opera house. During these heady days of the early 20th century, Texadans were known for their moonshine, setting up stills that were almost impossible to find. The island's colourful history is well exhibited in the Texada Island Heritage Museum, now in two locations—on your left as you come off the ferry from Powell River and in the school building in Van Anda.

## GETTING THERE
The ferry from Powell River to Blubber Bay makes 10 daily 35-minute round trips. For more information obtain a BC Ferries schedule or contact BC Ferries. KD Air has daily flights to Gillies Bay on Texada from Vancouver, Port Alberni and Qualicum (see page 320).

## SERVICES AND ACCOMMODATION
Most of the services on Texada are in Van Anda, toward the north end of the island (8 kilometres from the ferry). These include an inn with a restaurant and bar, a grocery store, service station and laundromat, a coffee shop and the Texada Branch of the First Credit Union, which offers full-service banking on weekdays. There is free Wi-Fi in the hotel and the coffee shop, and free public computers at the gas station. The RV park offers clean showers and a laundromat. Gillies Bay (20 kilometres south of the ferry) has a popular restaurant, a grocery store that sells takeout food and has an ATM, and a library with free public computers and Wi-Fi with a sufficiently strong signal

to be accessed in the library parking lot when the building is closed. Shelter Point Regional Park (604-486-7228) has an excellent beach, 52 campsites, hot showers, a telephone and a concession stand in the summer. There's a farmer's market in the Gillies Bay ballpark from noon to 2:00 p.m. every Sunday from June to October.

Primitive campsites can be found off forestry roads at Bob's Lake and Shingle Beach, and there are also some private campsites and RV sites on the island. There's also increasingly more accommodation in bed and breakfasts, cottages, a motel at Shelter Point and a hotel in Van Anda.

Information on Texada is available from the Powell River Visitors Information Centre, www.discoverpowellriver.com; 604-485-4701 or 1-877-817-8669. You can also get information on Texada from www.texada.org and www.thesunshinecoast.com/texadaisland.

## ESPECIALLY FOR WALKERS

Many easy walks are available for those not wishing to ascend one of Texada's peaks. In addition to the Shore and Road Walks outlined at the end of this chapter, try one of the following:

- Turtle Lake Trail (see hike 2)
- Spragge Road to Raven Bay (see hike 3)
- Gillies Bay Trails (see hike 5)
- Shelter Point Nature Trail (see hike 6)

## HIKES on TEXADA

Much of the hiking on Texada is on old logging roads, many of them now moss-covered and ingrown. Most hikes are on uninhabited Crown land on the southern half of the island.

Some trails are on private land managed by a company called Texada Island Forest Reserve. You will see many of the company's red-and-white signs with its telephone number and, often, a "No Trespassing" sign. A spokesperson for the company said that hiking was permitted on the land, but bicycles and motorized vehicles are strictly prohibited. Before using the land, call the company representative on Texada at 604-486-7772 to obtain permission.

One paved main road (with changing names) extends from the ferry dock through Van Anda and Gillies Bay, ending 4 kilometres past Shelter Point. From there, Central Road (known locally as the High Road) is a good gravel road back to Van Anda. Bell Road runs southeast from Central

Road at its intersection with Shelter Point Road. Bell Road connects with many of the forestry roads in Texada's south end, and this is where the best hikes are located.

The hikes described here are listed roughly from north to south. Distances on Texada can be fairly long, so some kind of transportation is almost essential. None of the hikes described are within walking distance of the ferry.

None of the hikes described here are in 900-hectare South Texada Provincial Park, which includes Mount Shepherd, or 35-hectare Anderson Bay Provincial Park, which includes a small island and a peninsula and is on Texada's southeastern shore. I chose not to include these parks as a four-by-four vehicle or a boat, as well as almost a whole day, is required just to get to them.

Much of the information for this chapter was made possible by Texada's master trekker, John Dove. John came to Texada more than 40 years ago to work as a geologist. He has hiked the island from end to end and knows the trails intimately, especially since he is responsible for creating many of them. John welcomes visitors to the island's hiking club, the Texada Trekkers, which has an outing every Saturday and another one mid-week (usually Tuesday or Wednesday). All you have to do is show up at 10 a.m., usually at the parking area in the Gillies Bay ballpark, but sometimes at the Royal Canadian Legion in Van Anda. For more information, call John at 604-486-7100 or email jdove@prcn.org. If you're on the island, check the community bulletin boards in the Van Anda post office and the Gillies Bay Store.

## 1. PIPELINE HIKE ★

| | |
|---|---|
| Trail length | Up to 31 kilometres one way |
| Time required | Variable |
| Description | Fairly level hike along pipeline right-of-way |
| Level | Easy |
| Access | The natural gas pipeline runs the length of the island and the right-of-way can be accessed in many places, including along Central Road, about 4 kilometres south of Van Anda. Yellow signs identify the pipeline path and red-ribboned sticks mark its route. |

| Cautions | No vehicles, including mountain bikes, are allowed on this grassy corridor. Walk with care, as there are open ditches and gravel barriers, in places. Some sections of this trail north of the cemetery in Van Anda are on private property. Do not trespass on these signed sections. |
|---|---|

Walking along this pipeline is not unlike walking along a hydro right-of-way cut through the forest. Nevertheless, the countryside is pretty. Don't walk farther than you wish to return, since this is not a circular route.

## 2. TURTLE LAKE TRAIL ★★

| Trail length | 3-kilometre loop |
|---|---|
| Time required | 75 minutes |
| Description | Pretty hike through forest and along a lake and stream. Some old growth and small waterfalls. |
| Level | Easy to far end of lake, then moderate with a few steep spots |
| Access | From Van Anda Post Office drive or walk south along Prospect Street for about 500 metres until you reach an old logging road continuing in the same direction. The hike starts here. |

This hike is in the area of the old Cornell gold mine. The section of trail around the pretty little lake was developed by Van Anda's postmaster, John Wood. This description was written by John and his sister Susan.

Walk along the old logging road for about 8 minutes until you reach a foot trail beside the ravine. This trail leads to a small bridge crossing Van Anda Creek at its outflow from Turtle (a.k.a. Emily) Lake. The trail then follows an old railway bed along the east side of the lake. If you have binoculars, you may be able to observe western painted turtles sunning themselves on floating logs.

Walk past the end of the lake and look for an old road leading off to the right away from the main trail. Follow this for about 4 minutes and then turn onto a flagged route angling downhill above the west side of the lake. The trail veers away from the lake to access the last old-growth near Van Anda before crossing Van Anda Creek via a mossy log (old bridge). The trail then turns right onto an alder-lined logging road and returns to the start of the hike.

## 3. SPRAGGE ROAD TO RAVEN BAY ★★

| | |
|---|---|
| Trail length | About 3 kilometres each way |
| Time required | 35–40 minutes each way |
| Description | Pleasant hike through mixed forest |
| Level | Easy |
| Access | Spragge Road is a short road to the east of Gillies Bay Road, about halfway between Van Anda and Gillies Bay. Park at the end of Spragge Road. You will see a private property on the right. Turn left onto a dirt road. You will almost immediately see a gate to another private property on the left. Take the old logging road just to the right of this gate. |
| Caution | Be very careful to respect the private property in this area. |

The logging road descends to pond-like Case (or Spragge) Lake, which it follows for a short distance. It then climbs a small hill to the left. There are several offshoots along the way but the main trail is wide and unmistakable. After about 20 minutes of pleasant downhill walking, you will come out on Central Road. This is as far as I walked. However, I'm told that if you walk left (north) along Central Road for a few hundred metres, you will find another old logging road heading right (east). (If you are driving from Van Anda, this point is about 5 kilometres from the town or 1.6 kilometres past the Imperial Limestone Company quarry.) About 20 minutes walking along this road will take you to Raven Bay on Texada's east side.

## 4. Mount Pocahontas ★★★

| | |
|---|---|
| Trail length | 2.5 kilometres each way |
| Time required | About 1 hour up, 45 minutes down |
| Description | A climb to a fine lookout that provides outstanding 360-degree views |
| Level | Moderate; some steep sections |
| Elevation | 533 metres, although your climb is only about half this |
| Access | The logging road to Pocahontas Bay runs off Central Road about 8.5 kilometres from Van Anda (on the left) or 6.2 kilometres from the intersection of Shelter Point Road if you're coming from the southeast. Park about 800 metres along this logging road, where a rough road goes off to the right. The hike starts here. |

The trail follows an old logging road for most of the way. While the surrounding forest is fairly young, there are many rocky outcrops along the left side as you climb and some mossy areas on the right. You'll pass large patches of evergreen huckleberry, many different varieties of fern, and both white and jack pine.

Continue straight on the road for about 40 minutes until it begins to descend. At this point look for a trail to the left. Red metal squares on the trees mark the trail, which becomes increasingly steep as you approach the site of the first forestry lookout in BC. The views from here are spectacular. On a clear day you will see as far as Savary Island to the north and Hornby and Denman islands to the west. This lookout is not the true summit of Mount Pocahontas; the summit lies to the south, with its six radio towers and thick forest cover limiting the views.

To visit another nearby viewpoint with an excellent outlook to the south and east, return to the main road and continue along it as it descends from the junction. Take the very next side road on the left and, after about 10 minutes, take the first turn on the right. This rough track leads up to the start of a short flagged trail on the left just as the track starts downhill. A less-than-5-minute climb brings you out on a grassy ridge high above Malaspina Strait.

## 5. GILLIES BAY TRAILS ★★

| | |
|---|---|
| Trail length | 5–10 kilometres, depending on route taken |
| Time required | 1–2 hours, depending on route taken |
| Description | Trails on old forestry roads through mixed forest |
| Level | Easy |
| Access | Take the section of School Road opposite the Gillies Bay grocery store and park at the field. Follow the logging road until you see a sign for Texada Island Forest Reserve. |
| Cautions | As this hike is on private land, first obtain permission to hike by calling Texada Island Forest Reserve (604-486-7772). The company accepts no liability should any mishap occur. |

This network of logging roads criss-crosses an area of second-growth alder and fir. There are some low, wet areas. Most of the roads go nowhere in particular but one leads to a bluff with a good picnic spot and a view over Gillies Bay. Another road leads to a beaver-dammed lake that contains painted turtles, while School Road (really just an old logging road, most of the way) is a 5-kilometre walk to Central Road, due east of Gillies Bay.

*This photo of "downtown" Gillies Bay provides some idea of how little Texada's ambience has changed over the years.* Craig Carpenter

## 6. SHELTER POINT NATURE TRAIL ★★★

| | |
|---|---|
| Trail length | 1 kilometre each way, plus additional forest trails |
| Time required | 30 minutes each way, plus 45 minutes if you try all the forest trails |
| Description | A very pretty hike through old-growth forest and along the ocean |
| Level | Easy |
| Access | The south side of Shelter Point Road at the entrance to the park |

This delightful hike on a well-manicured trail follows a bank along the water. The forest is fairly open, with some lovely old-growth trees and frequent glimpses along the trail of the ocean and the beach below. You will find several accesses to the beach, some of which are rather steep. There are also some fine benches to sit on and enjoy the view.

*The view looking northeast from Black Mountain toward Jervis Inlet and the mainland mountains.* John Dove

The trail loops to the left at the Ponderosa (a spot on the beach where a road access comes in on the left). At this point you can choose to continue by the trail (which is still flat, although slightly rougher than the first section), return by the beach (if it's low tide), or take the road until it crosses Davie Bay Road, where you turn left to return to your starting point. If you follow the beach and the tide is out, look for the low stone walls of the old aboriginal fish traps, which can be clearly seen at the south end of the hike.

Several forest trails join the nature trail here and there. If you decide to hike these too, you will add about another 1.5 kilometres to your outing.

## 7. BLACK MOUNTAIN ★★★

| | |
|---|---|
| Trail length | 4 kilometres |
| Time required | 90 minutes |
| Description | A trail through mixed forest to a fine viewpoint |
| Level | Moderate; some steep sections |
| Elevation | 545 metres; elevation gain 165 metres |
| Access | The trailhead is 3 kilometres from the junction of Bell Road and Hydro East. Heading south, take the turnoff on your left to Hydro East and almost immediately turn left (north) again at an unsigned road. The trailhead is farther along this road on the right and is marked with a cairn. |
| Cautions | This piece of Crown land has been tagged for logging, and although the trail will still be possible because it is outside of the cutting area, much of the forest may be gone and the road rebuilt by the time you arrive. |

Walk along the logging road for about 10 minutes until you see a cairn on your left. (At time of writing there were also four trees in a tight row there.) Follow the red flagging through the Crown land up the south flank of the hill heading mainly to the east. You will pass a lovely stand of white pine and some hairy manzanita before reaching viewpoints. Two have views to the south, but the last viewpoint on the trail has the most expansive view to the north—of Nelson and Hardy islands and to the southeast as far as Mount

*Texada Trekkers like to boast that they hike 52 weeks of the year, and they do run into snow sometimes even though the hike may have started at a lower elevation where the precipitation was just rain or sleet.* John Dove

Baker in Washington State on the clearest days. If you explore the area, you will find several viewpoints here. When you are through exploring, follow the marked trail back the way you came.

## 8. MOUNT DAVIES ★★★★

| Trail length | 4 kilometres |
|---|---|
| Time required | 2 hours |
| Description | A very enjoyable hike along a diverse trail through old-growth forest to two sensational viewpoints |
| Level | Moderate; some steep sections |
| Elevation | 760 metres; elevation gain 150 metres |

| | |
|---|---|
| Access | From the junction of Shelter Point, Central and Bell roads, take Bell Road south for 9.3 kilometres to a fork and then take the left road toward Bob's Lake. (Do not turn right to the BC Hydro reactor.) From here, drive 1.3 kilometres to a second junction, where you turn right into Texada Forest Service Road 5829 Branch 09, known locally as Cook Bay Road because it leads to Cook Bay. (A sign here directs you to the Anderson Bay Pipeline Route.) Continue for 2 kilometres to the intersection of Texada Forest Service Road 5829 Branch 02 (Thompson Road) and turn right. Drive for another 100 metres and park on the left side of the road. The flagged trailhead (several round boulders and a small cairn) is just a little farther down the same side of the road as the parking area. |

This 35-minute trail to the summit of Mount Davies passes through mixed forest with pine needle and moss ground cover. The well-flagged trail (red surveyor's tape) circles the mountain and provides views at the top. Along the way, you will pass massive moss-covered boulders from which ferns and other plants manage to grow.

About 15–20 minutes along the trail, you will pass a trail on the left (east). This trail passes through old growth, a wet area and a viewpoint on Bloody Mountain (a local name). Try this on your way back. For now continue to the summit.

The top of Mount Davies provides magnificent 360-degree views. To the south is Lasqueti Island and to the west are Hornby and Denman islands. You can even see Chrome Island light station to the south of Denman. To the north are the mainland mountains. You also have good views of the huge expanse of Texada Island in both directions.

It will take you about 15 minutes to descend to the flagged trail to Bloody Mountain, so named because a Texada Trekker once cut a finger here and bled profusely for a few minutes. This trail meanders through lovely old-growth forest and soon reaches a large lily pond where beaver live. After hiking for about 25 minutes, you'll reach another trail (marked with a cairn) that leads to a viewpoint.

The 20-minute (there and back) detour to the viewpoint is well worth the time and effort. It crosses a logged and replanted area before reaching the viewpoint. Here you are looking across Sabine Channel over Jedediah, Paul and Jervis islands to the northeast of Lasqueti Island. You can see Mount Shepherd to the southeast.

Once you return from the viewpoint to the main Bloody Mountain trail, it's only another 5–10 minutes down to the Texada Forest Service Road 5829 Branch 09 (the Cook Bay Road). Turn left (north) on the road and continue to an intersection where you will again turn left (northwest). At a third junction, take the left fork once again, which will put you back on Texada Forest Service Road 5829 Branch 02 (Thompson Road), about 100 metres from where you parked.

## 9. MOUNT GRANT ★★★★

| | |
|---|---|
| Trail length | 4 kilometres |
| Time required | 1.5–2 hours |
| Description | A superb trail with many fine views north and south of Texada Island |
| Level | Moderate; some very steep sections |
| Elevation | 755 metres; elevation gain: 135 metres |
| Access | From the junction of Shelter Point, Central and Bell roads, take Bell Road south for 9.3 kilometres to a junction, then take the left fork toward Bob's Lake. (Do not turn right to the BC Hydro reactor.) Continue 1.6 kilometres (past another turnoff) and park on the grass off the right side of the road (Texada Forest Service Road 5829 Branch 03). Walk back about 60 metres to the flagged trailhead on the right (north side of the road). |

You'll reach a junction about 5 minutes from the trailhead. You can choose to go either way, as this is a loop trail. I recommend turning right and have followed this route in the following description. The climb is more gradual this way, although the descent from the summit is steeper.

The trail up follows a logging road east-southeast around the mountain. Along the way you'll pass white, jack and ponderosa pine. Plants to look for along this trail include juniper, Labrador tea, adder's tongue, grape fern and ground cedar.

After you have walked for about 20 minutes, take a flagged trail heading off to the left (northeast). (At time of writing the logging road was blocked here with tree limbs to indicate that you are not to continue along it.) The new trail, which heads steeply uphill, is well marked with red flagging. You'll soon reach a viewpoint from which you can see Denman and Hornby islands to the west. After another 10 minutes you'll reach another viewpoint providing views of Nelson and Hardy islands and Jervis Inlet to the northeast. This view is even more spectacular from the summit. It took us an hour to reach the top, but we spent time examining some rare plants that are distantly related to ferns.

The trail down from the top is steep. Its descent begins in a southwesterly direction. Soon you will reach a cairn, indicating a change of direction to the north. This trail is well flagged. Shortly after this, you will see a side trail to the right. It's a short detour to a spectacular viewpoint atop a rocky outcrop. The rest of the return trail descends steeply, and you can easily return to the starting point in about 40 minutes.

## 10. TWIN PEAKS ★★★

| | |
|---|---|
| Trail length | 3 kilometres |
| Time required | 60 minutes |
| Description | A steep trail with many fine views north and south of Texada Island |
| Level | Moderate; some very steep sections |
| Elevation | 786 metres; elevation gain 205 metres |
| Access | From the junction of Shelter Point, Central and Bell roads (7.2 kilometres from the Gillies Bay ballpark), turn right on Bell Road and continue south for 9.3 kilometres to another junction and take the left fork toward Bob's Lake and Anderson Bay. (Do not turn right to the BC Hydro reactor.) Turn left at the next two junctions, continuing to follow the signs for Anderson Bay. The Twin Peaks trail access is at a road junction 17.4 kilometres from the first junction mentioned above, on the gas pipeline's forest road. |

Walk to your right (south) along the pipeline road for about 15 minutes until you see a cairn on your left. This is the beginning of the trail, which initially passes through open ponderosa pine forest. The trail marked by red ribbons soon begins its steep climb. After about 30 minutes of climbing, you'll see a cairn on your left indicating the side trail leading to the north peak. It will take you about 15 minutes to get to it and then to return to the main trail. This viewpoint is lower than the south peak (776 metres), but offers wide-angle views of Hornby, Denman and Lasqueti islands.

Once you have regained the main trail, continue on to the south peak, where you'll be rewarded by views both north to the Sunshine Coast and Nelson Island and south to Jedediah, Jervis, and Lasqueti islands. Return the way you came.

# SHORE AND ROAD WALKS

*John Dove—trail maker, trailblazer, guide and naturalist—is responsible for creating many of the island's trails.*
Craig Carpenter

**Erickson Beach:** There is a very short beach walk along Erickson Beach to the east of the government dock in Van Anda.

**Sanderson Trail:** This trail along the Gillies Bay shore parallels Sanderson Road and runs from the RCMP station on Gillies Bay Road to Balsam Avenue (off Sanderson Road). You can access the trail from several of the beach accesses off Sanderson Road (opposite Balsam Avenue, Ash Street or Oak Street) or from the access beside the RCMP station. The trail weaves in and out along the shoreline in front of houses and passes through blackberry bushes that drip with the luscious fruit in August. You might consider walking one way along the trail and then returning along the road. The trail provides sweeping views of the large bay.

*Wetland near Twin Peaks.*

**Shelter Point Regional Park beach access:** This beach is a lovely place to walk at low tide.

**South of Davie Bay:** Unfortunately the wonderful beaches and islands of Davie Bay are now accessible only by water. However, you can park at the hydro station south of Davie Bay and walk on the beach for some distance to the south to reach the mouth of Stromberg Creek. Here there is a rustic footbridge, a small waterfall and pool, and a tiny beach. The road can be used to circle back to the hydro station. If you walk south for about 3 kilometres on the forest road just above the hydro station, you'll reach the quiet unattended campground at Shingle Beach. Facilities here include picnic tables, piped water and toilets.

## AND IF YOU PADDLE . . .

Texada's position in the middle of the Strait of Georgia means that it is more exposed than most of the islands described in this book. Waves and wind can build up in the strait and create dangerous conditions on both sides of

*Seals bask on the rocks near Favada Point on Texada Island.*

Texada. Sabine Channel has quite strong currents that create steep seas. This, combined with Texada's few bays and inhospitable shores, makes paddling here more difficult—and dangerous—than on many other Gulf Islands. I recommend that only experienced paddlers, or paddlers in the company of a guide, use the launches described below. I have not launched from any of these accesses, although I have kayaked to the southwestern shore of Texada from Jedediah Island (about a 20–30-minute paddle).

**Van Anda:** You can launch from the government dock in Van Anda or from the Texada Boating Club's ramp or docks in Sturt Bay to explore Texada's northeastern shore.

**Raven Bay:** This is another launch site for visiting Texada's northeastern shore.

**Pocahontas Bay:** From here you can explore Texada's eastern shore.

**Sanderson Road:** There are beach accesses opposite most of the side roads that intersect Sanderson Road. While they give you access to Gillies Bay, the bay dries out at low tide, thus limiting the time when you can use these accesses.

**Shelter Point Regional Park:** This is a good place to launch and will allow you to explore the Texada shore both to the north and south.

**Hydro West:** This is a good place to launch but there is limited parking. If you paddle northwest to Davie Bay, there are several islets to visit along the way.

**Shingle Beach:** You can launch from the beach at this forestry site. It will give you access to the south Texada shoreline, as well as the opportunity to paddle north to Davie Bay.

**Anderson Bay:** This is an excellent place to launch and to camp, but you need a four-wheel-drive vehicle to reach this part of the island. Much of Anderson Bay is provincial park.

**Big Beach:** This combination paddle and moderate-to-steep hike, suggested by John and Susan Wood, is for the adventuresome who also have a long, full day to spend doing it. Paddle about 7.6 nautical miles (14 kilometres) from the Shelter Point boat launch to Big Beach, a sloping gravel crescent beach 60 metres wide facing west-northwest (49° 43' 43" N, 124° 37' 24" W). After admiring the rare giant chain fern at the north end of Big Beach, follow the orange ribbons up the steep cliff and inland for about 10 minutes to reach a junction with a loop trail. Turn left and follow the coastal trail. After about 45 minutes you will be on the cliffs overlooking Cabin Cove. Follow the trail down to the beach, and after another 20 minutes turn right onto the old logging road to return to where you started. About 20 minutes along, watch for a side trail on the left leading uphill to a dramatic viewpoint. A steep ravine provides access to high open bluffs of arbutus and juniper with a view over the expanse of ancient forest and across to Hornby and Denman islands and the mountains of Vancouver Island. Shortly after leaving the viewpoint side trail, turn right off the old logging road onto a well-marked path to complete the loop.

# Thetis

*T*hetis is the smallest island accessed by ferry that is discussed in this book and, except for about 14 kilometres of public road and 19 kilometres of shoreline, everything on Thetis is private. Most of its 10.4 square kilometres are forested, with some farmland, meadows and wetlands. While several large landowners have kept much of the island from being developed, new lots have been created by a recent strata development near the centre of the island. However, the community plan requirement that new lots be a minimum of 4 hectares in size will limit the number of new lots that can be created in the future.

Although serviced by a ferry, many visitors to Thetis are boaters who spend much of their time in and around the two popular marinas in Telegraph Harbour, where most of the island's services are found. Those who venture inland find a small, tranquil island that has changed little over the decades.

*A view of Capernwray Harbour Bible Centre from the beach at Preedy Harbour, Thetis Island.* Veronica Shelford

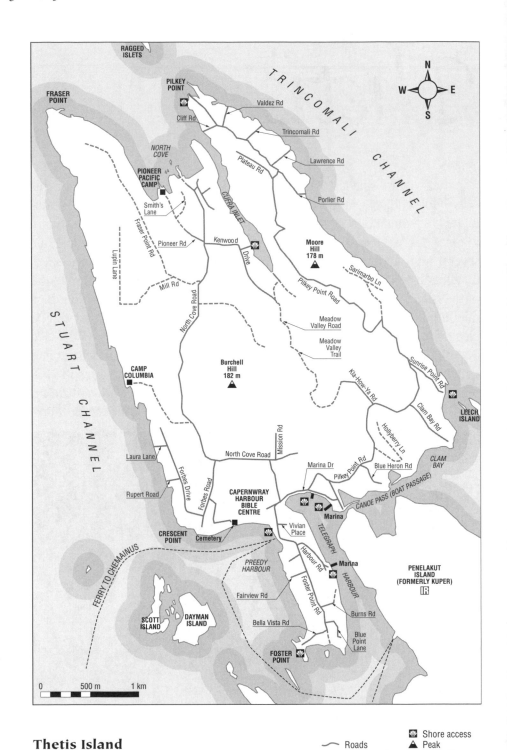

**Thetis Island**

Roads
Private roads

Shore access
Peak
Indian Reserve

Like other Gulf Islands, Thetis has attracted a wide variety of strong-minded, independent individuals, including writers, craftspeople and recluses of all stripes. The permanent population of about 370 swells in summer months with the seasonal residents who own cottages here. While hiking is curtailed by private property on Thetis, its serene roads are delightful to explore on foot or by bicycle.

## HISTORY

Thetis Island was named after the British frigate H.M. *Thetis*, which operated in the Gulf Islands under Captain Augustus I. Kuper between 1851 and 1853. Thetis and Kuper (now Penelakut) Island were once divided only by tidal flats. A channel was dredged between them to allow boats passage. This channel, now known as Canoe Pass, was originally about 2 metres deep at low tide but has since silted in and become much shallower.

Almost all of Thetis's early European settlers were from Great Britain, including its first resident, William Henry Curran, an Irishman who felled trees and sold them to the Chemainus sawmill in the 1870s. Two pioneering families—the Hunters and the Burchells—arrived in the early 1890s and soon owned almost all the island between them. The Hunters eventually donated land to the Intervarsity Christian Fellowship, which now operates the Pioneer Pacific summer camp here. The Burchells ran a successful store and farm, where the Capernwray Harbour Bible Centre now stands. In 1904 Alfred Heneage and his sister Eveline Mary bought land on Thetis. Eveline grew lavender crops, which she distilled into perfume, and Alfred grew a fine vegetable garden. In keeping with island tradition, Alfred left the land to the Anglican Church, and it became Camp Columbia, another summer camp for children. Rupert Forbes arrived with his family in 1905. He built small boats, which were admired for their workmanship and lovely lines. Today the Forbes home—Overbury Farm Resort—is still in the family. Thetis grew slowly and by 1914 had a population of only 70, most of whom supported themselves by growing vegetables for the Chemainus market.

## GETTING THERE

There are 12 daily ferry crossings between Thetis Island and Chemainus on Vancouver Island; the voyage takes between 30 and 50 minutes depending on whether it goes via Penelakut Island as well. For more information obtain a BC Ferries schedule or contact BC Ferries. Seair Seaplanes and Tofino Air fly to Thetis from the Vancouver airport (see page 320).

## SERVICES AND ACCOMMODATION

Limited groceries can be purchased at the two marinas in Telegraph Harbour and the Howling Wolf Farm Market. The Telegraph Harbour Marina also has a café/restaurant and gift shop, while the Thetis Island Marina has a restaurant, pub, post office and laundromat. There are several bed and breakfasts, cabins for rent, and a small resort, but no public campground on Thetis. Accommodation is listed on the community website at www.thetisisland.net. Note that in the summer there is often a water shortage on Thetis.

## SHORE AND ROAD WALKS on THETIS

Thetis has no Crown land or public parks, and therefore no public hiking trails. However, the roads are pretty and have little vehicle traffic, making Thetis a pleasant place to spend a day walking or cycling. Perhaps the best shore walk is just north of the ferry dock. You can walk along Thetis's western shore from here for some distance at low tide.

Residents walk, with permission, on their neighbours' land, but these trails are not available to the general public. If you want to follow a trail to the island's interior or to access the shore, you must first ask the property owner's permission.

*A view of Pilkey Point, Thetis Island.* Carol Sowerby

Most of the walking is along either Pilkey Point Road or North Cove Road. If you walk up the hill from the ferry, you'll have the choice of turning right (east) along Pilkey Point Road or left (north) up North Cove Road.

**Pilkey Point Road (7 kilometres one way):** Before turning onto Pilkey Point Road, stop and enjoy the view down over Capernwray Harbour Bible Centre and the ferry dock. Take Pilkey Point Road east, skirting the head of Telegraph Harbour. Take a small detour by turning right down Marina Drive to the attractively landscaped grounds of the Telegraph Harbour Marina (about a 10-minute walk from the ferry).

Continuing along Pilkey Point Road, you'll pass a few farms, some boggy areas and stands of trees. Be prepared for a stiff climb as the road goes up Moore Hill, which provides some glimpses of the sea and the mountains on Vancouver Island. It will take you about 90 minutes to reach the end of Pilkey Point Road, where you'll find a public beach access. Pilkey Point is a popular place for residents to come on summer nights to picnic, swim and watch the sun set.

**North Cove Road (3.5 kilometres one way):** A few minutes walk from the ferry terminal, North Cove Road passes the Community Hall and the Thetis Island Elementary School (to the right). A little farther on you can make a

*Moore Hill, toward the northeastern end of Thetis Island, is the second-highest point on Thetis. Unfortunately for hikers, it is private land and you have to obtain permission from the landowners to use the trails here.* Veronica Shelford

worthwhile detour to the left onto Forbes Road and continue to St. Margaret's Lane (left again) and Thetis Island's historic St. Margaret's Cemetery. This pretty little graveyard, about 2.5 kilometres from the ferry terminal, contains the graves of many of the island's pioneers.

North Cove Road continues past Forbes Road about 3 kilometres to North Cove (where there is no public beach access). If you turn off North Cove Road onto Kenwood, you'll reach narrow Cufra Inlet, which stretches over 1 kilometre toward the centre of the island. Commercial clam beds and soft ground make it hard to walk along the inlet's banks, and the unwelcoming shoreline, with little human habitation, does not invite exploration.

**Foster Point (2 kilometres one way):** From the ferry it's possible to walk south along Foster Point Road for about 2 kilometres. At the end of the road (where it turns off into Buena Vista), you'll find a somewhat overgrown path that provides public access to Foster Point itself. From here you have good views south to tiny Hudson Island, east to Penelakut Island and west to Vancouver Island.

## AND IF YOU PADDLE . . .

If you wanted to circumnavigate Thetis Island, you'd be looking at about 11 nautical miles (18 kilometres), a good day's outing, including a stop or two for lunch and tea. Nearby Penelakut and Tent islands belong to the Penelakut First Nation.

There are only a few places to put in on Thetis since so much of the island is private. Here are a few suggestions:

**Preedy Harbour:** Try the beach or the public dock just south of where the ferry lands. This gives you access to Thetis's western shore and the cluster of small, but pretty islands just offshore. You can also paddle south and view the stunning sandstone sculpture on nearby Penelakut and Tent islands, and a little farther to the east, Valdes Island, much of which is owned by the Lyackson First Nation (three reserves).

**Telegraph Harbour:** You can launch from the public boat ramp (on the right just as you turn down Marina Drive) or, with permission, from one of the marinas in Telegraph Harbour. There's a small beach to the north of the Thetis Island Marina's store, which is very convenient. From here you can explore Telegraph Harbour and exit either by narrow Canoe Pass at its northern end or from the open end to the south. The former gives you access to Thetis's northern end, as well as Penelakut Spit on Penelakut Island and the cluster of privately owned islands north of Penelakut. The latter gives you access to the Penelakut Island shoreline and Thetis's western shore. Note that while Canoe Pass can be very shallow at low tides, it only dries completely at the lowest tides.

**Sunrise Point Road (east shore) and Pilkey Point (northeast shore):** I don't recommend these beach accesses mainly because the previous accesses are so handy. Sunrise Point gets you on Thetis's eastern shore, and Pilkey Point puts you on the north shore with possibilities of exploring, at high tide, some of shallow Cufra Inlet, which cuts into the island for some distance.

*Approaching Telegraph Harbour from the south, Penelakut Island is on the right and Thetis on the left.* Carol Sowerby

# Marine Parks

*M*arine parks provide recreational opportunities for boaters throughout the year. Most of them also provide safe overnight anchorages, camping, picnic tables, fresh water and outhouses. They don't usually have extensive trail networks, although most of them have some trails, often along beautiful shoreline.

The marine parks described in this chapter are administered by either BC Parks or Parks Canada as part of Gulf Islands National Park Reserve (GINPR). The areas described in this chapter are accessible only by private boat or passenger ferry. Marine parks on or near islands discussed elsewhere in this book are described in the chapters devoted to those islands. For example, Tumbo Island (GINPR) is discussed in the chapter on Saturna Island.

The provincial marine parks and the islands that are part of GINPR are all on small islands, have at least 3–4 kilometres of trails and can be reached by either a private passenger ferry or a relatively short paddle. Parks that are more interesting as destinations for experienced paddlers than they are for hikers are not described here. BC Parks includes more detailed information about its marine parks on its website, www.env.gov.bc.ca/bcparks. Information on areas of GINPR can be found on the Parks Canada website, www. parkscanada.gc.ca/gulf.

The following rules should be observed in all marine parks:

- All wildlife and cultural heritage is protected and should be left undisturbed.
- There are no disposal facilities; take out all your garbage.
- Where mooring buoys are provided, no more than one boat should be moored to a buoy; rafting of boats is not allowed.

*Marine parks are idyllic places to camp and enjoy the best of the Gulf Islands, including spectacular sunrises and sunsets.*

- Fresh water is not always available, so bring your own.
- Cutting trees is not allowed.
- In provincial marine parks where no camping facilities are provided, onshore camping is sometimes permitted (check the services available for the park you're going to); in GINPR camping is allowcd only in designated campsites.
- Campfires, including hibachis and propane campfires, are not allowed in GINPR (except in Prior Centennial Campground on Pender Island and McDonald Campground on Vancouver Island). In other parks where campfires are allowed, follow the usual precautions. Fires are permitted only in designated fire rings, as these islands receive little rain and are very dry. At times open fires may not be allowed on any of the islands. Watch for campfire bans posted by the Ministry of Forests.
- Quiet hours are from 10 p.m. to 8 a.m. Excessive noise is not permitted at any time.
- Boats are prohibited from discharging sewage or grey water while travelling through or while moored or anchored in marine parks.
- Dogs may not be permitted in some areas; check first. When they are permitted, they must be leashed to protect wildlife, sensitive plants and other visitors. You must also clean up after them.

*Marine parks are wonderful places to kayak. The kayak allows you to see some of the fantastic rock formations and driftwood sculptures that you cannot see from the trails.*

- The consumption of alcohol is permitted only in your campsite.
- Firearms are prohibited.
- Barbecues can be used only on the ground, unless a barbecue attachment is provided on the picnic table.

## 1. JEDEDIAH ISLAND MARINE PROVINCIAL PARK ★★★★

Jedediah Island lies in Sabine Channel between Lasqueti and Texada islands, and is accessible only by private boat. It is a popular destination for kayakers, who often reach it from either Lasqueti Island or Schooner Cove on Vancouver Island, where private boat operators offer kayak ferry service to the island.

Jedediah Island is named after the son of Lord Tucker of England, who sponsored a survey expedition of the Gulf Islands in the late 19th century. The island had only a handful of owners before Evan and Mary Mattice of Seattle, Washington, purchased it in 1949. In 1972 Mary and her second husband, Albert Palmer, retired to the island and lived there until they put it up for sale in 1990. The BC government bought it in 1995 with the help of many private donors, several environmental organizations and $1.1 million from the estate of the late Daniel Culver, a mountaineer from North Vancouver who died on his descent from the summit of K2.

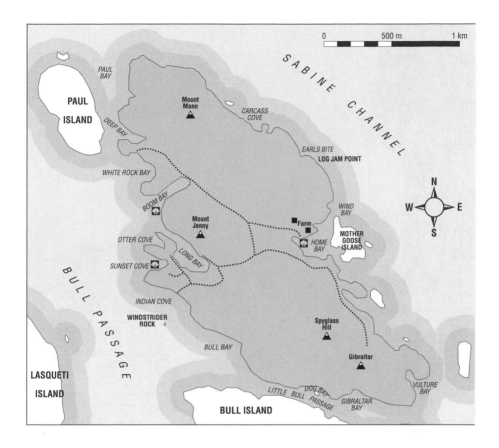

## Jedediah Island Marine Provincial Park

······· Trails
🔰 Shore access
▲ Peak

One of the largest island parks in the province (243 hectares), Jedediah contains mature Douglas-fir and arbutus and rocky outcrops. The island's homesites, farm fields and orchards are still evident, and feral sheep and goats live on the island.

Several good camping areas can be found near the shoreline around Long Bay and in the small bays on the east side of the island.

## HIKING/WALKING TRAILS

The 3.5 kilometres of walking trails cross the island and connect Jedediah's many bays. The main trail passes through old-growth forest to an open field, linking up with several other trails. Animal trails meander through open forest and reach the island's peaks.

*Home Bay, Jedediah Island. This house was built by a Mr. Foote of Vancouver, who purchased the island soon after it was Crown-granted in 1885. The house was occupied until 1990, most recently by the last owner, Mary Palmer, who bought the island with her first husband in 1949.* Craig Carpenter

## 2. NEWCASTLE ISLAND MARINE PROVINCIAL PARK ★★★★

Newcastle Island in Nanaimo Harbour is 336 hectares in size. From May to September you can reach it by a 10-minute foot-passenger ferry from Maffeo–Sutton Park, just north of downtown Nanaimo (behind the Civic Arena) on Highway 1. The ferry runs between about 10 a.m. and 5 p.m., with additional later sailings in the high season. At time of writing the Nanaimo Harbour Ferry (1-877-297-8526; www.nanaimoharbourferry.com) operated the service. Outside of summer months you can take a water taxi to the island. Private boats can anchor in Mark Bay or tie up at the wharf, where there are berthing facilities for more than 50 boats.

Middens remain from the residents of two Salish villages, which were deserted by the time coal was discovered here in 1849. Newcastle Island shares a name with the famous northern English coal town, and for 30 years coal was mined here. Sandstone quarried on the island between 1869 and 1932 was used in buildings such as the San Francisco mint and for pulpstones used in paper mills. From about 1910 to 1941 Newcastle was home to a small settlement of Japanese who operated a herring saltery, cannery and shipyard.

In 1931 the Canadian Pacific Steamship Company acquired the island and built a dance pavilion, tea house, picnic areas, soccer field and wading pool. The company successfully competed with the Union Steamship Company's similar operation on Bowen Island by bringing pleasure-seekers on one-day outings from Vancouver. Until World War II, Vancouvcrites regularly flocked to the island on Sunday outings and company picnics. In 1955 the island bccame the property of the City of Nanaimo, and in 1961 it was established as a provincial marine park.

Newcastle Island is one of BC's most developed marine parks. The dance pavilion has been restored and is now a visitor centre, complete with displays and a restaurant. There are individual and group campsites, picnic facilities, washrooms with coin-operated showers, pit toilets, picnic and barbecue shelters, an adventure playground, soccer field, swimming areas and about 20 kilometres of well-developed trails. The park also contains food lockers for campers to protect food from the marauding bands of raccoons that live on the island. In 2010 BC Parks began a program of rebuilding some of thc island's damaged or dangerous infrastructure, so some sections of the park might be closed when you visit. Check the BC Parks website or www. newcastleisland.ca for up-to-date information.

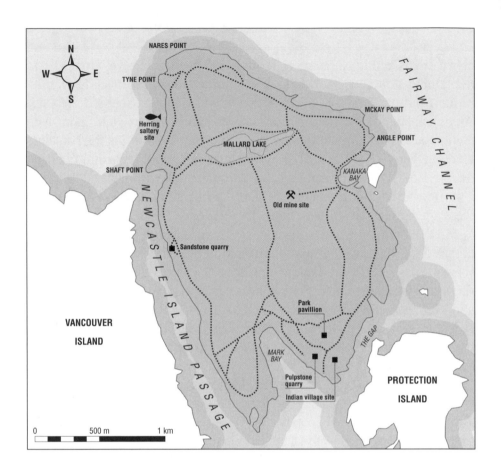

**Newcastle Island Marine Provincial Park**

········· Trails

## HIKING/WALKING TRAILS

You can walk all around and through the centre of the island on 22 kilometres of trails. Along the way you will pass sandstone cliffs, sandy gravel beaches, middens, the remains of Newcastle's industrial past and even a small lake. The caves and caverns along the shoreline were reputedly used for burials by the Coast Salish. From Newcastle you have many fine views of the mainland mountains and of Vancouver Island. Among the animal life are blacktail deer, otters, rabbits, raccoons and squirrels, as well as muskrats and beaver on Mallard Lake. The forest contains Garry oak, dogwood, arbutus and Douglas-fir.

*Newcastle Island is a microcosm of Gulf Islands history, having been the site of a centuries-old Salish village, a coal mine and a sandstone quarry from 1869 to 1932, and a pleasure resort from 1931 to 1955, when as many as 1,500 people at a time came from Vancouver to picnic and party.* Mark Kaaremaa

## 3. Pirates Cove Marine Provincial Park ★★★★

Pirates Cove on De Courcy Island is about 16 kilometres southeast of Nanaimo. Only 38 hectares on the southeast tip of the island are in the park; the rest of the island is privately owned.

De Courcy Island has a mystique because of its association with Edward Arthur Wilson, a cult leader known as Brother XII. Despite being the subject of several books, the details of Wilson's life are sketchy and will probably never be completely known. It's generally agreed that after extensive travels he came to British Columbia from England in 1927 as the leader of a theosophist cult called the Aquarian Foundation. Fuelled by the donations of his followers, Brother XII built a commune first in Cedar, south of Nanaimo, and then on De Courcy and Valdes islands. In time he began to psychologically and physically abuse his followers. They in turn took him to court to recover their financial contributions. The resulting lawsuits and counter-lawsuits made headlines in the Nanaimo newspapers. In the end Brother XII disappeared mysteriously with Madame Zee, his female partner. His legendary hoard of gold also disappeared.

In addition to the usual coastal plants, Pirates Cove contains Rocky Mountain juniper, satinflower and poison oak (you'll want to avoid this

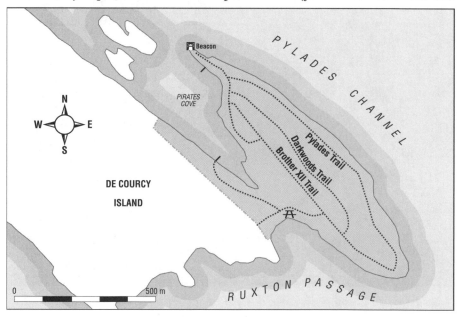

**Pirates Cove Marine Provincial Park**

one, so stay on the trails). Pipsissewa, a low-growing evergreen plant with pink flowers and leathery, shiny leaves, is abundant on the park's east side in June and early July. Among the park's animal inhabitants are blacktail deer, river otters, mink and raccoons. Offshore, look for harbour seals, Steller and California sea lions, porpoises and killer whales. Wilson's warblers, Pacific-slope flycatchers, black oystercatchers, white-crowned sparrows, bald eagles and great blue herons are among the birds most frequently sighted on the island.

## HIKING/WALKING TRAILS

There are about 5 kilometres of trails in Pirates Cove. The Pylades Trail (3 kilometres), along the cliff above the eastern shore of the island, provides good views of Pylades Channel and the sandstone rocks on Valdes Island

*Pirates Cove, De Courcy Island. The natural shelter of this well-protected little harbour probably led to its name and definitely accounts for its popularity with boaters. The hiking trails follow the shoreline of the cove and continue along Pylades Channel, circumnavigating the park.* Mark Kaaremaa

to the east. It ends at the tip of the rocky peninsula at the entrance to the cove. From here you can return by either the Darkwoods Trail (1 kilometre) through the centre of the park or the Brother XII Trail (800 metres) that follows the eastern shore of the cove. At the beginning of these return trails you will find excellent views of both the cove and the boats that frequent this popular anchorage. All the trails are well established and easy to follow.

A short, unnamed trail leads from the beach on the south side of the park to camping spots and picnic tables along the western edge of the park. You'll find a freshwater pump and outhouses in the camping area.

## 4. PRINCESS MARGARET (PORTLAND ISLAND), GINPR ★★★★

Princess Margaret is south of Salt Spring Island, west of Moresby Island and about 3 kilometres north of the Saanich Peninsula. It can be reached by private boat, water taxi or a 45-minute paddle from one of the launch sites near Sidney, or from launch sites on Salt Spring Island.

The 575-hectare island was used by First Nations people for many years, and evidence of their use remains. In the mid-1800s the Hudson's Bay Company contracted up to 400 Hawaiian workers (known as Kanakas) to work in the company's fur and timber businesses and some of these people settled on the island. They stayed until 1907 and are remembered by such place names as Kanaka Bluff and Pellow Islets (to the east of Princess Margaret). A remnant orchard exists at Princess Bay.

The island had several owners over the years, one of the most memorable being Frank A. Sutton, a one-armed ex-soldier, who bought the island in 1928 to raise horses. Sutton constructed a large stable, planted an orchard and planned to build a hotel, a golf course and 30 summer cottages. However, he had to give up the island the following year when the stock market crashed, taking his money with it. In 1957 Portland Island became the property of the province, and it was gifted to Princess Margaret when she visited BC the next year. She was good enough to return it to the province in 1967, when it became a park named in her honour. In 2003 it became part of GINPR.

There are many small islands around Portland. Brackman Island to the southwest, also part of GINPR, is a Special Preservation Area and is accessible only with prior written permission from Parks Canada (see page 320). The other neighbouring islands are privately owned.

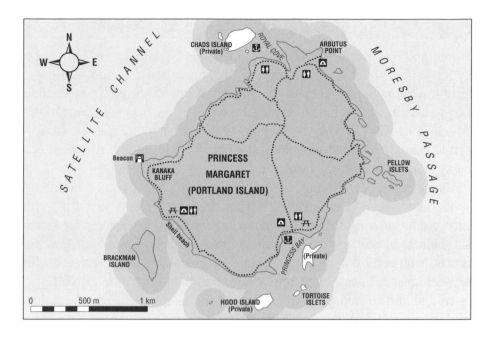

**Princess Margaret (Portland Island)**

.......  Trails     🔺 Camping
🛥 Moorage     🚩 Lighthouse
🚻 Washrooms     🪑 Picnic site

There are two anchorages off Portland, one in Royal Cove and the other in Princess Bay. (A trail connects them.) Camping is allowed in the open field at Princess Bay, on Shell Beach and at Arbutus Point. Outhouses and picnic tables are available at camping areas. No fires are permitted at Princess Margaret.

## HIKING/WALKING TRAILS

About 10 kilometres of hiking trails (four separate trails) run along the circumference of the island and cross north-south and east-west as well. You will see the fruit trees that have survived from when people lived here. You may also find Rocky Mountain juniper and yellow-flowering cactus on rocky outcrops, as well as arbutus and Garry oak trees south of Princess Bay. The island's growth is still sparse in places as a result of feral sheep (removed in the 1980s) and the large population of indigenous blacktail deer (which remain). You will also pass a beautiful shoreline, including Royal Cove, where you may see mink, river otters and such shore birds as oystercatchers, great blue herons and glaucous-winged gulls. Bald eagles and turkey vultures are commonly spotted in the sky, along with the occasional red-tailed hawk.

## 5. SIDNEY SPIT (SIDNEY ISLAND), GINPR ★★★★

Sidney Spit is at the northern end of Sidney Island, 5 kilometres (25 minutes by ferry) from the town of Sidney on Vancouver Island. A foot-passenger ferry leaves the Sidney dock at the bottom of Beacon Street from Victoria Day to Labour Day. At time of writing it was run by the Alpine Group (1-800-647-9933 or 250-474-5145; www.alpinegroup.ca/companies/alpine-sidney-spit-ferry.html). You can also reach the park by private boat (the park has many mooring buoys) or by water taxi.

Called Sallas Island by officers of the Hudson's Bay Company in about 1850, Sidney Island was renamed by Captain George Henry Richards, who surveyed the area in 1859. A year later when the island was offered for sale at six shillings an acre, few people wanted to buy. Today most of Sidney Island is private property, but the northern third—approximately 400 hectares, with an additional 223 hectares of foreshore/marine area—is part of GINPR.

In addition to hiking there are opportunities for excellent swimming, birdwatching and camping on Sidney Spit. Bring your own drinking water as the water provided, while drinkable, can be very salty.

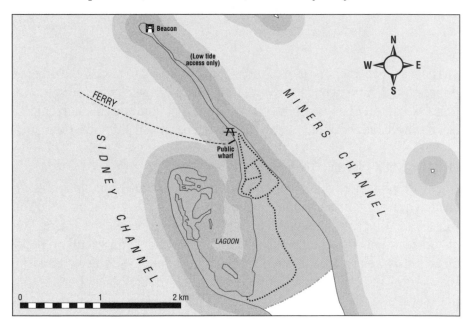

**Sidney Spit**

*Sidney Spit is a long sandy finger of land extending far into the sea.* Parks Canada

## HIKING/WALKING TRAILS

Several hiking trail loops exist. One leads south to the campsites and the site of the Sidney Island Brick and Tile Company, which functioned in the early 1900s and employed about 70 men. There is a viewing and interpretive sign platform off this trail by the Sidney Lagoon, a popular birdwatching area especially in the spring. You can also explore the more than 20 kilometres of Sidney Spit's sandy beaches, although you are requested to stay on the beach and intertidal areas and off the vegetated portions of the spit, which are Special Preservation Areas. It will take you about two hours to walk from the dock to the beacon at the end of the long spit and back.

## 6. WALLACE ISLAND MARINE PROVINCIAL PARK ★★★

Wallace Island is located in Trincomali Channel, midway between Galiano and Salt Spring islands (about a 20-minute paddle from either). You can get here by private boat or water taxi from Salt Spring. The park covers 72 hectares.

Jeremiah Chivers, a Scot, lived on Wallace by himself from 1889 to 1927, when he died at the age of 92. He planted a garden and orchard, bits of which are still visible. In 1946 Americans Jeanne and David Conover bought the island, built a home and, ultimately, a small resort. Some of the resort's cottages and the Conover home can still be seen on the island. Conover sold the island in 1966 but it did not become a park until 1990. There are still a couple of private cottages and a small piece of private property on the east side of Princess Cove; the privacy of these property owners should be respected.

Wallace Island is a great place to visit in the off-season, especially in the spring when the island is covered with wildflowers, the bald eagles are nesting and there are plenty of harbour seals on the rocky islets to the west. You may also see blacktail deer, river otters and mink. Steller and California sea lions are sometimes sighted in the winter.

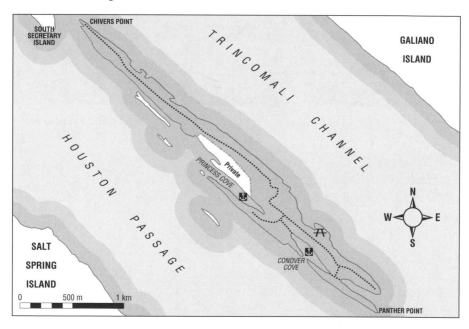

## Wallace Island Marine Provincial Park

⋯ Trails     🚢 Moorage
⋯ Park boundary     🛉 Picnic site

*David Conover's recreation centre with the constantly expanding collection of boat names carved on driftwood by visiting mariners.*

The park is a very popular destination for boaters, especially in the summer months. There are protected anchorages in both Conover Cove and Princess Cove. (Conover Cove also has a small dock.) There is camping on the island, picnic tables, outhouses, a picnic shelter and fresh water, which must be boiled before drinking. Fires are not permitted on the island.

## HIKING/WALKING TRAILS

There are several trails here. The 4-kilometre main trail runs down the centre of the island from Panther Point (named after a ship that went aground here in 1874) in the southeast to Chivers Point in the northwest. It passes through lovely woods and provides access to Conover Cove and the public side of Princess Cove on the way. Side trails lead to some of the many beautiful, sheltered coves around the island. Among the many excellent spots for picnics, Chivers Point is perhaps the loveliest. The main trail passes by the remnants of David Conover's resort, which make interesting exploring. There have been plans to renovate them for some future park use, but nothing has been done for years. The trail also passes an old garden area, complete with the remains of farm equipment.

*The ever-varied sandstone shoreline contains many treasures like this intricate sculpture.*

# Resources

Information sources change very quickly in today's world. There are increasingly greater amounts of information available on the Internet, including topographic maps and up-to-date hiking information. The resources provided here are merely suggestions of what is and what will be available. So be creative and supplement these suggestions with the latest resources you can find on your own. If you want more information about a specific park or nature reserve, try Googling/searching its name, perhaps followed by the words "Management Plan"; you'll be amazed at the treasure trove of information you'll find.

## BOOKS

Andersen, Doris. *Evergreen Islands: A History of the Islands of the Inside Passage*. Vancouver: Gray's Publishing/Whitecap Books, 1979.

Assu, Henry, with Joy Inglis. *Assu of Cape Mudge: Recollections of a Coastal Indian Chief*. Vancouver: University of British Columbia Press, 1989.

Baron, Nancy, and John Acorn. *Birds of Coastal British Columbia*. Vancouver: Lone Pine Publishing, 1997.

Bovey, Robin, Wayne Campbell, and Bryan Gates. *Birds of Victoria and Vicinity*. Edmonton: Lone Pine Publishing, 1989.

Cannings, Richard, and Sydney Cannings. *British Columbia: A Natural History*. Vancouver: Greystone Books/Douglas & McIntyre, 1996.

Cannings, Richard, Tom Aversa and Hal Opperman. *Birds of Southwestern British Columbia*. Surrey, BC: Heritage House, 2005.

Carrick, Douglas. *The Eagles of Hornby Island: My Tree-top Neighbours*. Surrey, BC: Hancock House, 2008.

Darwin, Betty J., and Patricia J.M. Forbes. *So You Want to Know About Lasqueti Island: A Visitor's Guide to Its Past and Present*. Parksville, BC: Parks West Printing and Stationery, n.d.

Elliott, Marie. *Mayne Island and the Outer Gulf Islands: A History*. Mayne Island, BC: Gulf Islands Press, 1984.

Fladmark, Knut R. *British Columbia Prehistory*. Ottawa: National Museum of Man, National Museums of Canada, 1986.

Fletcher, Olivia. Hammerstone: *A Biography of Hornby Island*. Edmonton: NeWest Press, 2001.

Hamilton, Bea. *Salt Spring Island*. Vancouver: Mitchell Press, 1969.

Hill, Beth, and Ray Hill. *Indian Petroglyphs of the Pacific Northwest*. Saanichton, BC: Hancock House Publishers, 1974.

Howard, Irene. *Bowen Island, 1872–1972*. Bowen Island, BC: Bowen Island Historians, 1973.

Isbister, Winnifred A. *My Ain Folk: Denman Island, 1875–1975*. Courteney, BC: E.W. Bickle, 1976.

Isenor, D.E., E.G. Stephens and D.E. Watson. *Edge of Discovery: A History of the Campbell River District*. Campbell River, BC: Ptarmigan Press, 1989.

Kahn, Charles. *Salt Spring: The Story of an Island*. Madeira Park: Harbour Publishing, 1998.

Kirk, Ruth. *Wisdom of the Elders: Native Traditions on the Northwest Coast*. Vancouver: Douglas and McIntyre/British Columbia Provincial Museum, 1986.

Lewis-Harrison, June. *The People of Gabriola: A History of Our Pioneers*. Gabriola Island, BC: June Lewis-Harrison, 1982.

Ludvigsen, Rolf, and Graham Beard. *West Coast Fossils: A Guide to the Ancient Life of Vancouver Island*. Rev. ed. Madeira Park: Harbour Publishing, 1997.

McCloskey, Erin, and Gregory Kennedy. *British Columbia Nature Guide*. Edmonton: Lone Pine Publishing, 2010.

Murray, Peter. *Homesteads and Snug Harbours: The Gulf Islands*. Ganges, BC: Horsdal and Schubart, 1991.

Palmer, Mary. *Jedediah Days: One Woman's Island Paradise*. Madeira Park, BC: Harbour Publishing, 1998.

Parker, Gill, ed. *Hiking Trails 3: Northern Vancouver Island*. 10th ed. Victoria, BC: Vancouver Island Trails Information Society, 2008.

Pojar, Jim, and Andy MacKinnon, eds. *Plants of Coastal British Columbia*. Edmonton: Lone Pine Publishing, 1994.

Sept, J. Duane. *Common Wildflowers of British Columbia*. Sechelt, BC: Calypso Publishing, 2002.

Sept, J. Duane. *Common Birds of British Columbia*. Sechelt, BC: Calypso Publishing, 2003.

Smith, Elizabeth, and David Gerow. *Hornby Island: The Ebb and Flow*. Campbell River, BC: Ptarmigan Press, 1988.

Snowden, Mary Ann. *Sea Kayak the Gulf Islands*. Vancouver: Rocky Mountain Books, 2010.

Steward, Elizabeth. *Galiano: Houses and People—Looking Back to 1930*. Galiano Island, BC: Elizabeth Steward, 1994.

Taylor, Jeanette, and Ian Douglas. *Exploring Quadra Island: Heritage Sites and Hiking Trails*. Quathiaski Cove, BC: Fernbank Publishing, 2001.

Thompson, Bill. *Texada Island*. Powell River, BC: Powell River Heritage Research Association, 1997.

Walbran, John T. *British Columbia Coast Names: Their Origin and History*. Vancouver: Douglas & McIntyre, 1971.

## MAPS

Road maps for individual islands can usually be obtained from local real estate offices, tourist offices and chambers of commerce. Marine charts are widely available in bookstores and map stores.

A wealth of map information is available on the Internet, including topographic maps. For example, the Capital Regional District (CRD) provides maps with great detail for its area on its very user-friendly website: http://viewer.crdatlas.ca/public. You can also order topographic maps online from the GeoBC Crown Registry and Geographic Base Branch, www.basemaps.gov.bc.ca, and through other non-government websites, although I find some of these websites difficult to navigate.

The following outlets are excellent sources for topographic and recreation maps, marine charts and guidebooks:

- Crown Publications, 563 Superior St., Victoria, BC V8V 9V7; 1-800-663-6105 or 250-387-2432/6409 or 250-356-6778; www.crownpub.bc.ca
- Nanaimo Maps and Charts, 8 Church St., Nanaimo, BC V9R 5H4; 1-800-665-2513 or 250-665-2513
- ITMB (International Travel Maps and Books) Publishing Ltd., 12300 Bridgeport Road, Richmond, BC V6V 1J5; 604-273-1400; www.itmb.com

The following hard-copy maps are a few that I've found useful:

- The National Topographical Series (NTS) (1:50,000), individual topographic maps of the Gulf Islands prepared by Natural Resources Canada. For information, visit http://maps.nrcan.gc.ca/topo_metadata/index_e.php. The maps are available from the three outlets listed above.
- Terrain Resource Information Management (TRIM) maps (1:20,000). These are produced in Integraph Design Format (IGDS) and are available from the outlets listed above.
- *Canadian Topographic Maps, 92B14: Gulf Islands* (1:50,000). Published by ITMB.

## ACCOMMODATION

Information on accommodation is available on the islands' tourist websites, which are referenced in each chapter. You can also obtain some information on accommodation from British Columbia Approved Accommodation, Tourism BC's free, annual booklet, which you can obtain from Travel Info-centres or by calling 1-800-435-5622 (toll free) or 604-435-5622 in the Vancouver area, or by visiting Tourism BC's website, www.hellobc.com.

## SOURCES OF INFORMATION

BC Ferries: 1-888-223-3779; www.bcferries.com.

BC Ministry of Forests, Mines and Lands, PO Box 9525, Station Provincial Government, Victoria, BC V8W 9E2; 1-800-663-7867; www.gov.bc.ca/for/.

BC Parks, 1-800-663-7867; www.env.gov.bc.ca/bcparks.

BC Tourist Information, 1-800-435-5622; www.hellobc.com.

Capital Regional District Parks, 490 Atkins Avenue, Victoria, BC V9B 2Z8; 250-478-3344; www.crd.bc.ca/parks.

Comox Valley Regional District, Parks and Recreation Department, 600 Comox Rd., Courtenay, BC V9N 3P6; 1-800-331-6007 or 250-334-6000; www.comoxvalleyrd.ca.

Fisheries and Oceans Canada, 1-866-431-3474; www.pac.dfo-mpo.gc.ca/psp.

Gulf Islands National Park Reserve (GINPR), 1-866-944-1744 or 250-654-4000; www.parkscanada.gc.ca/gulf.

Gulf Islands Water Taxi, 250-537-2510.

Harbour Air, 1-800-665-0212 or 604-274-1277; www.harbour-air.com.

KD Air, 1-800-665-4244 or 250-752-5884 (Gillies Bay); www.kdair.com.

Lasqueti passenger ferry, Western Pacific Marine, 604-681-5199, 604-605-6018 or 250-927-0431; www.westernpacificmarine.com.

Newcastle Island passenger ferry (Nanaimo Harbour Ferry), 1-877-297-8526; www.newcastleisland.ca/index.php?page=14.

Penelakut First Nation Band Council, Penelakut Island, 250-246-2321.

Regional District of Nanaimo, Recreation and Parks Services, 6300 Hammond Bay Road, Nanaimo, BC, V9P 6N2; 1-888-828-2069; www.rdn.bc.ca.

Saltspring Air, 1-877-537-9880 or 250-537-9880; www.saltspringair.com.

Seair Seaplanes, 1-800-447-3247 or 604-273-8900; http://seairseaplanes.com.

Tofino Air, 1-800-665-2359; or 250-247-9992; www.tofinoair.ca.

Tsawout First Nation Band Council, 7728 Tetayut, Saanichton, BC; 250-652-9101.

# Acknowledgements

A book like this cannot be written by one person alone. I have had help from and am indebted to a great many people. For economy of space I am citing here mainly the people I have consulted for this edition. I would also like to thank the professional, efficient staff at Harbour Publishing, especially managing editor Anna Comfort, copy editor Margaret Tessman, book designer Martin Nichols, book cover designer Teresa Karbashewski and cartographer Nick Murphy, who each made significant contributions to the book.

The following remarkably helpful island consultants provided information and read the draft manuscript of this edition of the book to cull errors: Ian Stuart, Wil Hilsen, Sue Hern (Bowen); Andy Ellingsen, Sabina Leader Mense, Beth Rees, Vicki deBoer, Ruth Riddell (Cortes); Louise Bell, J. Thornton, Annie Corddry (Denman); John Gambrill, Tom Cameron, Carol Ramsay, and Lesya Fesiak and Joan Michel of the Regional District of Nanaimo Parks Department (Gabriola); Jerry Azevedo, Don Anderson and Ken Millard (Galiano); Doug Carrick, Tony Law (Hornby); Pat Forbes, Jack Soule (Lasqueti); Peter Askin (Mayne); John Chapman (North and South Pender); Judy and Richard Leicester, Lannie and Ralph Keller (Quadra); Dan Dickmeyer, Gernot Gessinger, Philip Grange, Mark Haughey, Fred Powell, Brian Radford, Simon Rook, Kees Ruurs, Nieke and Kees Visser (Salt Spring); Michel Bourassa, Athena George, Jacques Campbell, Jim Campbell (Saturna); John Dove, John Wood, Susan Wood (Texada); Veronica Shelford (Thetis).

I would also like to thank Judy Norget for continuing to review my material and creating maps for me; Carolyn Stewart and Todd Shannon of Parks Canada for reviewing the chapters that contain information on the Gulf Islands National Park Reserve; and Joe Benning, Drew Chapman, Ron Quilter, Dylan Eyers and Dave Forman of BC Parks for reviewing the manuscript for their areas of interest. Thanks also to the many people I interviewed, to the photographers who allowed their work to be reproduced and to the members of the Salt Spring Trail and Nature Club who introduced me to some of the finest Gulf Islands hikes.

# Index